# CONCEPTUAL STILL LIFE PHOTOGRAPHY

By Robyn Selman

Representative **GLENN PALMER-SMITH**: "Imagine it's 1905 in Columbus, Ohio. You're sitting in a room behind lace curtains. You can see out, but no one can see in. Through the window you see a Fuller Brush salesman coming up the walk. When he taps on the door you don't have to answer it. That's phone mail.

"The old way of calling someone up and going to see them doesn't exist anymore. Go try to do a cold call. Leave a message on phone mail and see if anyone calls you back. If they do, it'll make the *Guiness Book of World Records*. Phone mail basically took the telephone conversation out of existence.

"There are only three ways to create business today. One is through referrals—word of mouth from existing clients. A second is is to get exposure in magazines. The third way is advertising, which makes promotional pieces more critical than they ever were.

"In other words, you're back in Columbus, Ohio in 1905. Only this time you do want to buy a hair brush. So you open up the yellow pages and you call Fuller Brush. Now *you* need them, so you give them a call. That's how the magazines and promotional pieces work—like the yellow pages."

This edition of *Conceptual Still Life Photography* focuses on photography representatives—their relationship to today's market, their collaborative work with photographers. For more than a year now, we've been hearing the words *recession, cut back, lay-off, small budget*. We hear them on the East Coast and the West. And we're hearing them from reps.

Reps are the messengers of change. What they see and hear in the marketplace is one of the photographer's most potent pieces of equipment, as important as camera and strobe. Without the rep's input, the photographer is shooting in the dark.

What happens in commerical photography when budgets shrink as they continue to do? Photographs change. Some reps suggest that the images that sell are scaled down, pared of embellishments and stylistic flourishes. Shades of meaning are traded in for direct contact. There was a time, not so long ago, when commerical photography could imitate art. This is not that time. Instead, this is a year of realism and perhaps even caution. It's a time when black and white images will become more saleable and right-between-the-eyes product illustration will make clients feel secure.

Meanwhile, other reps insist that creativity is not depressed although the economy is. Despite the economic blight, and even partially because of it, art directors are looking for superior originality and creativity. Whatever the case, all reps agree that creativity is called for in reps marketing strategies.

And of course there are some rep/photographer pairs who appear altogether unfazed by the nervous market. Perhaps because of remarkable talent, perhaps because of remarkable marketing, certain photographers are more in demand now than ever, commanding higher prices than ever. But that number is relatively small. Most of the reps we talked with were more than a little concerned about what will sell today. It's the question everyone wants answered, but—in the 90's anyway—might be afraid to ask.

While most reps talk about the responsibilty they feel to steer their talent in new, lucrative

directions, # DARIO SACRAMONE

talks about going in a new direction himself.

Not long ago, he began repping Christopher Lawrence, who is known primarily for shooting fashion still life for advertising, catalogues and editorial but was interested in moving into food. Sacramone, who is known as a rep of people and still life photography, had decided on the same direction.

"I went to food photography," Sacramone says, "because I think there's a good market for it in today's economic climate. There's been a general slowdown at the agencies for many reasons, but the bottom line is that the business has changed. A number of agency people have been let go. That means contacts have changed or left altogether. Budgets have fallen by the wayside. Today, a campaign is one ad. In the past, a campaign meant six or eight ads. The clients who are buying that much work now are food clients. Food sells.

"This is my first venture into the area of food photography—not that it's really any different. It's mostly a matter of research. You really have to be on top of the marketplace and respond to what's happening out there. Being computerized helps. I've got a great mailing list that I can change on the spot."

Though it's been less than a year that Sacramone has been working with Lawrence, the relationship feels familiar to both of them. "I chose Christopher because we had a great rapport over the telephone before we even met. When we did meet, my feelings were confirmed. But we took our time. I wanted him to meet the other reps that were out there so

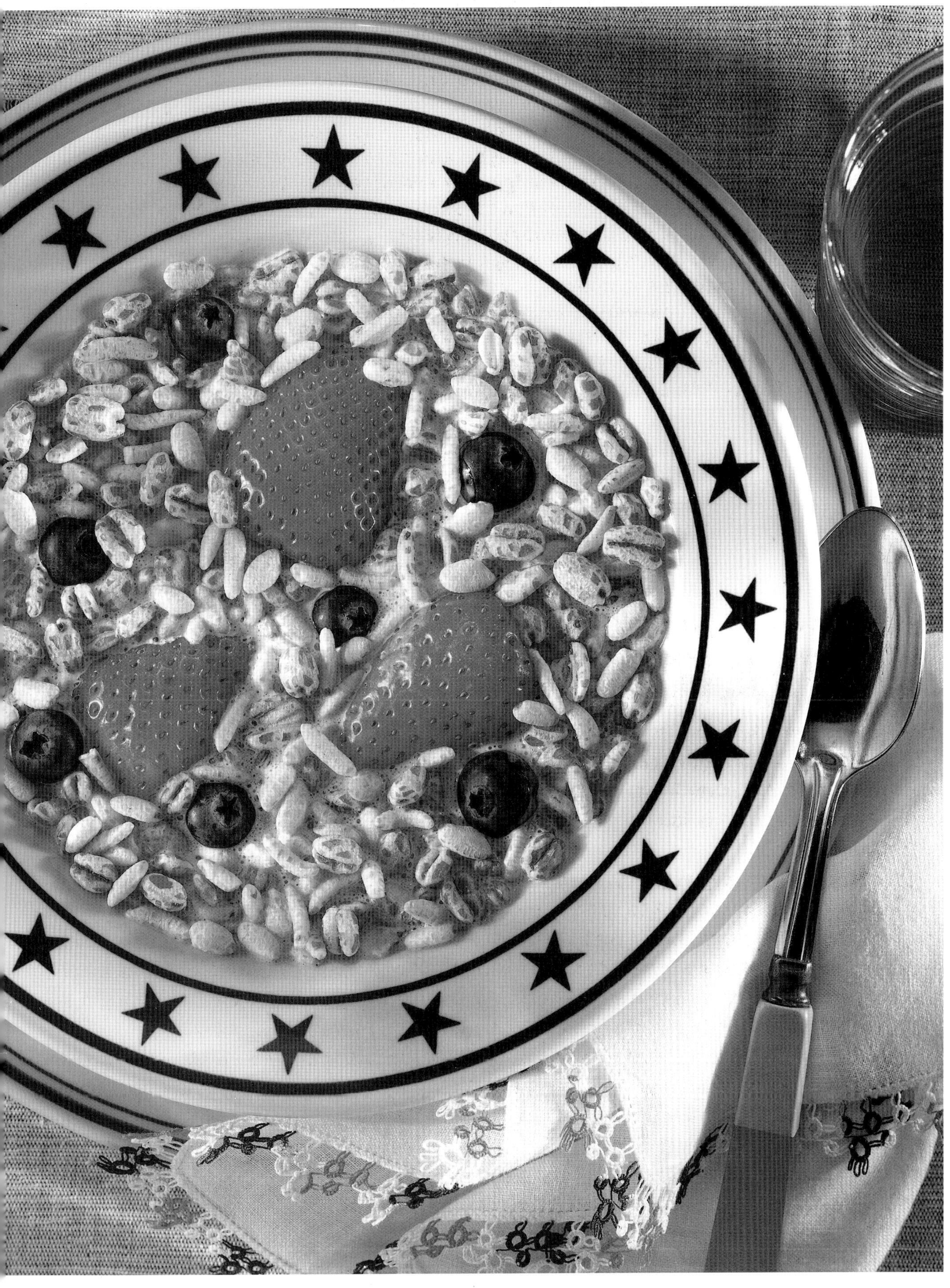

Photo © Colin Cooke represented by Robert Bacall

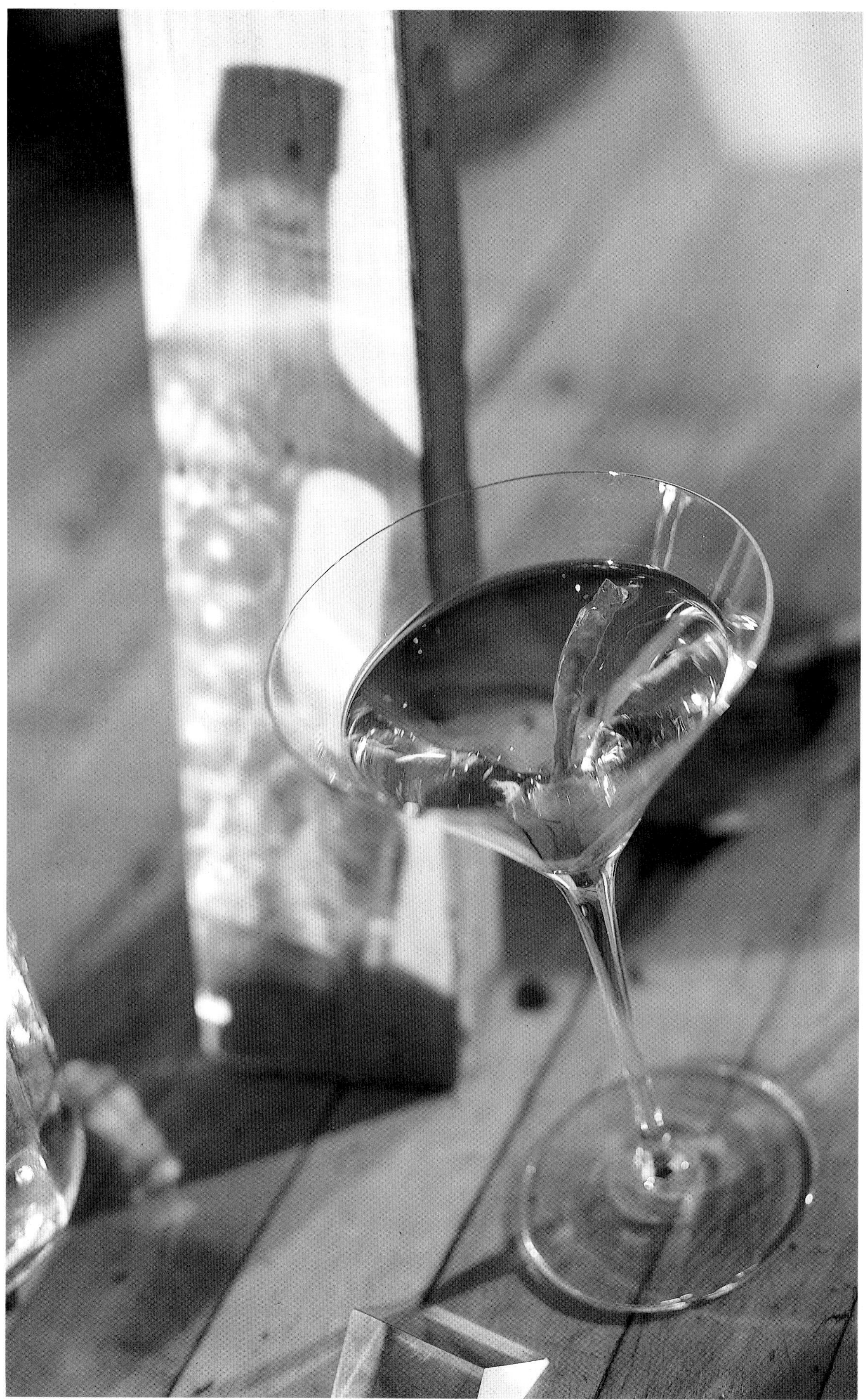

that he would be able to feel that he had made the  right choice for himself. What I liked about Christopher's photography is that the food is the star of the shot. Another thing that impressed me was that he already had an entire food portfolio prepared. That made me feel confident about him—he's a worker, he's aggressive. He produces lots of new work and that's very important today—to explore new things in the area you've chosen." Sacramone is obviously taking his own advice.

# ROBERT BACALL

calls it zeroing in: images with one product and fewer props. One of his photographers, Colin Cooke (who has recently worked for Seagrams, Schieffelin, Austin Nichols, Mastercard, Kraft General Foods and Lever Brothers), is heading toward a distinctively cleaner look.

That's a good tactic, according to Bacall. He sees an increasingly competitive climate in which individual photographers will have to work even harder to stand out.

"If there's one rule of thumb in a business with very few rules," Bacall says, "it's to adapt."

**GEORGE WATSON** suggests that where once images were trendy, they're now straight-forward. "Things seem to be going American, toward a hard-edged product sale, less romantic, more commercial looking. It seems as though the trend is to be more generic, to represent the product as it is, bare bones."

Watson's photographer Kan has built a reputation based on his expertise with liquids and cold beverages. Kan has shot Seagrams' Taos product for the two years it has been in test markets. As Watson says, "The idea of this photograph is to show the product first and foremost, because the product is new. Next, they wanted to illustrate how refreshing and light it is. The idea is that it's so light and cold that it comes up out of freezing arctic water on an iceberg."

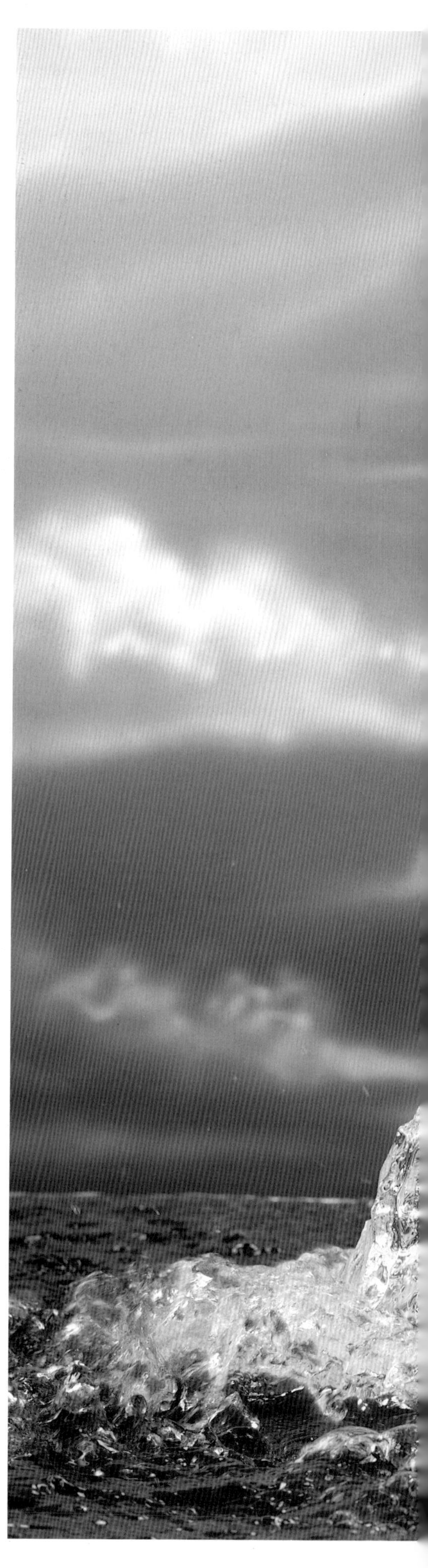

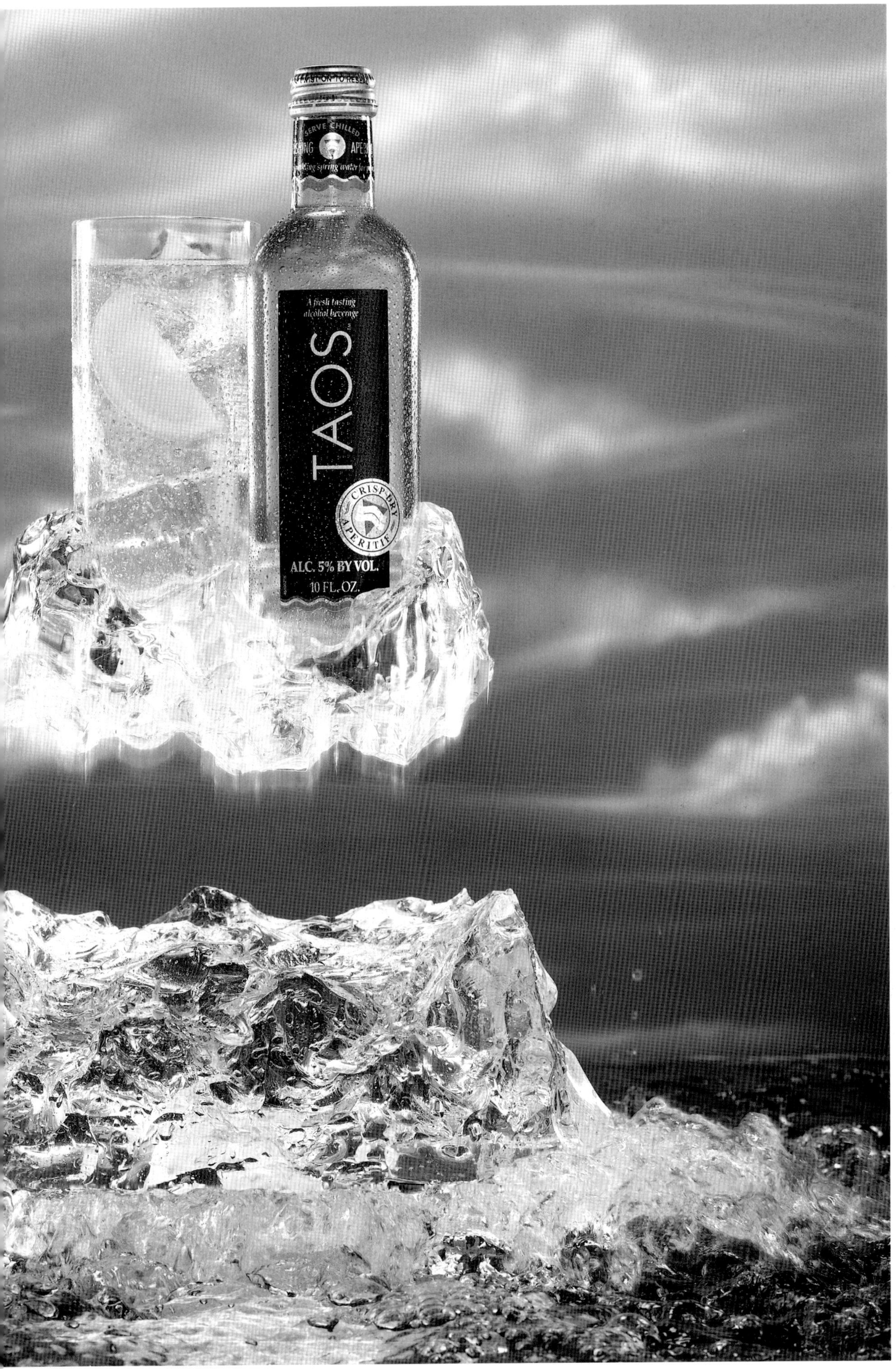
SERVE CHILLED
TAOS
A fresh tasting
alcoholic beverage
CRISP DRY
APERITIF
ALC. 5% BY VOL.
10 FL. OZ.

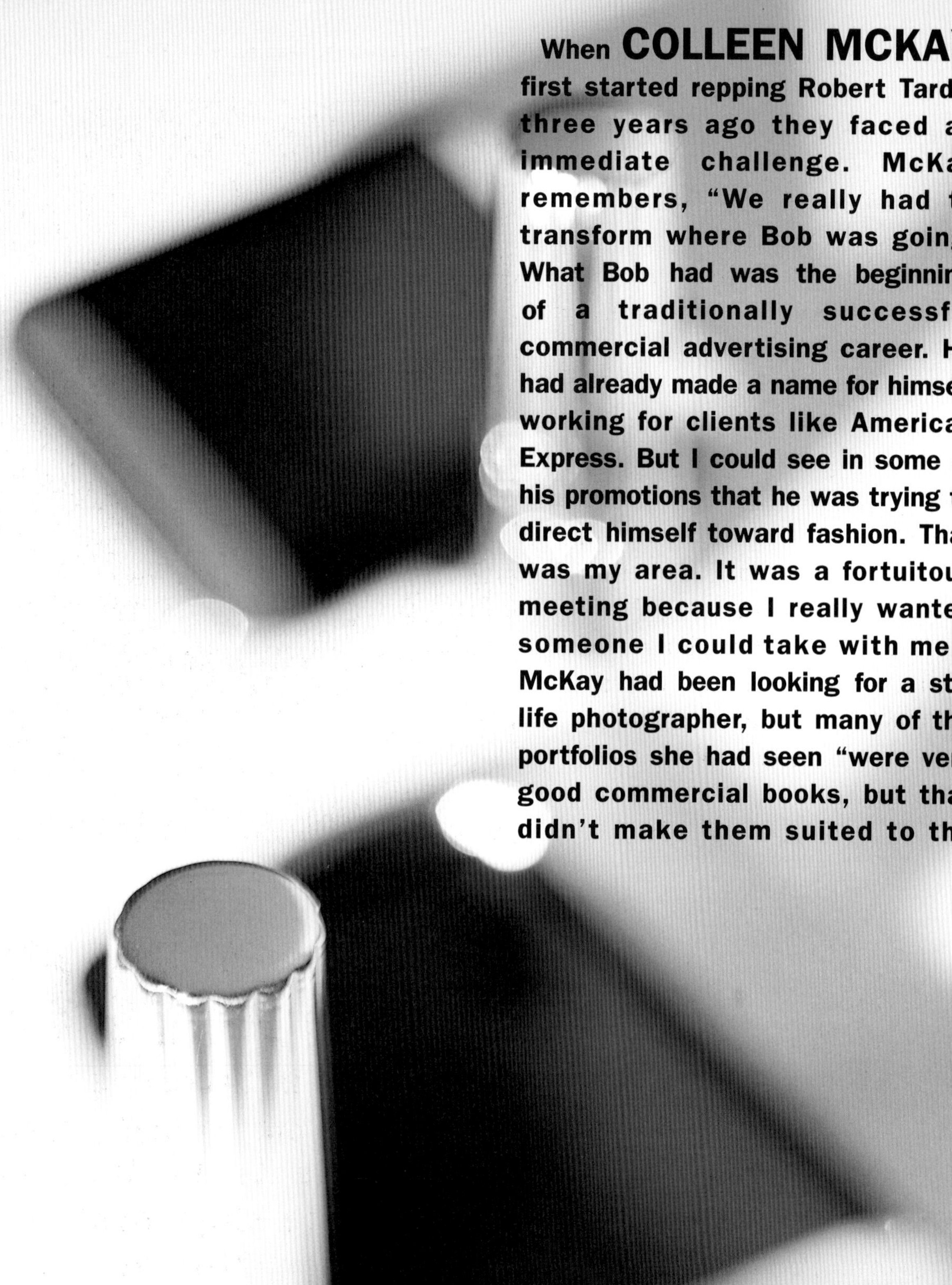

When **COLLEEN MCKAY** first started repping Robert Tardio three years ago they faced an immediate challenge. McKay remembers, "We really had to transform where Bob was going. What Bob had was the beginning of a traditionally successful commercial advertising career. He had already made a name for himself working for clients like American Express. But I could see in some of his promotions that he was trying to direct himself toward fashion. That was my area. It was a fortuitous meeting because I really wanted someone I could take with me." McKay had been looking for a still life photographer, but many of the portfolios she had seen "were very good commercial books, but that didn't make them suited to the

Photo © Robert Tardio represented
by Colleen McKay

fashion market. Fashion clients don't want to use advertising photographers—they want a more editorial look."

McKay took Tardio's work—images that put cosmetics together with lighting and gold—to all her existing clients. And how are she and Tardio doing now? "We're not feeling the cutbacks that other people are talking about. We're well positioned in the fashion and beauty markets which seem to be traditionally recession-proof.

"I find people respond to the attitude and emotion in a shot. They want freshness without pretension, nothing that's overdone. The shots we've included in *NY Gold* are really representative of Bob's work. They have the technical ability that clients want, but they also have mood."

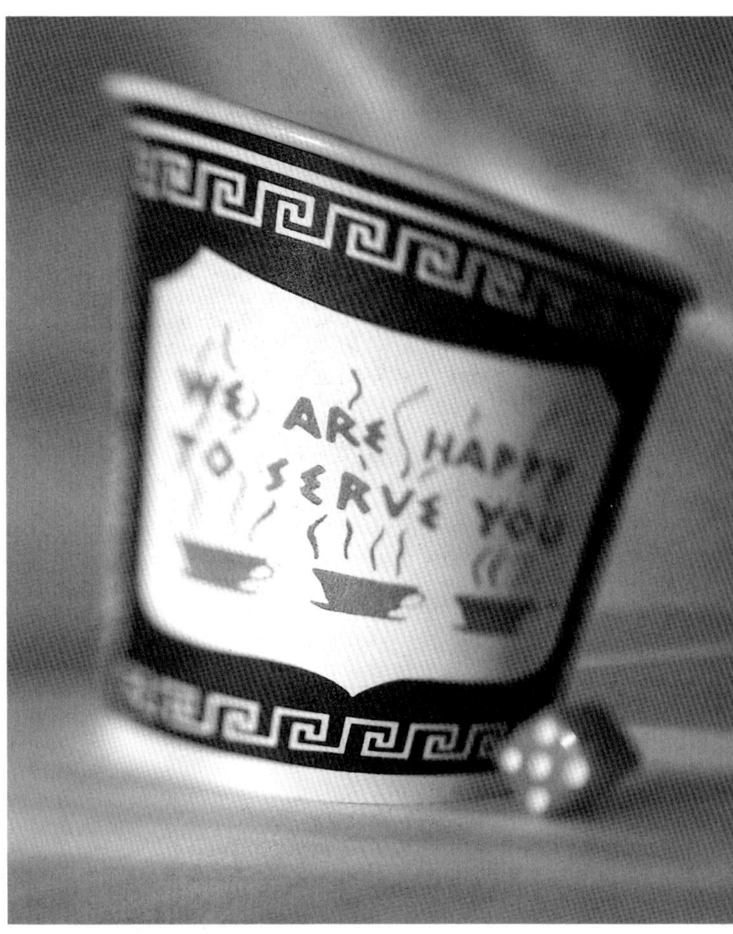
Photo © Stuart Heir represented by Jim Zaccaro


# JIM ZACCARO

thinks that the move toward natural light is becoming more popular than it was: "That's not to say that the  strong graphic image  is being phased out, just that the two  tendencies seem to be coming together." That convergence plays right into photographer Stuart Heir's work. Zaccaro says, "The jobs we've been doing lately seem to be a blend—even if it's something to be photographed on seamless with the product as hero, clients still want a natural look."

Generally, Zaccaro and Heir try to show images in *NY Gold* that go a little further out than what they're actually selling. Zaccaro says, "The shot with the Brillo pad is a example of Stuart going a little further out. It's there to tease and intrigue the art director.

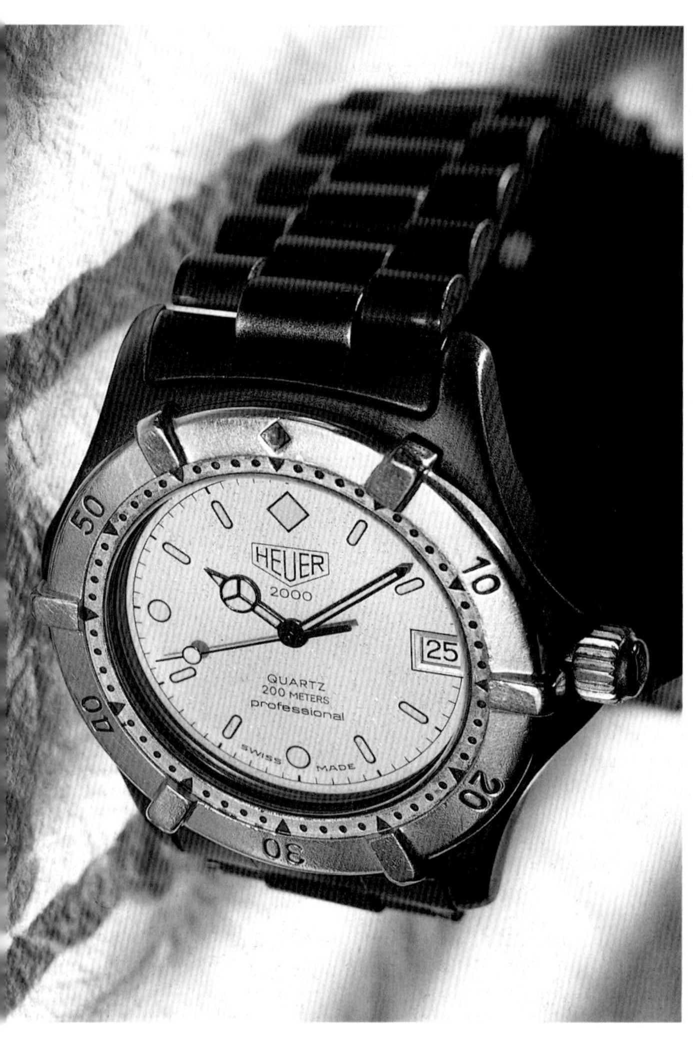

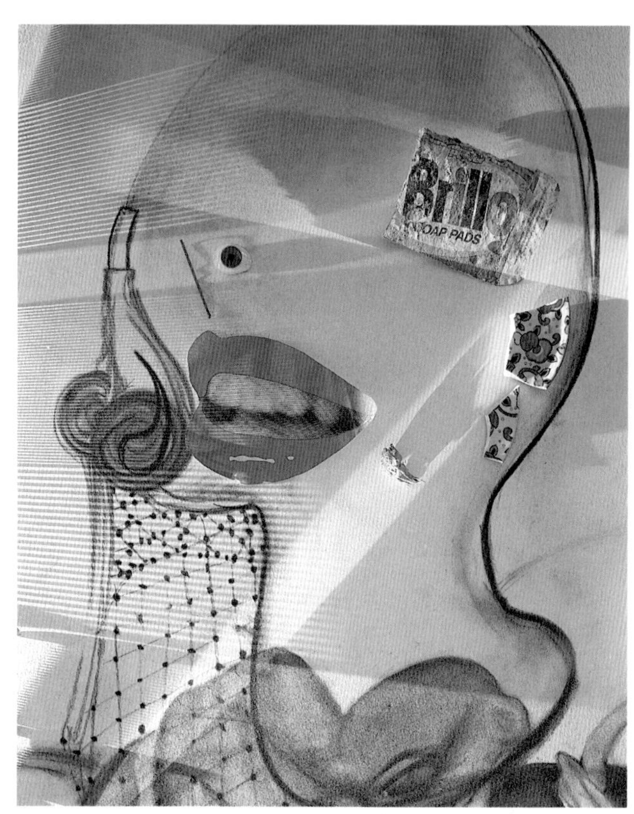


Photos © Stuart Heir represented by Jim Zaccaro

**The wristwatch is more realistic. Somewhere in the middle is the coffee cup."**

**"One of the things I had to do with Stuart when we first got together was to bring him back a little bit. He was too far out. When photographers know  there's a lot of competition they tend to get a little too creative and less usable. While art directors appreciate creativity they have a job to do. They want to be certain there's some control to tap into."**

**When representative RALPH MENNEMEYER met photographer David Weiss, he was impressed. "I looked at David's book and it blew me away. It's that simple. I first saw David's book in June. In December, I still couldn't get his images out of my head. That's how I knew we'd work well together. I believed that much in what he does."**

**Mennemeyer and Weiss chose two images for *NY Gold* because they each suit different trends in the market. "If you think back to the 70's, the look was clean, black and plexi. There are still people who think that**

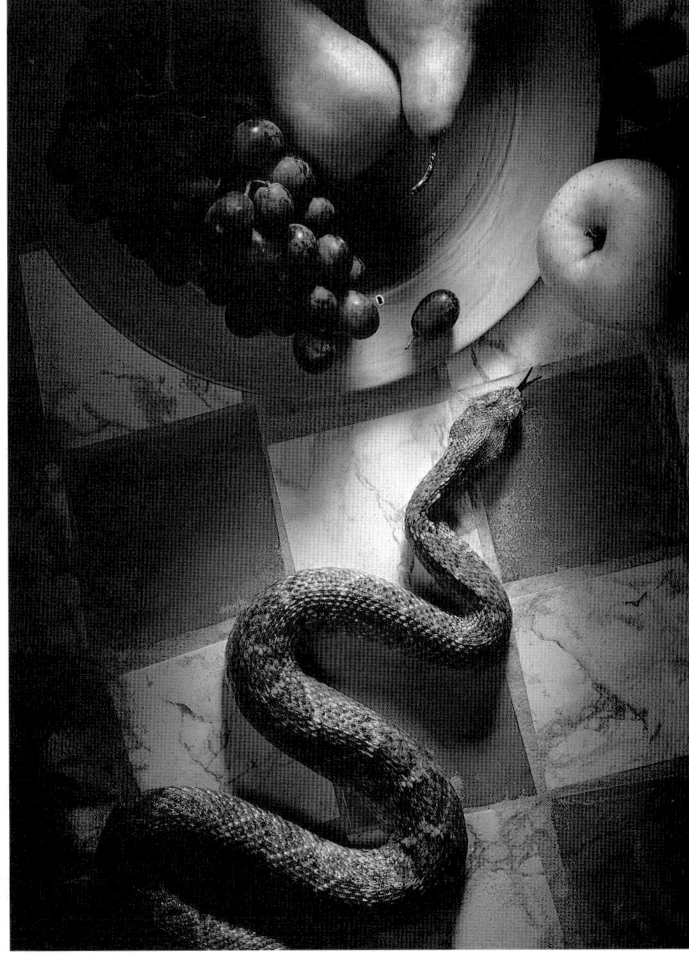

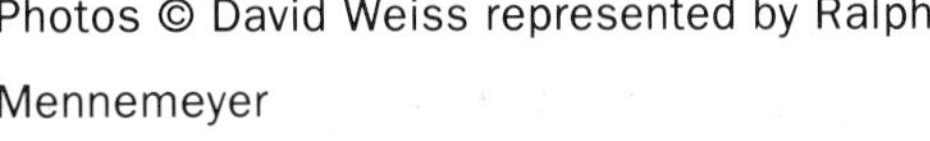

Photos © David Weiss represented by Ralph Mennemeyer

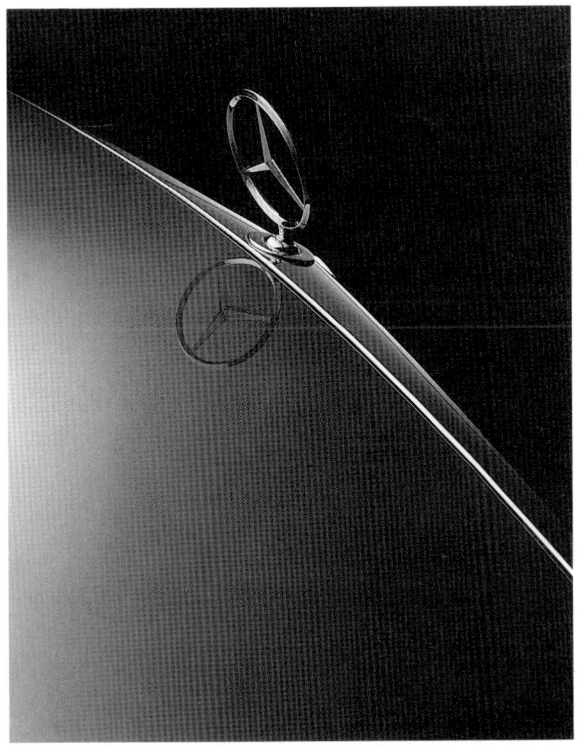

way, which is why a shot that's simple and well designed, like the Mercedes Benz ad, is in *NY Gold*.

"On the other hand, there are younger people—and not necessarily chronologically either—who are looking for something else, a more complicated picture where the tactile sense is very important, where color matters and lighting is just about everything. That's why we put in the snake shot. There's a unity between the two images: the light, the design and the diagonals. That's how we round out a presentation of what David does. There's a definite strategy at work here."

# ALISON KORMAN

began her repping career after a series of other jobs in her early twenties—including work in  a corporation, as a performance artist, and a graphic designer. "I wanted to work with artists and be independent. Repping was the only field where I could start with virtually no connections and very little capital. I could go with a phone and the sweat of my brow."

Ten years later, Korman, who reps photographer David Bishop, feels strongly that all the different jobs she had contribute to her repping. "My work in graphics helps me visually, my work as a performer helps me sell. One of the hard things about this business is that many people who do what I do have some artisitic background but because of the traditional rep/photographer relationship, they're unable to fully use it. It takes a sensitive and broad minded photographer to really recognize what a rep can offer. One of the reasons why my partnership with David works so well is that he's open enough to hear my input. And he's educated me tremendously about business, because he's a very good businessman. The rep is not just the business mind and the photographer is not just  the creative mind. That's just a way of dismissing one another."

As Korman explained that the sensitive, mindful coordination of artist and agent is crucial, the other aspect of the rep/photographer relationship made itself known: the phone rang constantly in the background. Korman explained what she sells in this market: "In the past, people were into cold, hard, slick images—things had to look just perfect. That's what the 80's were all about. But toward the end of the decade people started warming up.  They wanted images that were very soothing, comforting, like hot chocolate in winter. Back to mother as opposed to this slick power- light.

"David was on the vanguard of this movement with his photographs in simulated natural light. It was almost as if he had anticipated the trend and in some ways he had. He felt the same yearning. But now people are looking to come back into the world

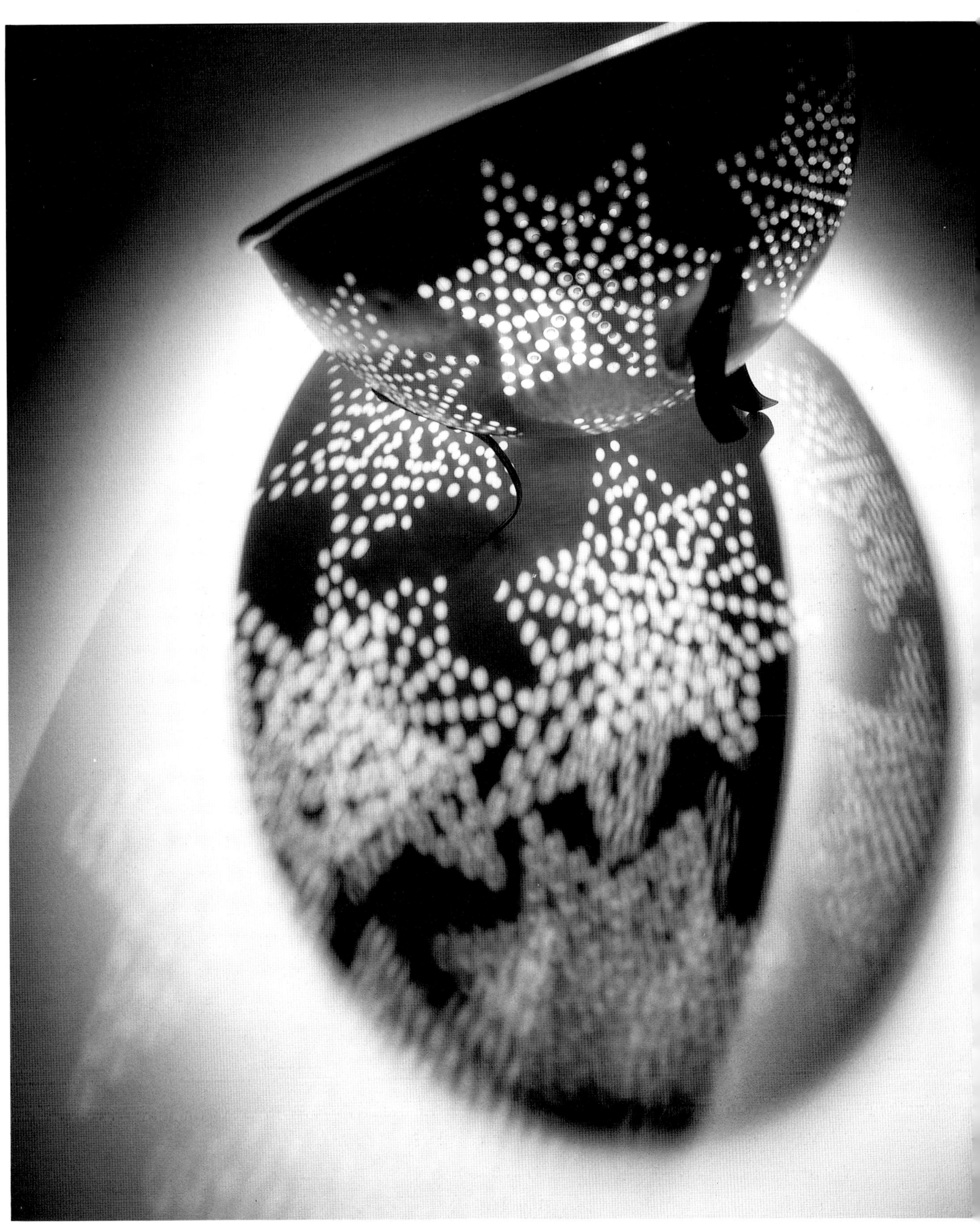

Photo © David Bishop represented by Alison Korman

yet go farther, so that same naturalism has become heightened. ”

These three still life images were all Bishop's personal work. Korman says that his personal work always leads Bishop's professional work, not the other way around.

“We tend to put a lot of personal work in David's ads. Particularly in the *Gold book*. When people are looking for something more commercial or safe, they tend to go to *The Black Book*. We're in there, too, but our ad varies slightly. Something like the airplane shot would never be right for the *Black Book*. In the *Gold Book*, we have room to tease, to titillate. Each of these shots has a quality that's surreal and dreamy. It's the light of heightened naturalism. You'll find us heading deeper in that direction for a while.”

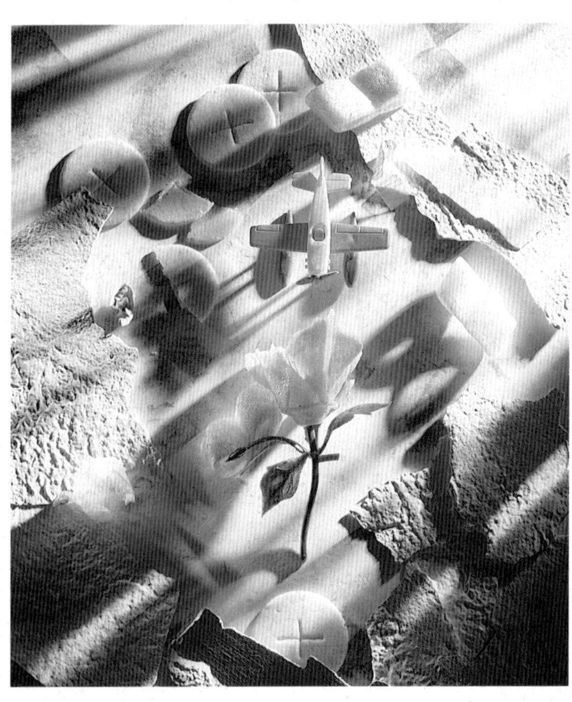

Photo © David Bishop represented by
Alison Korman

## GLENN PALMER-SMITH

says that “Two years ago everybody was trying to become very artistic. You saw a lot of birds nests, wire and feathers. The work was very self-consciously trying to be art instead of advertising. Now that the market's changed people are doing a very basic kind of photography which will sell product. When the market tightens like this it forces people to get in touch with the real reason they're in those studios taking pictures. There isn't as much room to massage the ego. You're there to provide a service.”

In the case of John Manno, adapting to this market doesn't seem like it will require much of a leap—he was an essentialist before it was fashionable, let alone a

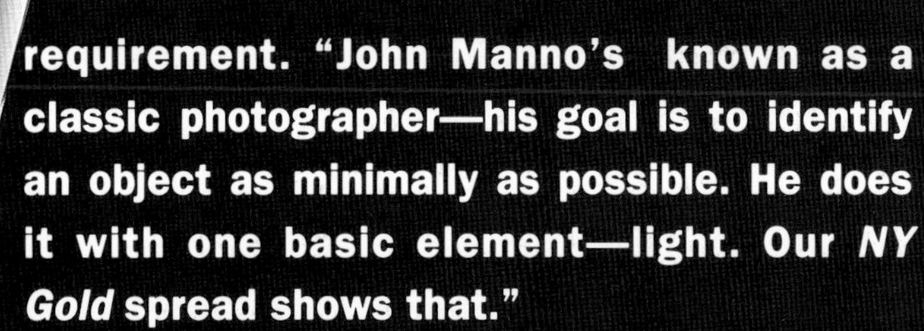

requirement. "John Manno's known as a classic photographer—his goal is to identify an object as minimally as possible. He does it with one basic element—light. Our *NY Gold* spread shows that."

On the relationship between photographer and rep Palmer-Smith says, "A marriage between a photographer and rep is as important as a marriage between a man and a woman. Maybe even more important, because your livelihood is wrapped up in it in a big, big way. So it follows that the way to make the decision about who to rep, after talent, is personality. John and I just clicked." When asked, "Given this market, is there something beyond the obvious to the rep's job?" Smith replied, "Cheerleader."

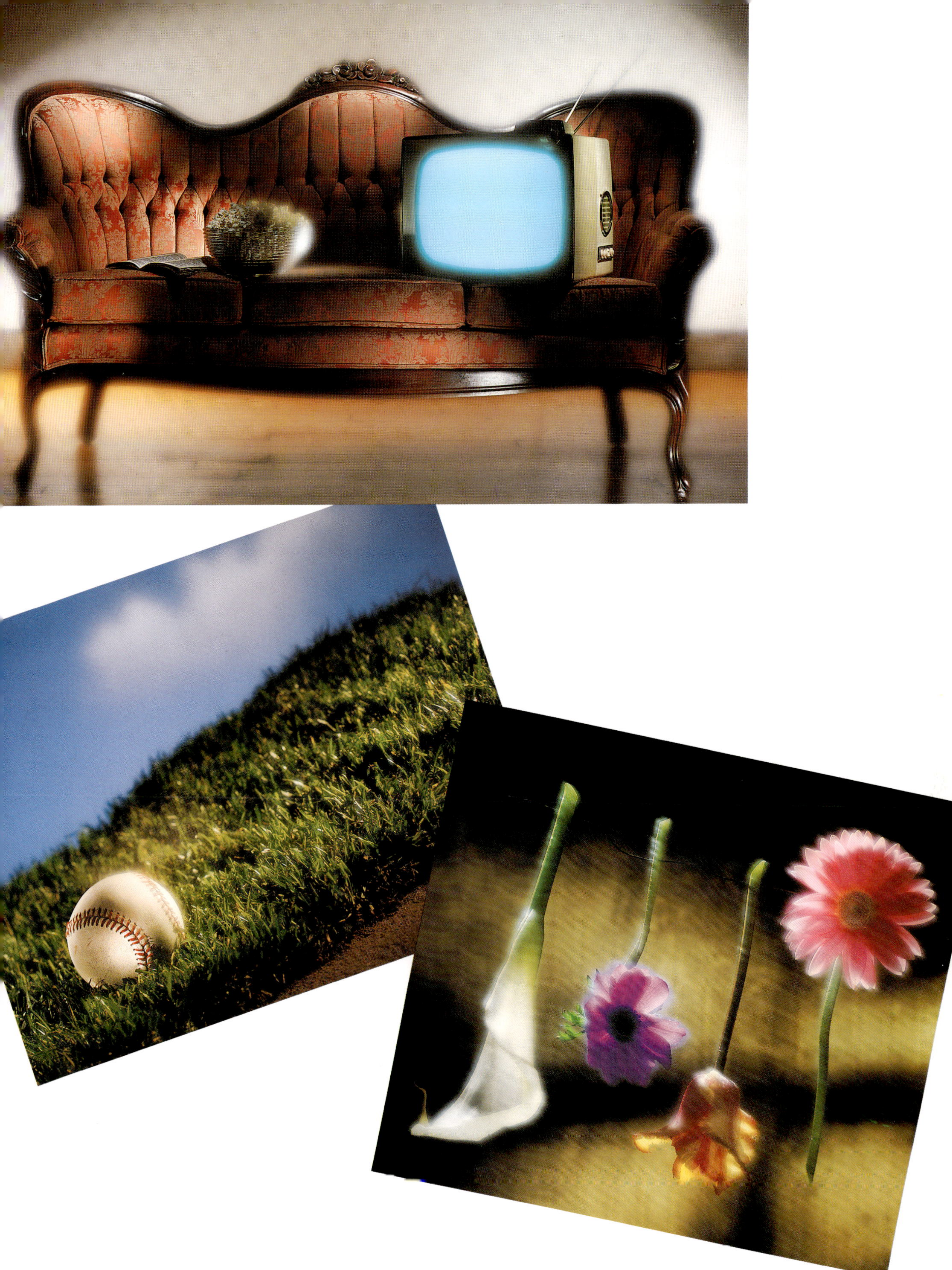

TONY CORDOZA  15 WEST 18 TH STREET  NEW YORK  212 243 8441

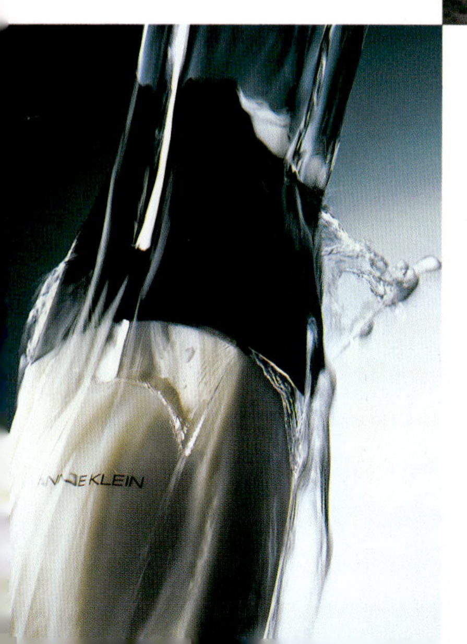

N KLEIN


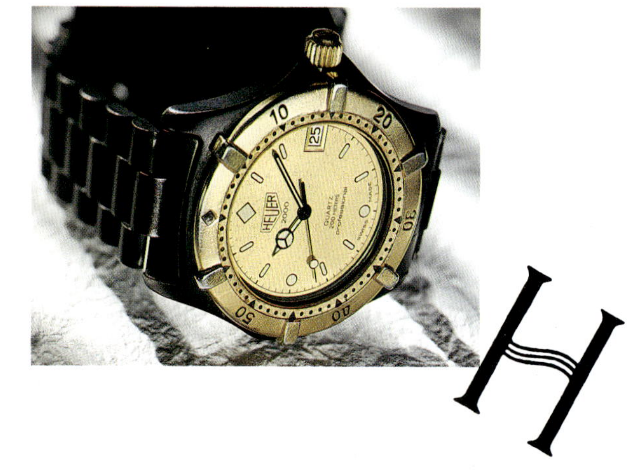

HEUER
2000
QUARTZ
200 METERS
professional
SWISS MADE

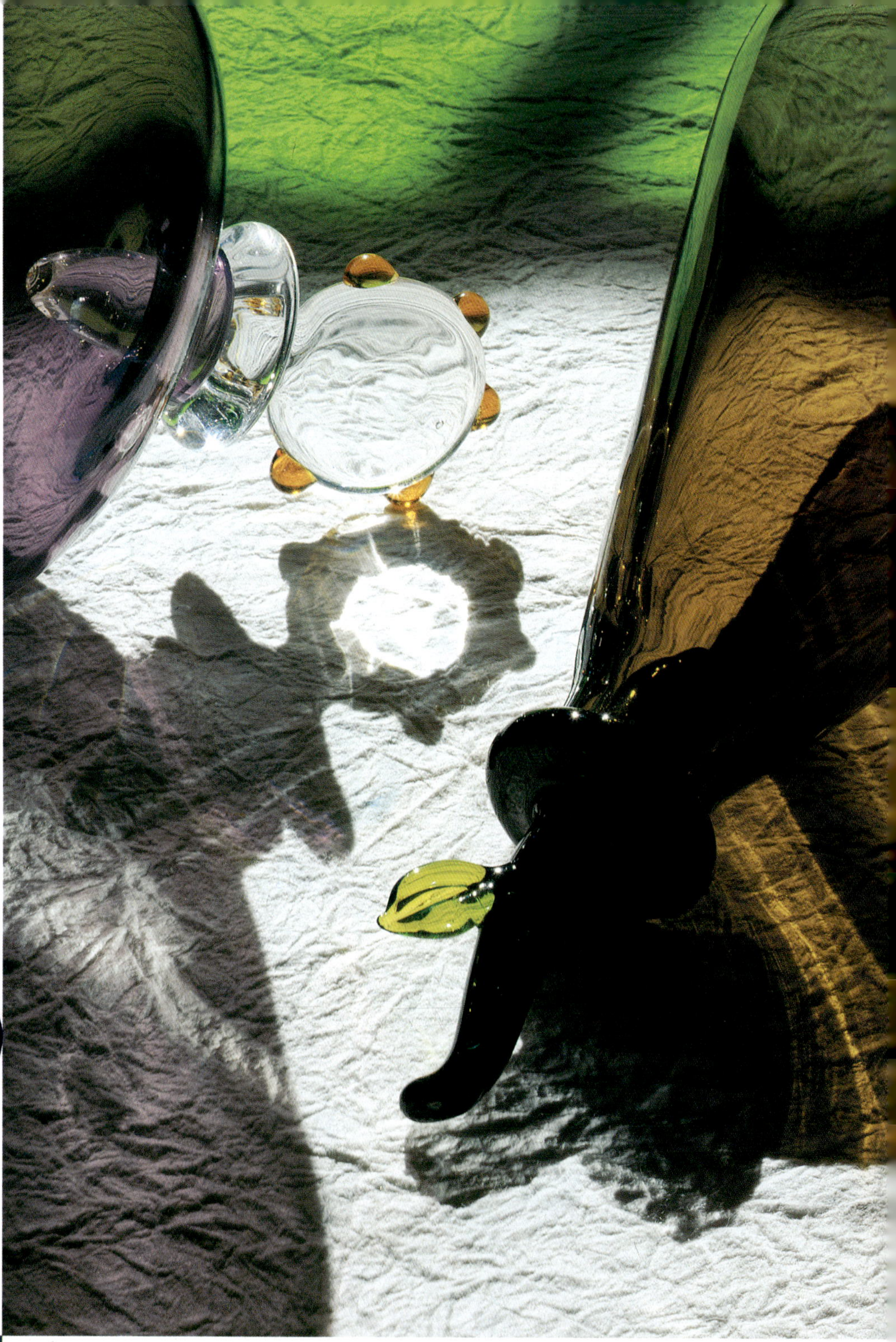

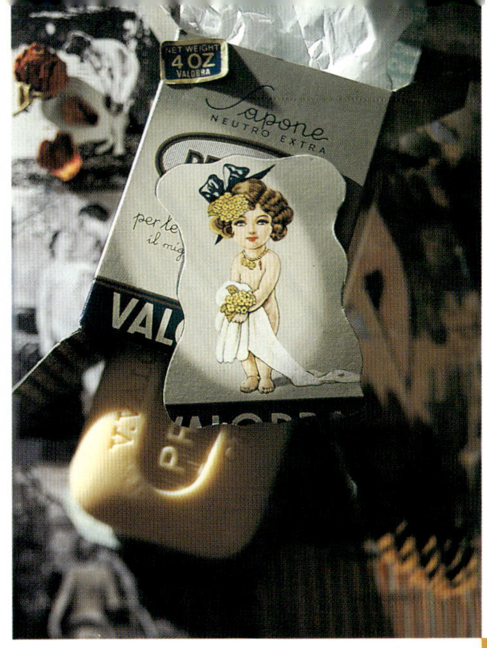
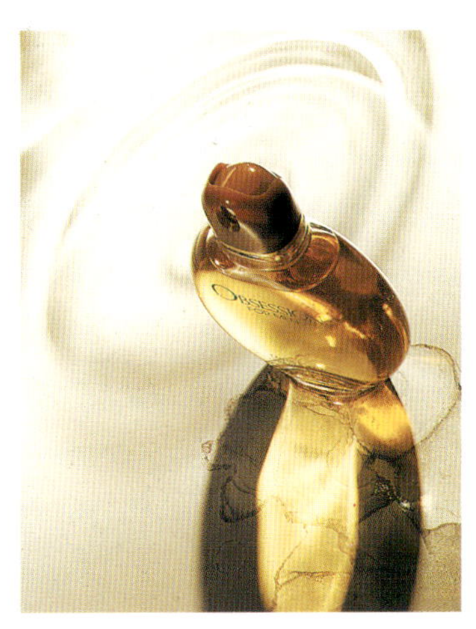
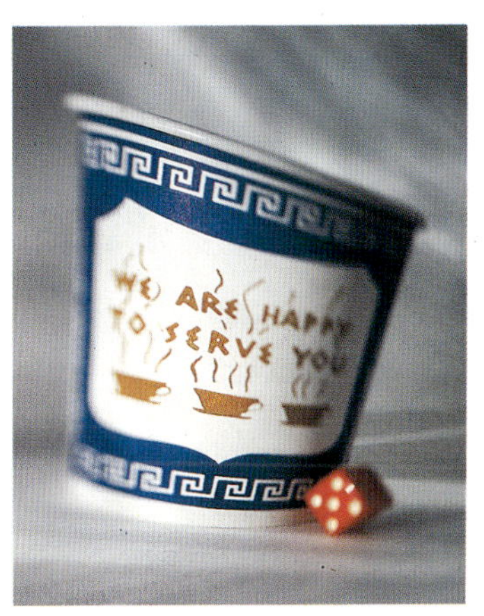
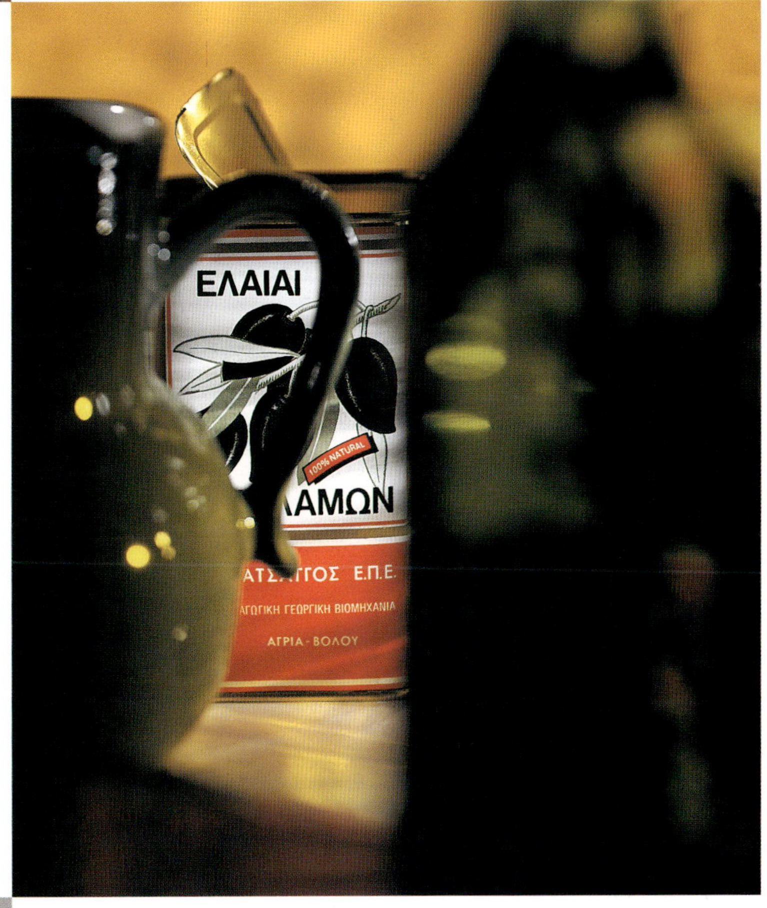
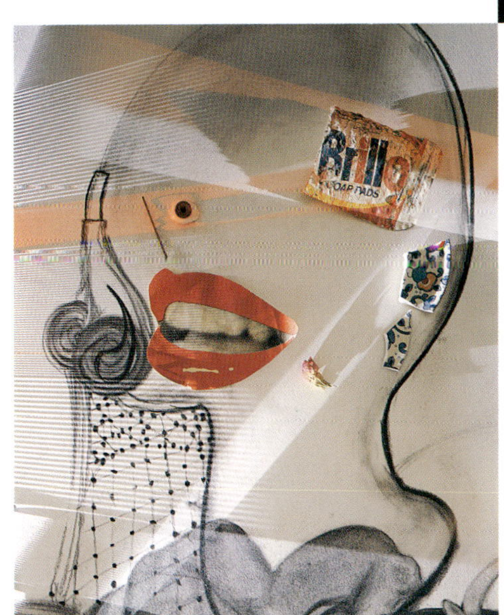

STUART HEIR

30 W. 22ND ST.
N. Y. C. ▪ 1 0 0 1 0
2 1 2 ▪ 6 3 3 ▪ 2 1 8 7
AGENT: JIM ZACCARO
2 1 2 ▪ 7 4 4 ▪ 4 0 0 0
FAX: 2 1 2 ▪ 7 4 4 ▪ 4 4 4 2

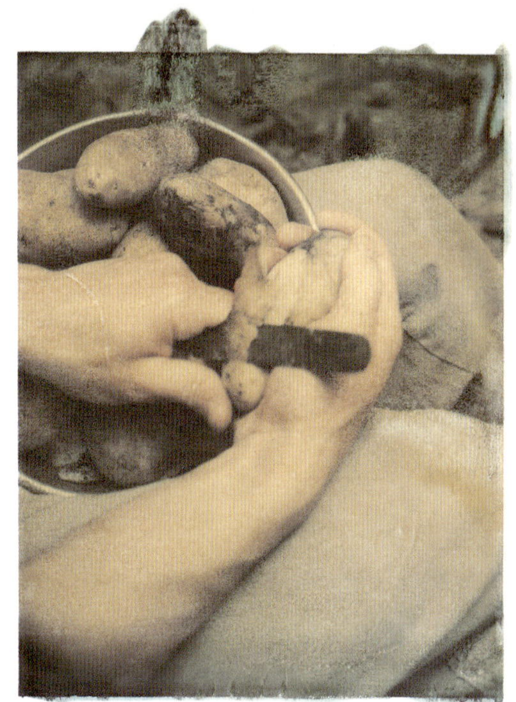

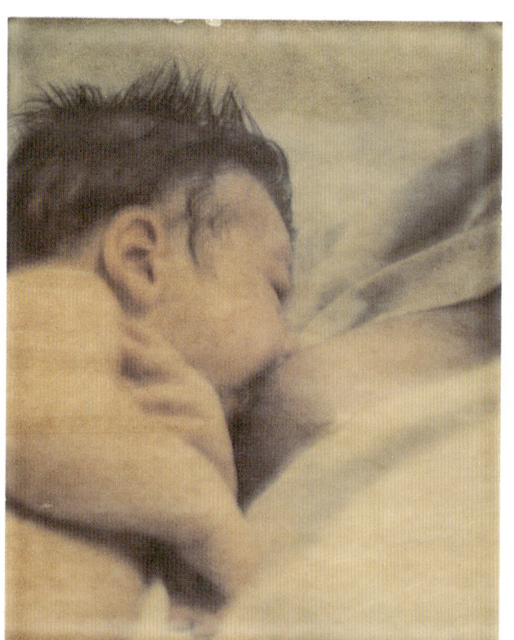

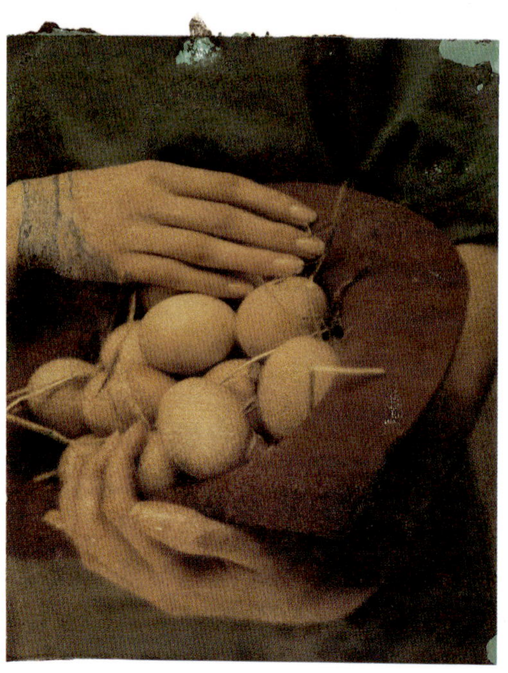

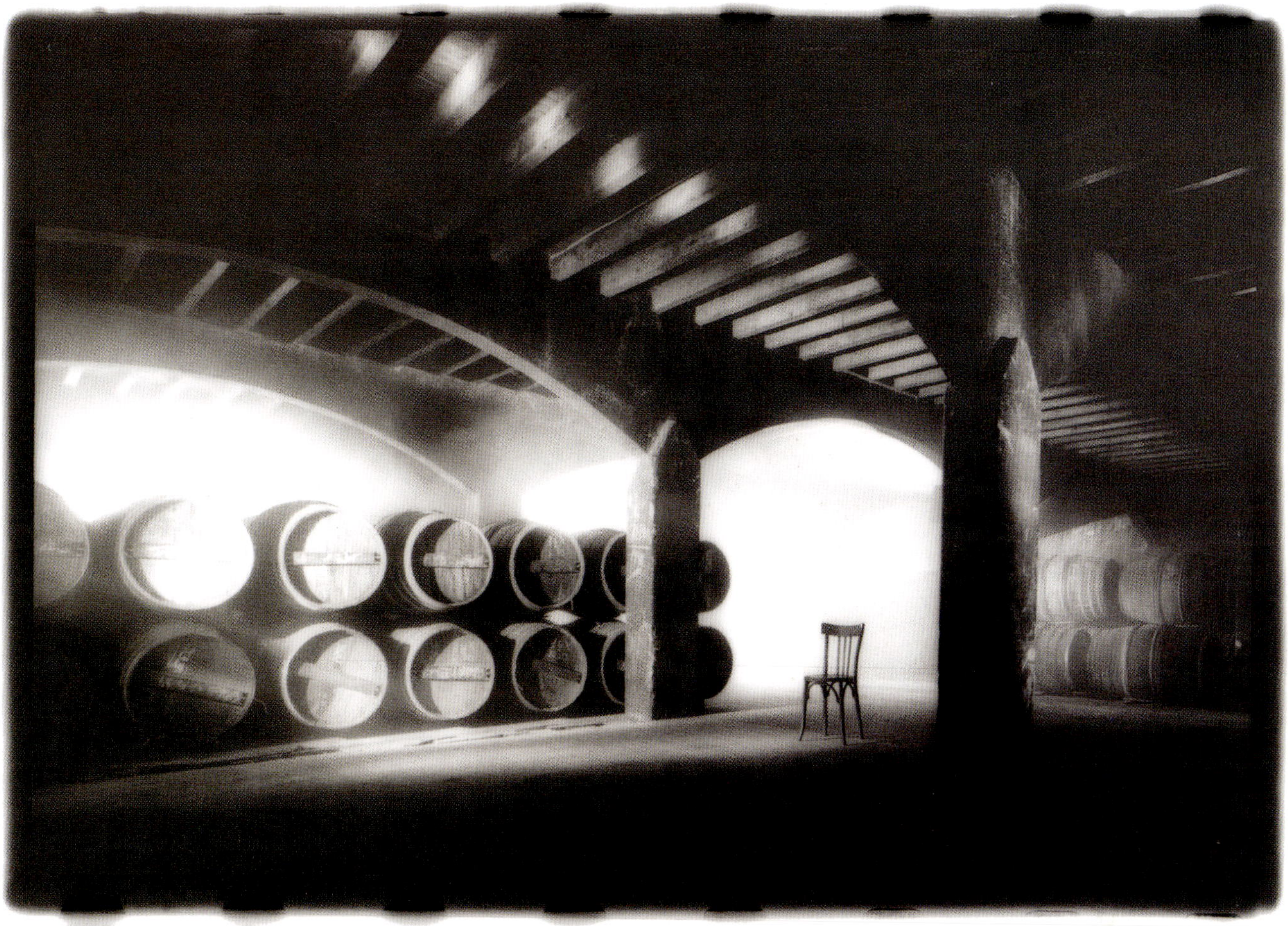

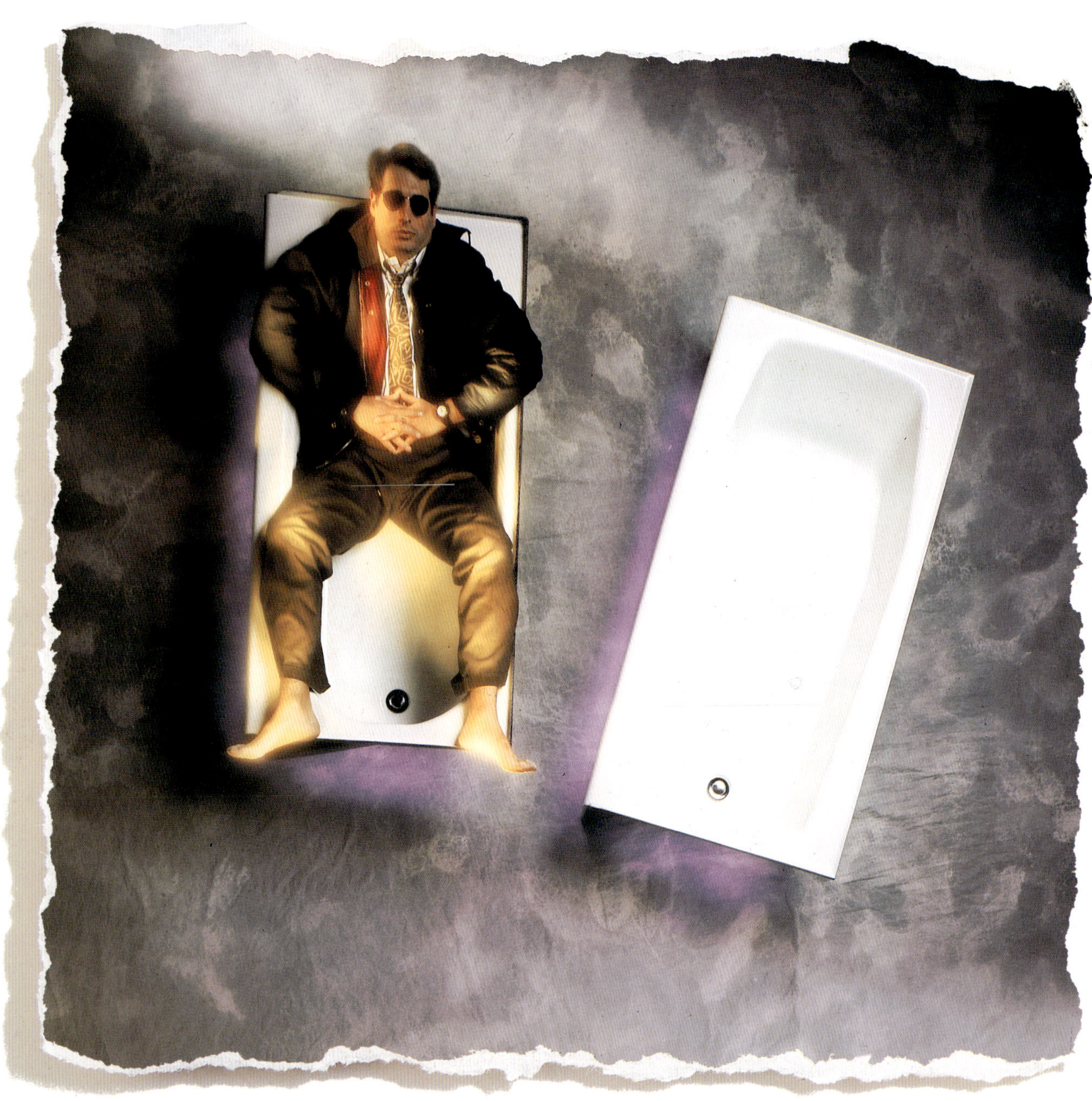

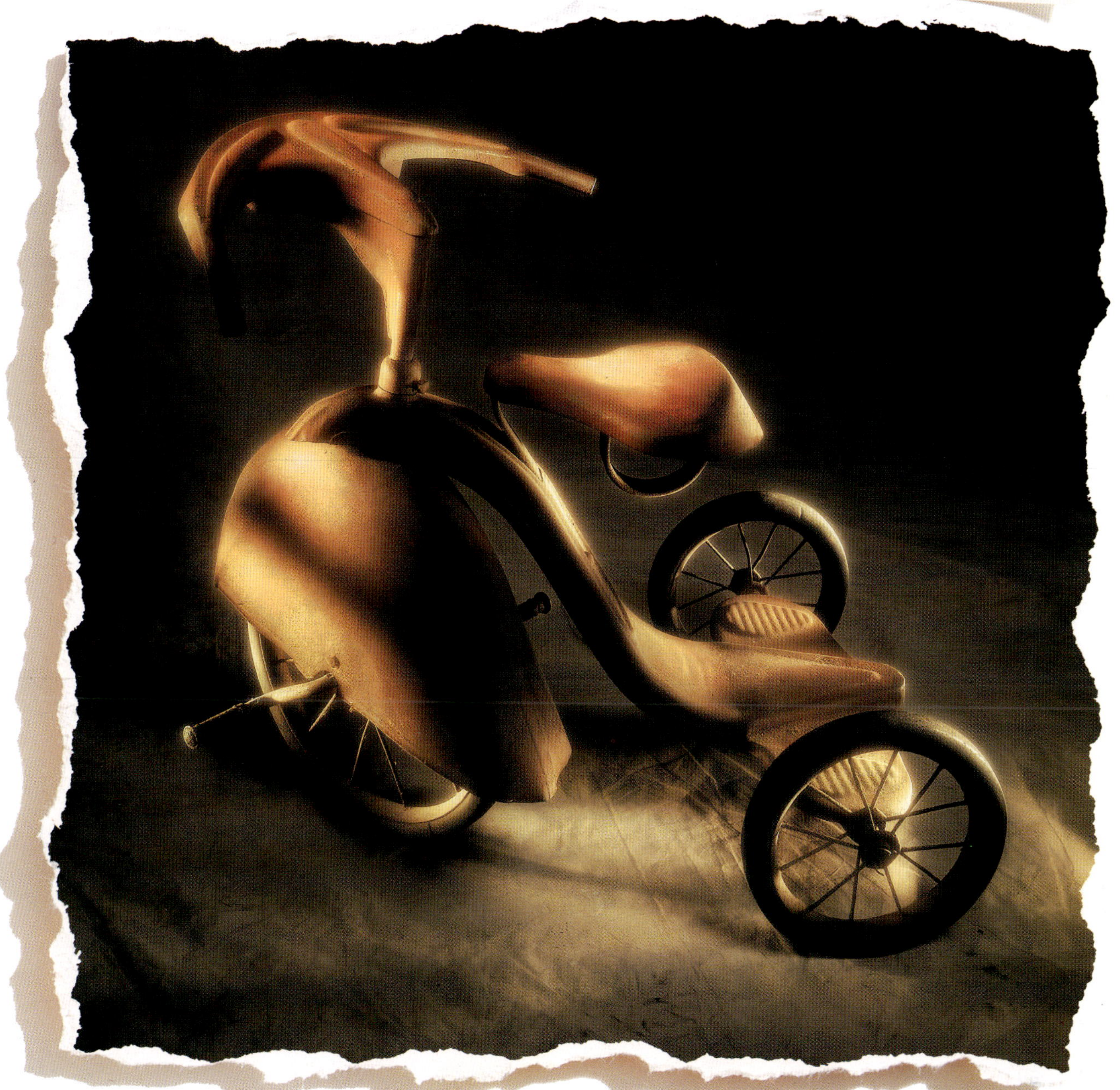


Jon Holderer Studio

37 West 20th Street • New York City 10011

STUDIO 212.620.4260

Represented By Wendy Hansen

212.684.7139

Jon Holderer

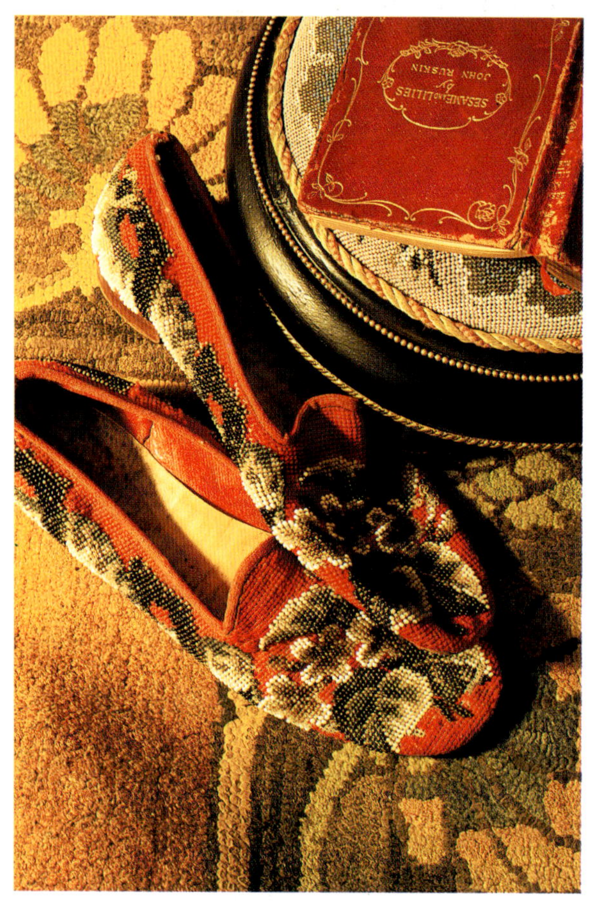

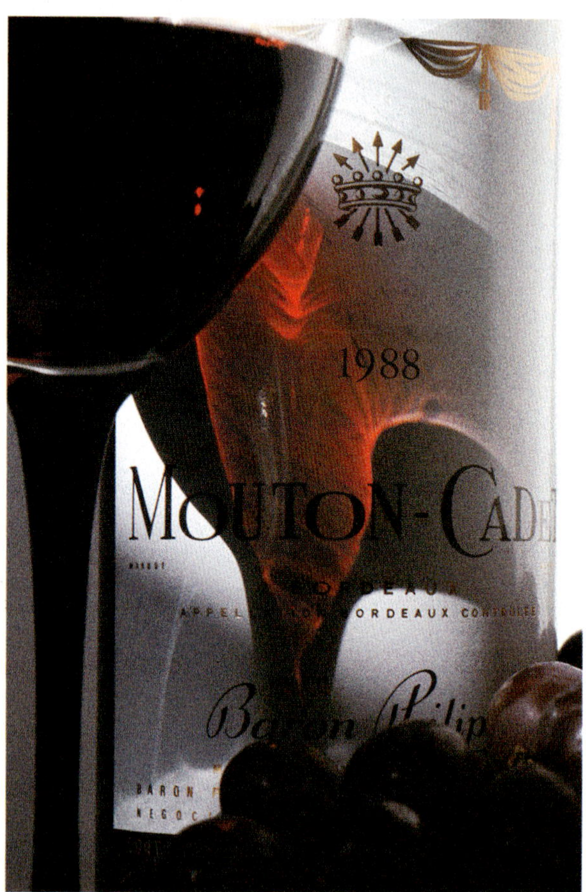



E D W A R D   A D D E O

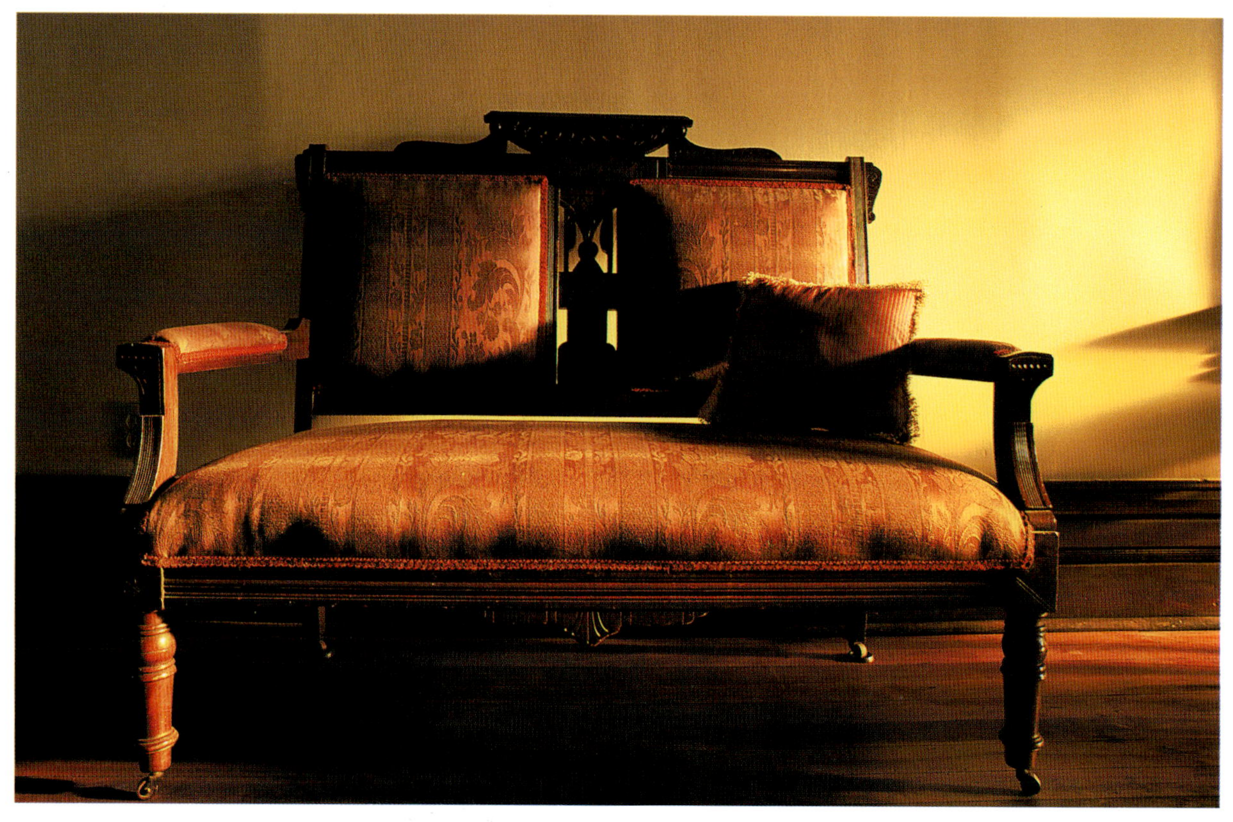

P H O T O G R A P H Y   2 1 2   9 3 2   9 1 2 0

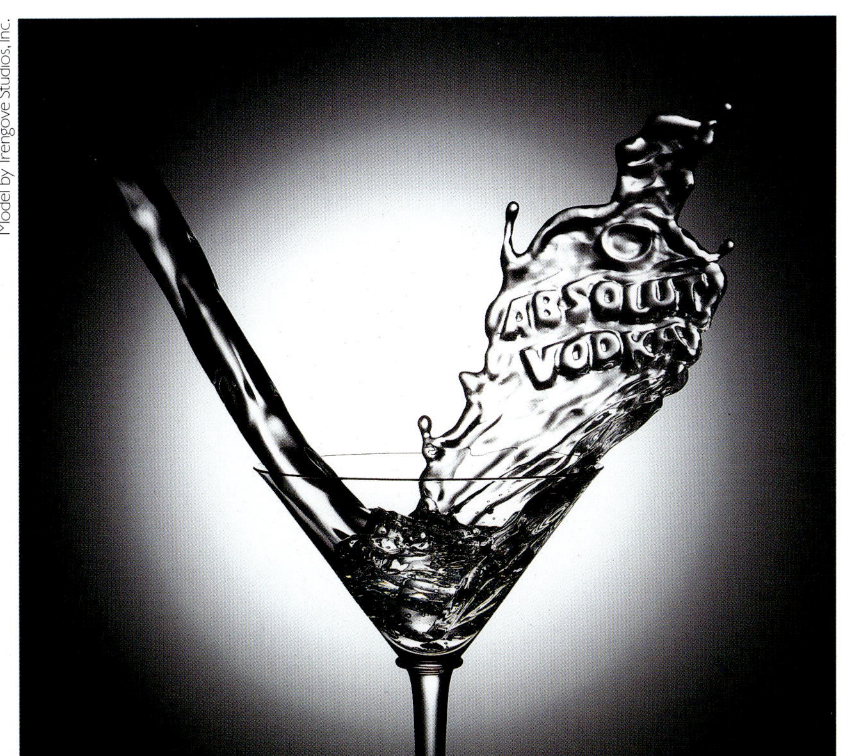


# Dan Wagner

212•481•0786

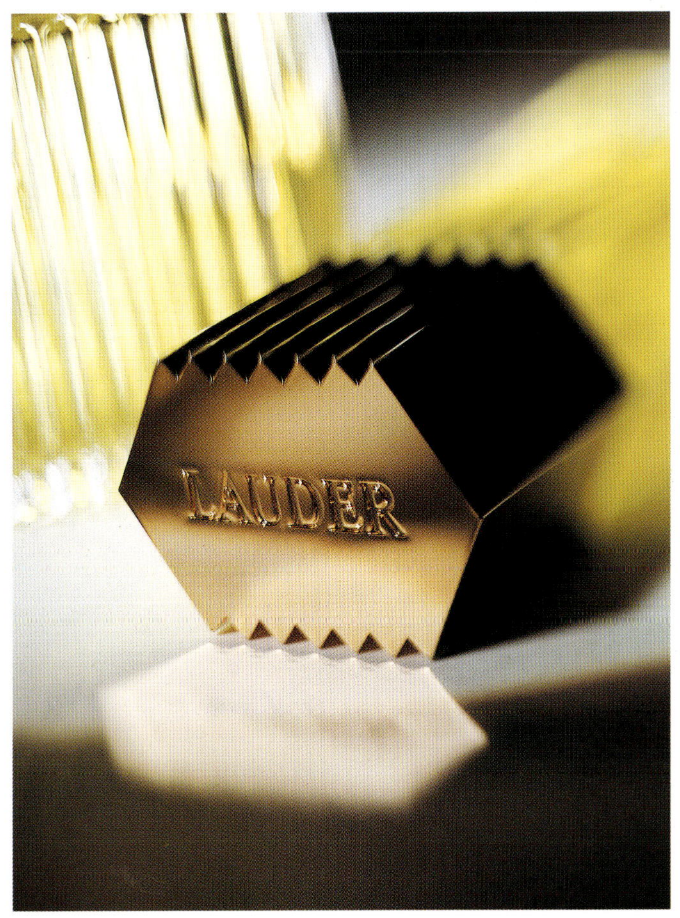

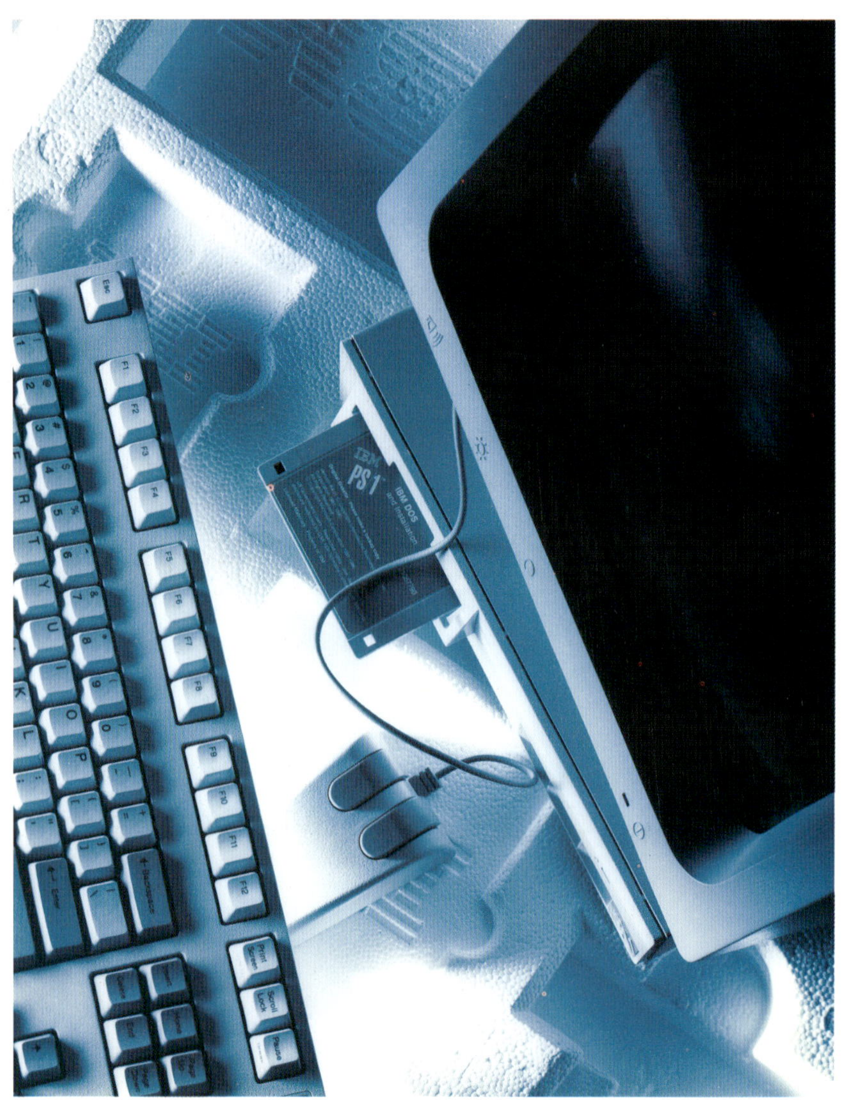

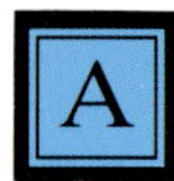

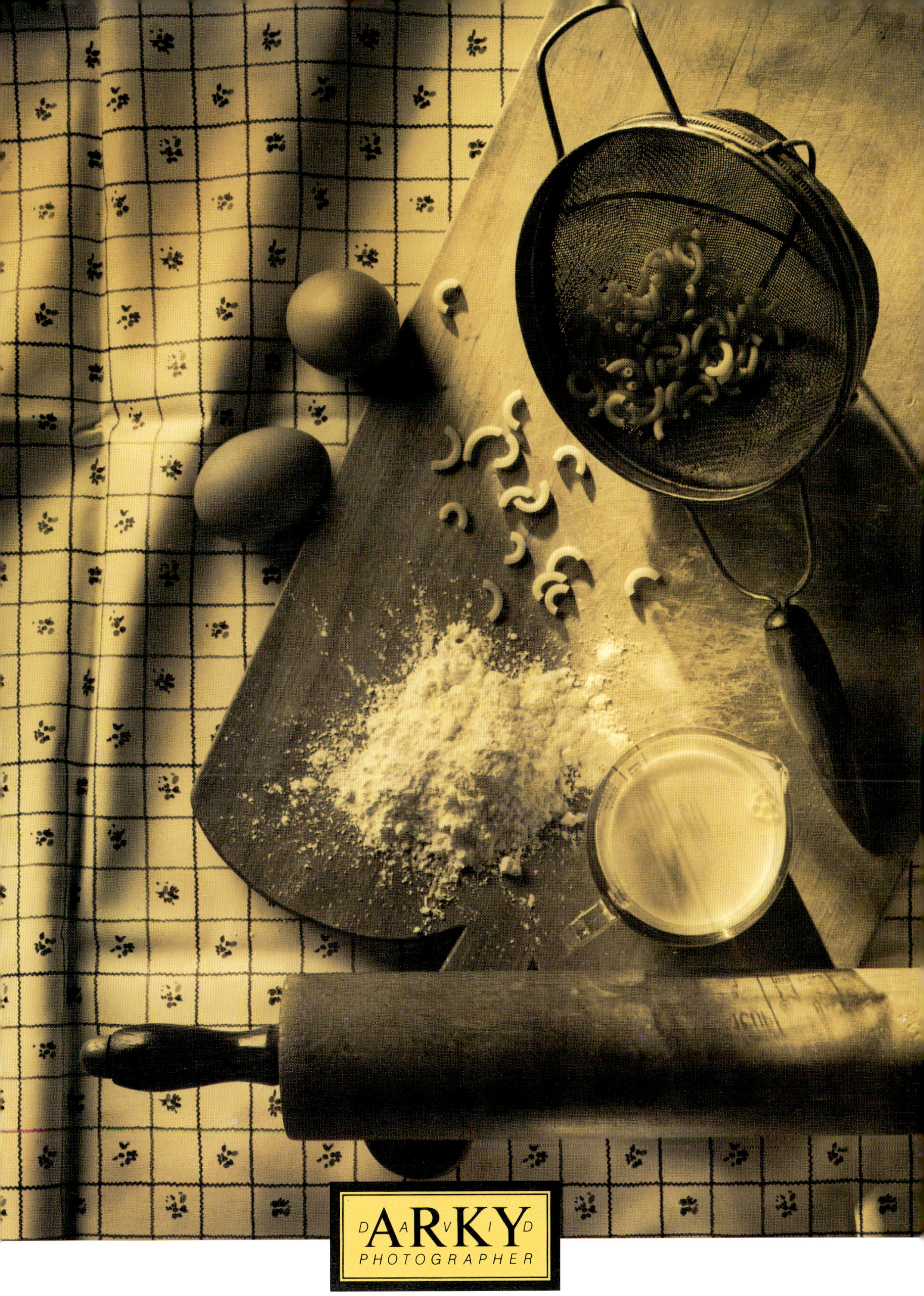
DAVID
ARKY
PHOTOGRAPHER
(212) 242-4760

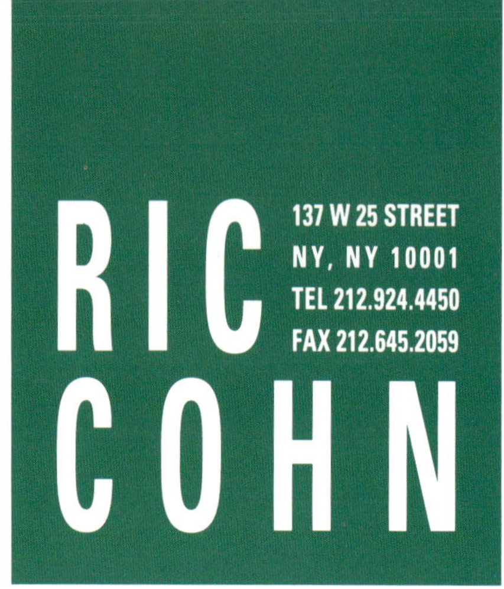


**CALL CAROL FOR PORTFOLIO OR TV REEL**

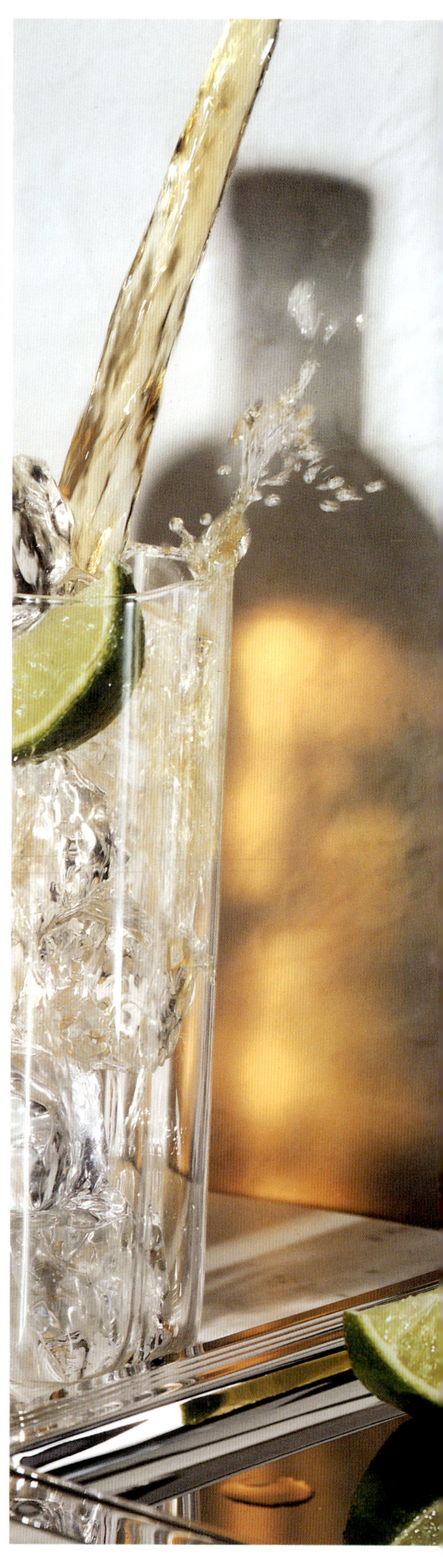

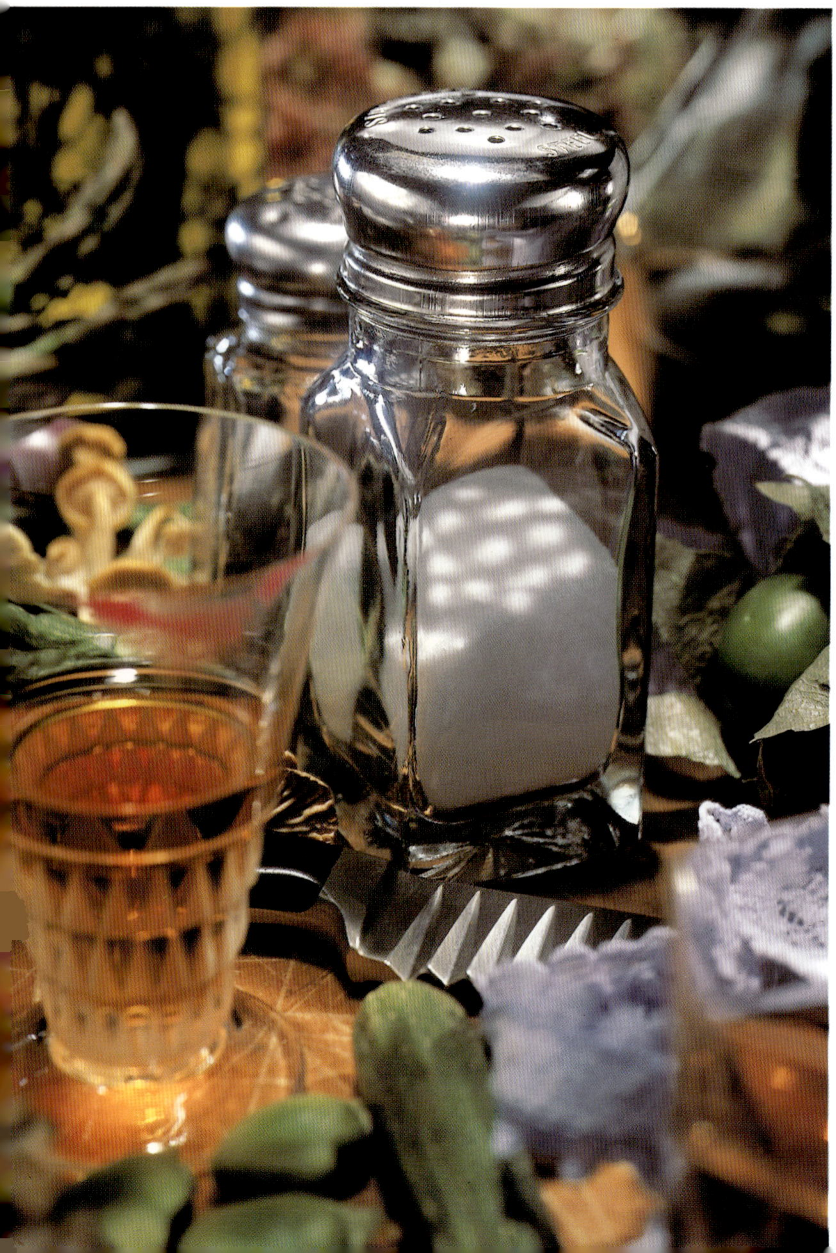

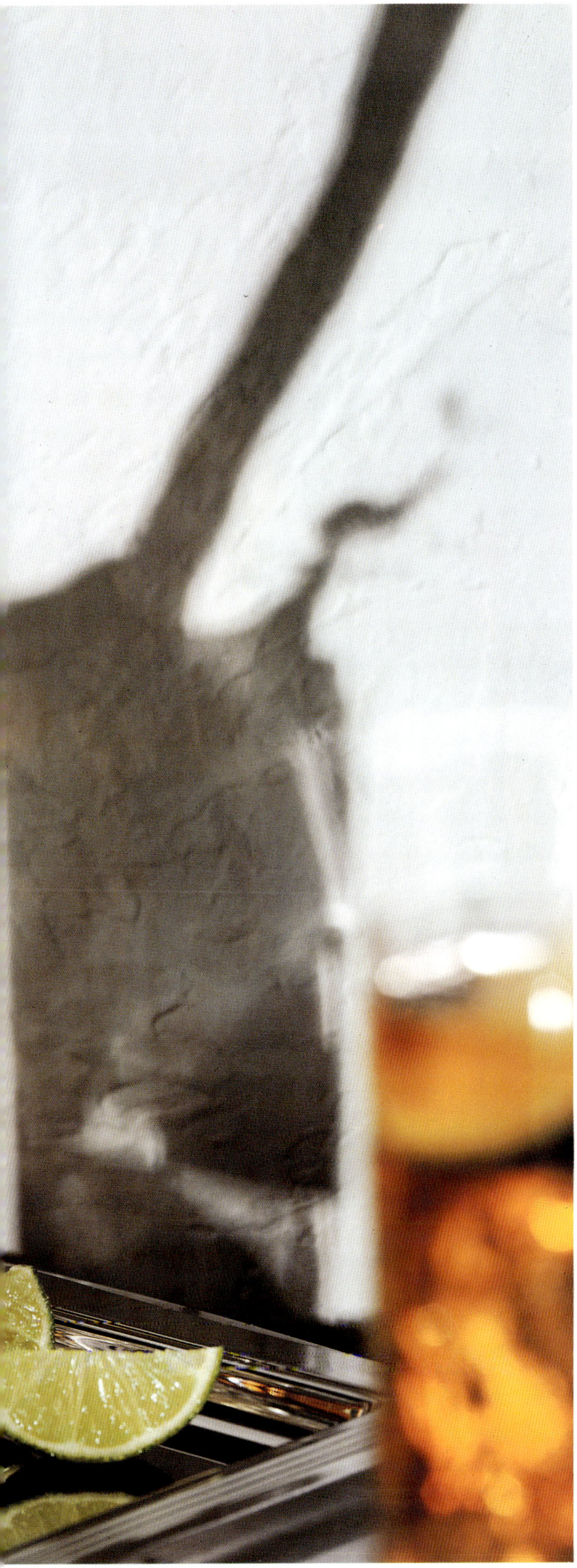

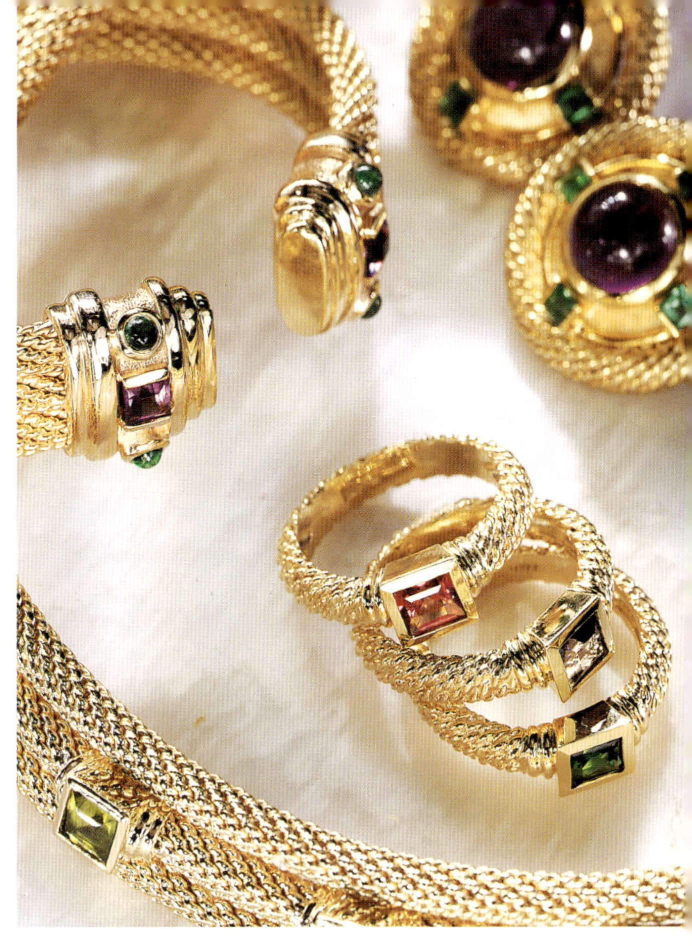

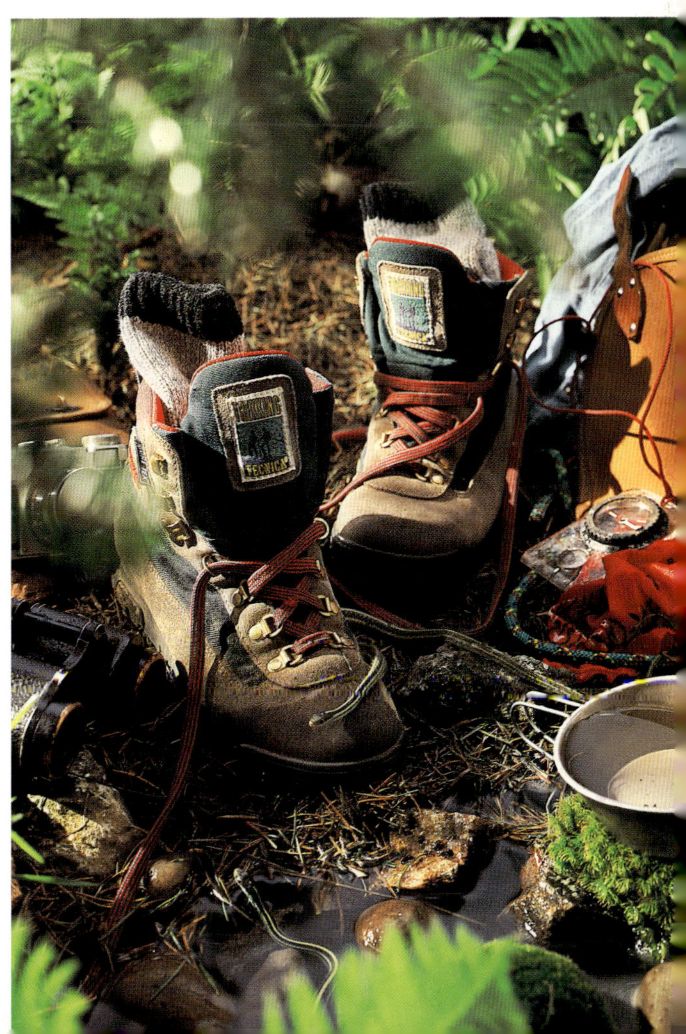

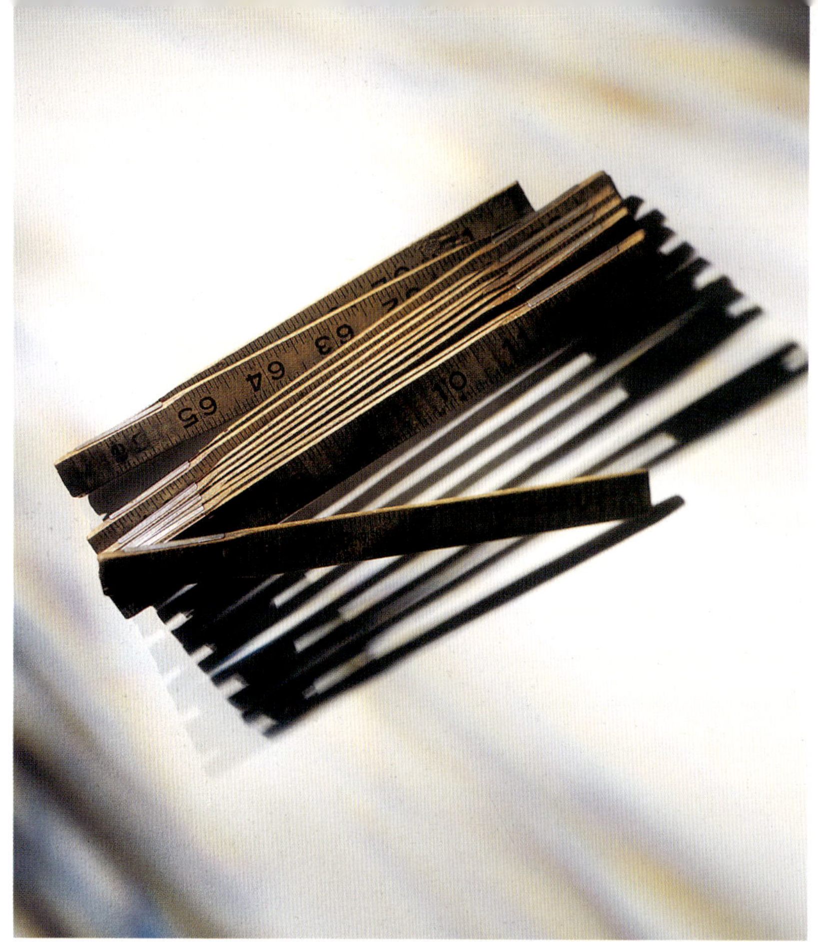

# DAVID BISHOP

*251 West 19th Street, New York 10011 212/929/4355*
*Represented by Korman & Company 212/633/8407*

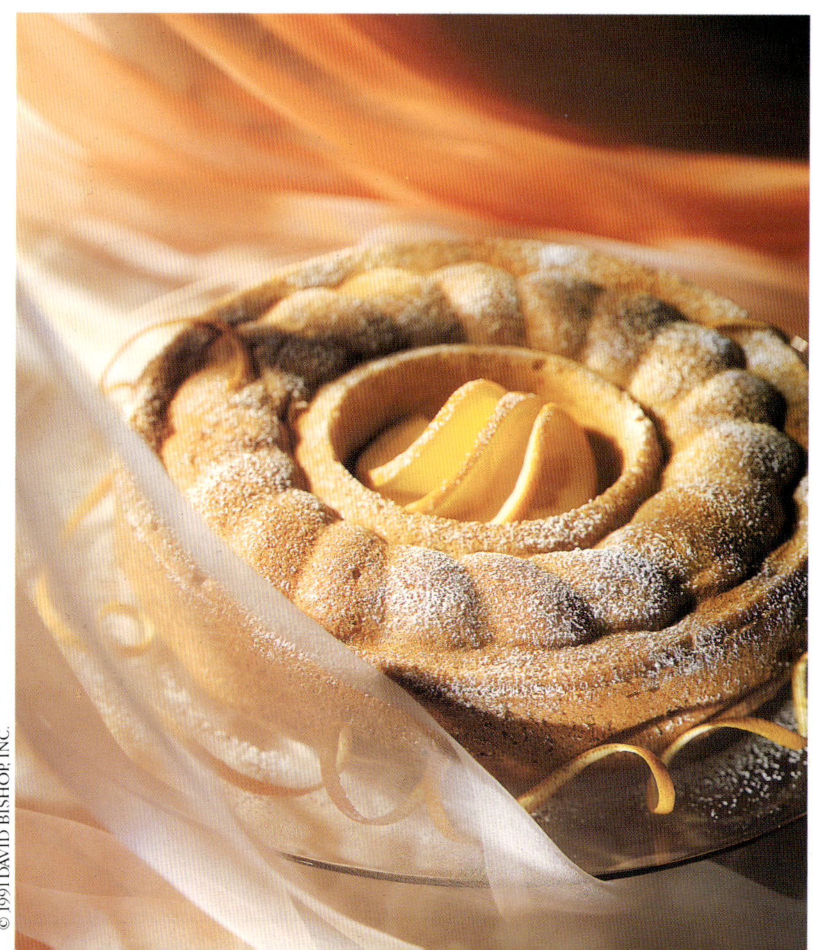

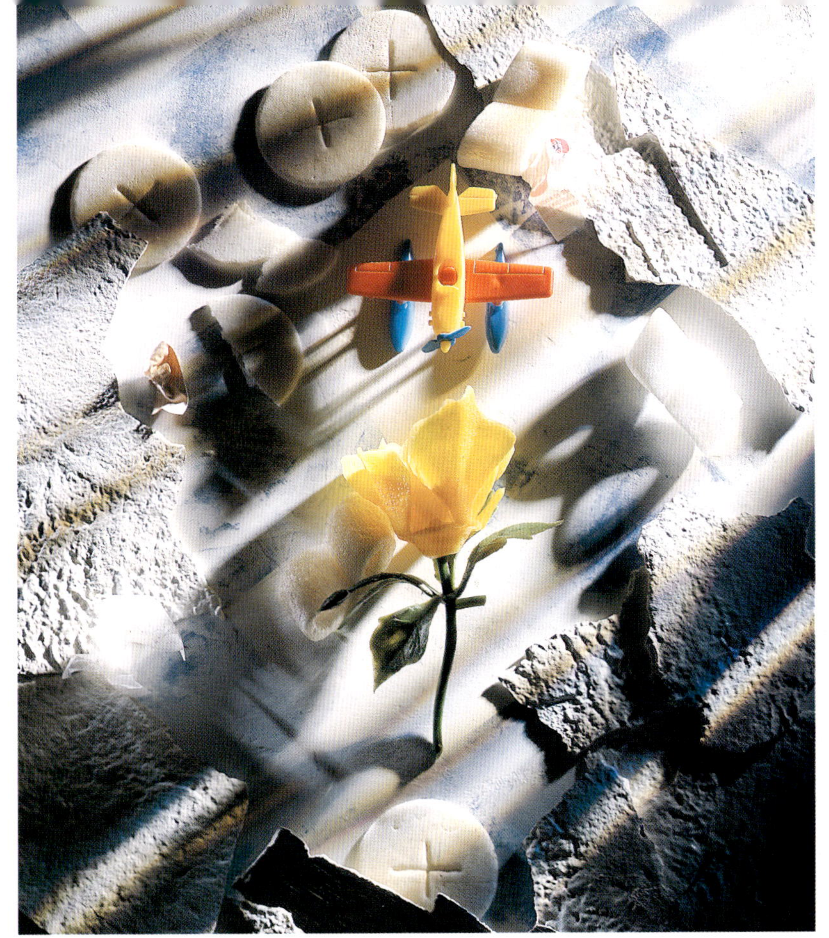

# DAVID BISHOP

*251 West 19th Street, New York 10011 212/929/4355*
*Represented by Korman & Company 212/633/8407*

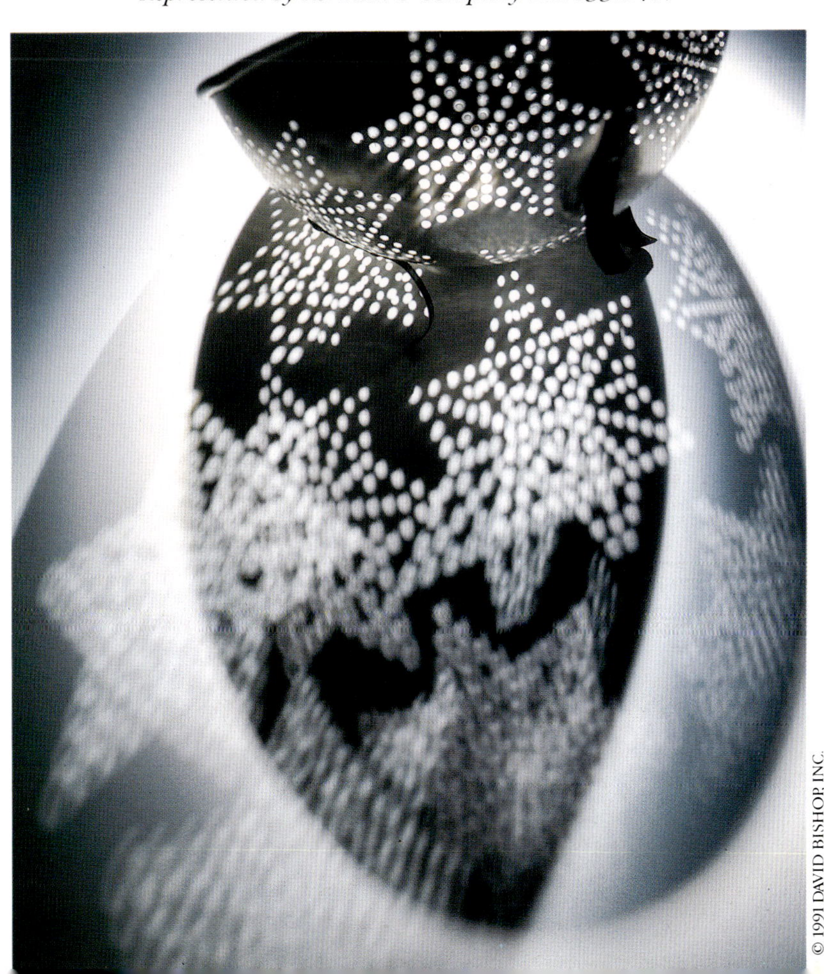

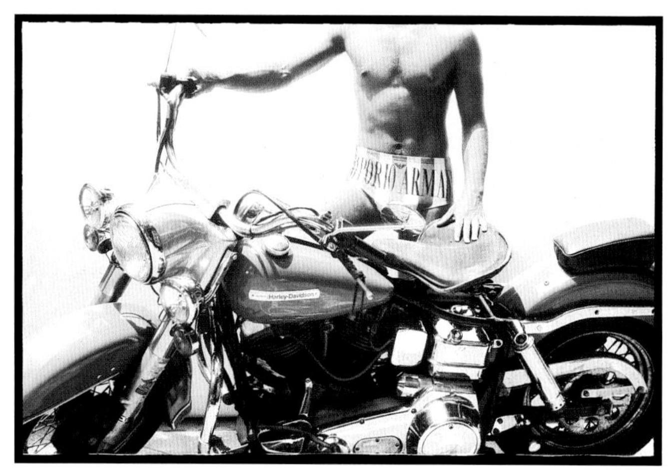

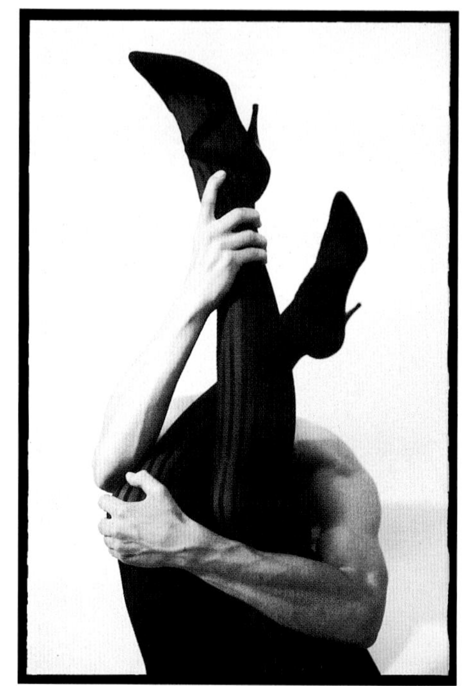

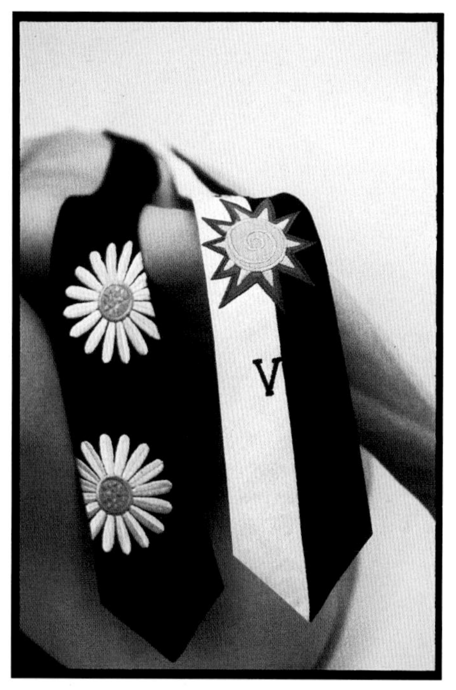

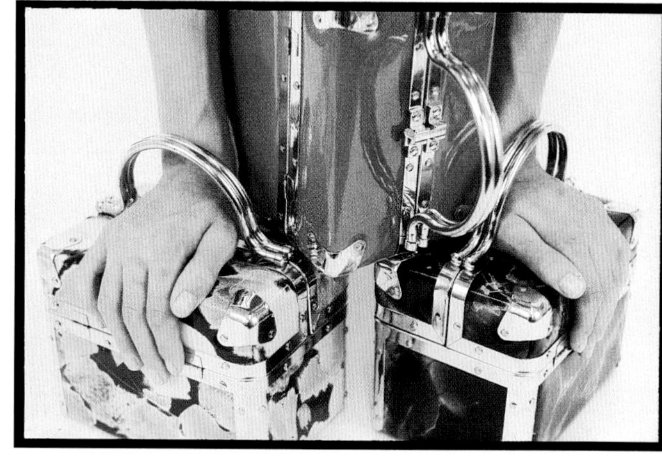

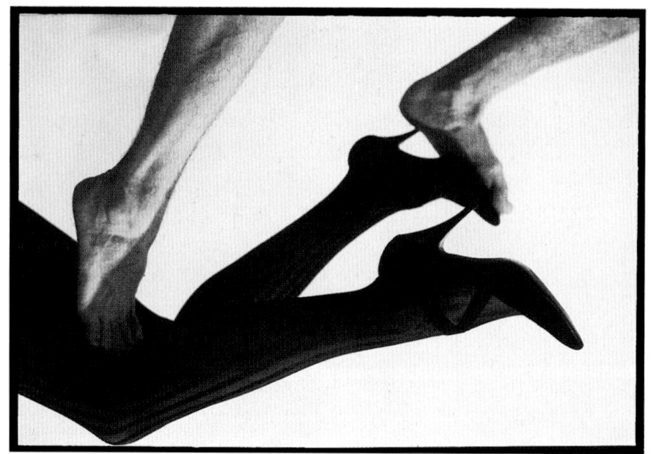

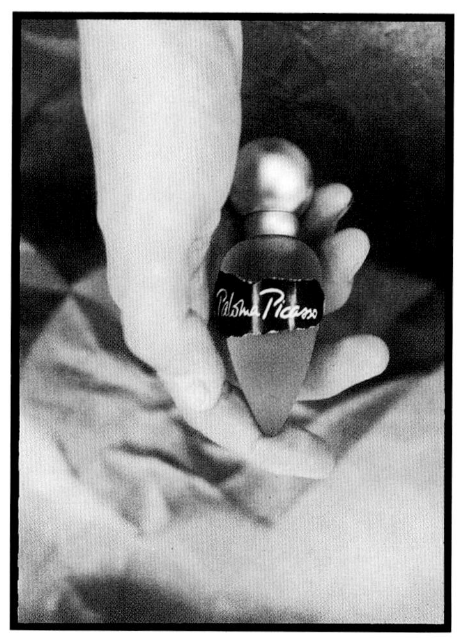

# CHRISTINA LESSA

2 1 2 . 9 7 9 . 0 3 7 3

JUNG LEE

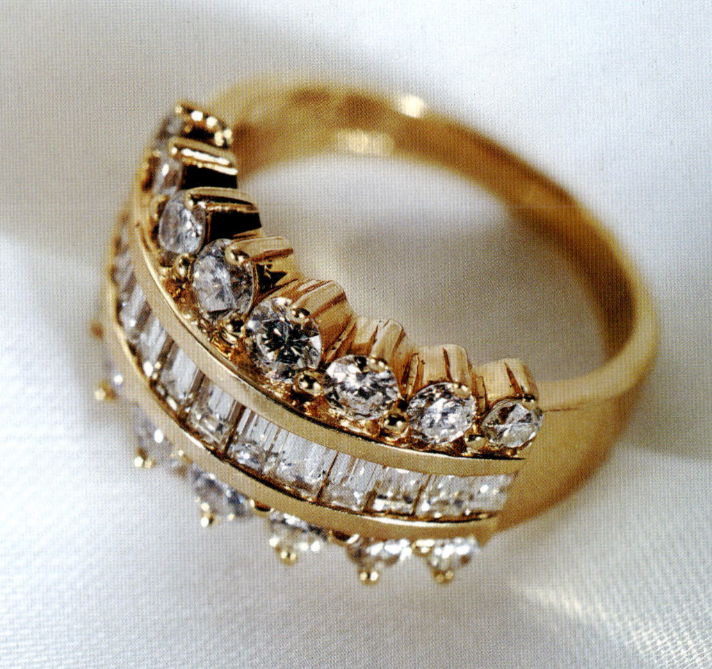

147  W.  25TH  ST.  N.Y.C.  10001•212-807-8107 FAX:  212-807-8142

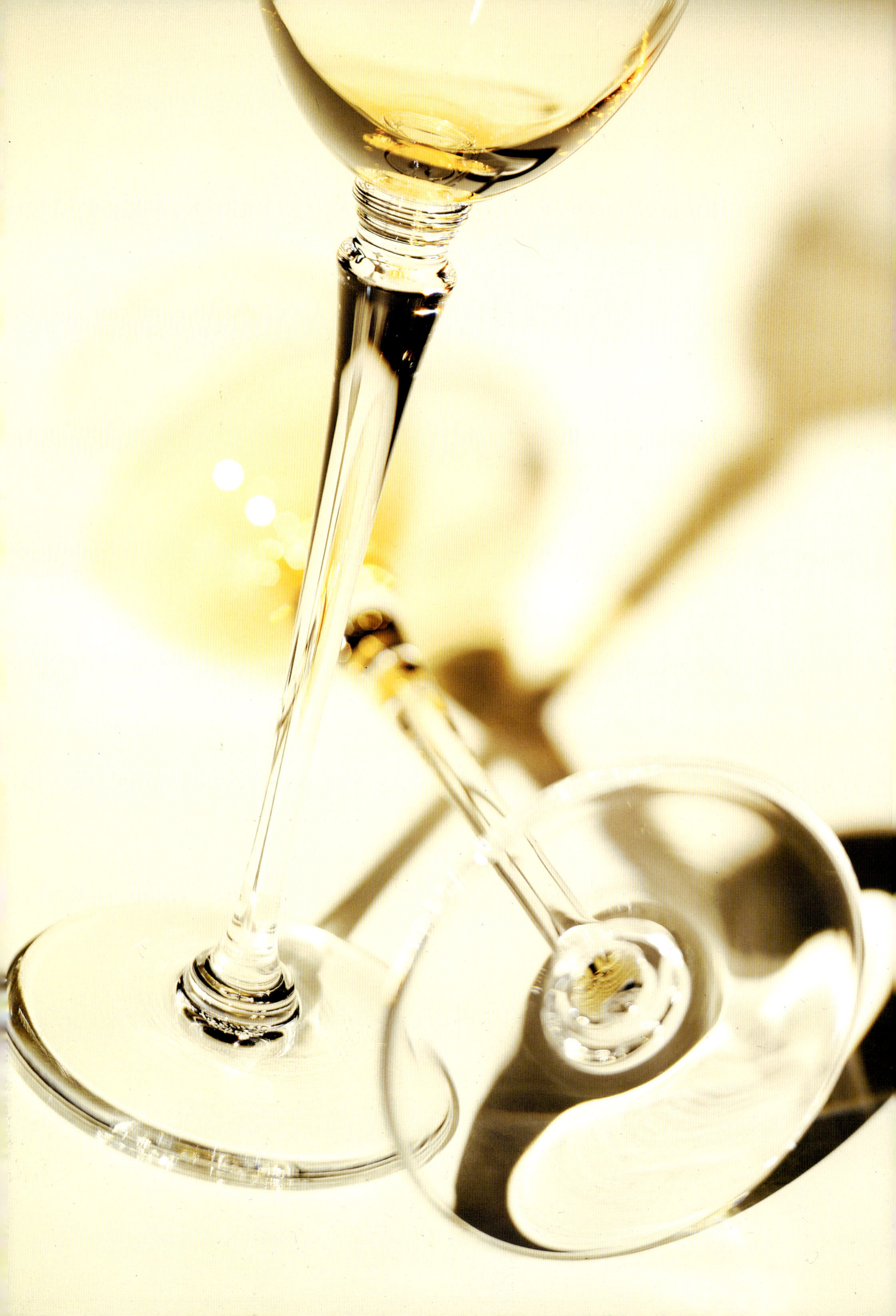

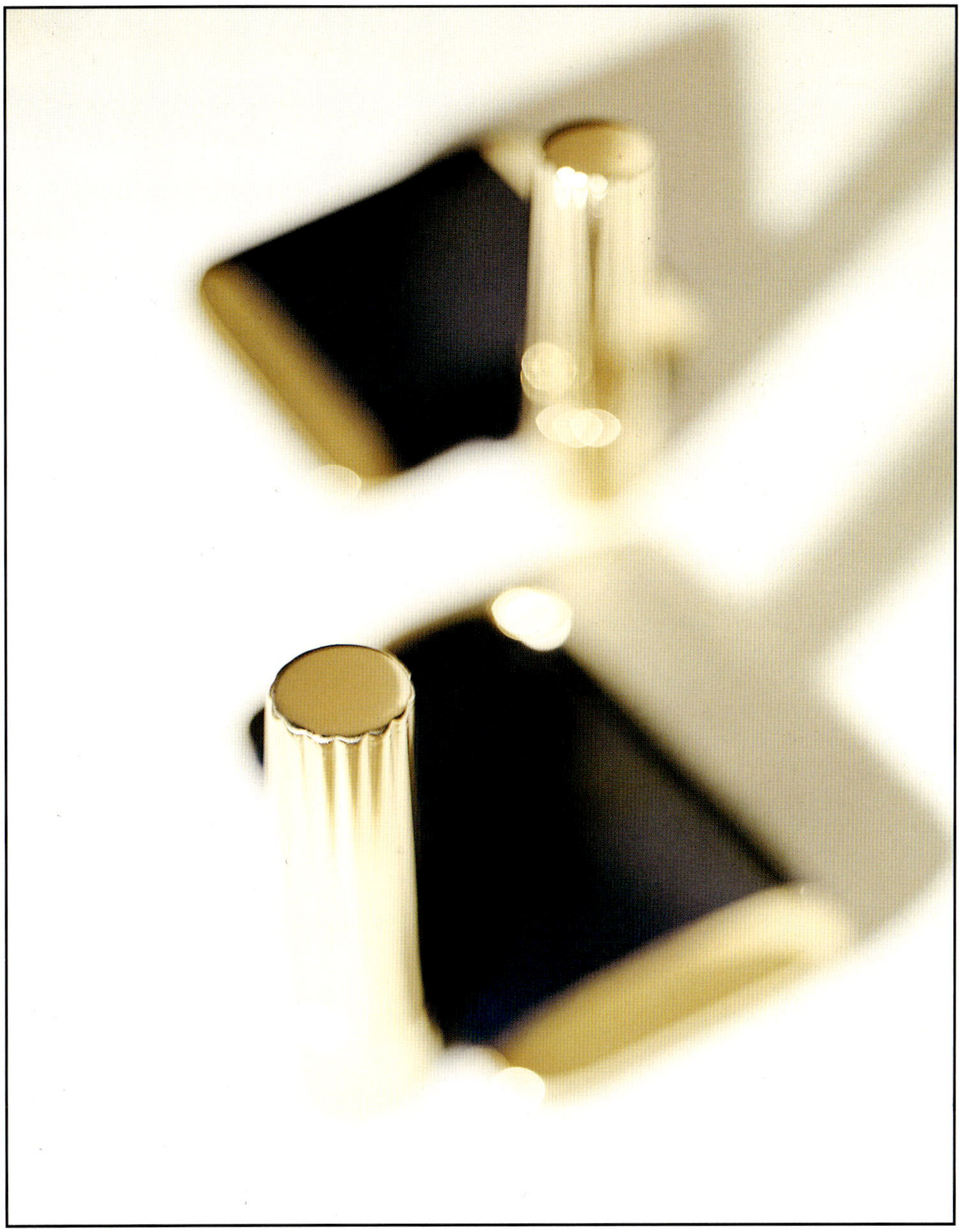

# ▪ R O B E R T   T A R D I O ▪

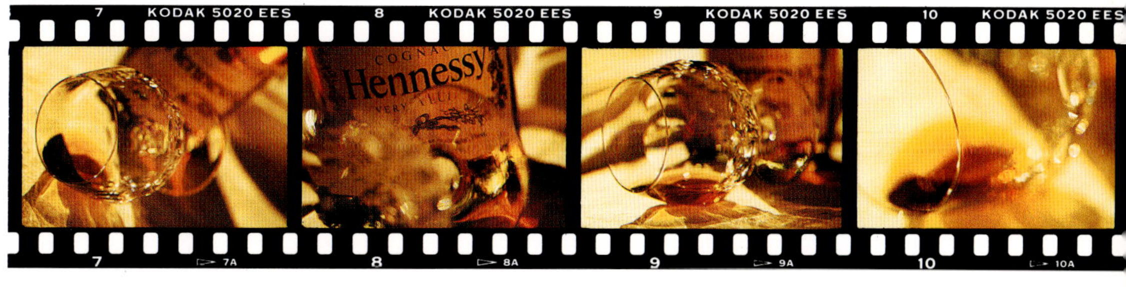

*Represented by Colleen McKay  212·598·0469*
*Studio: 212·463·9085*

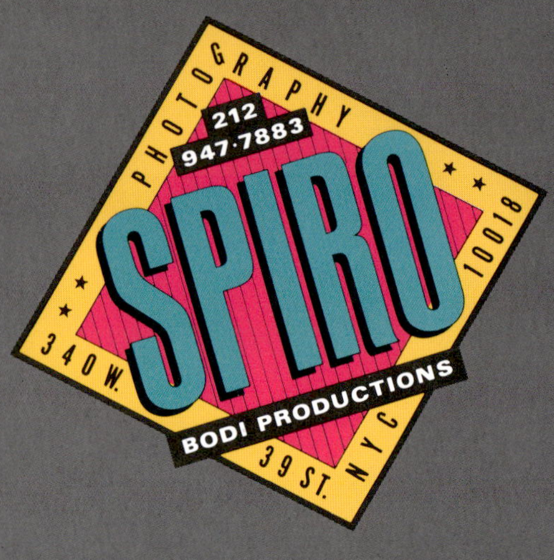


Going Fishing…

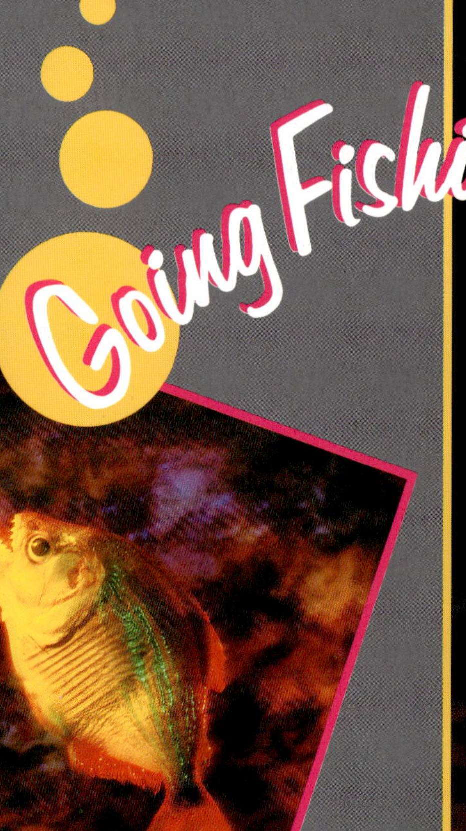

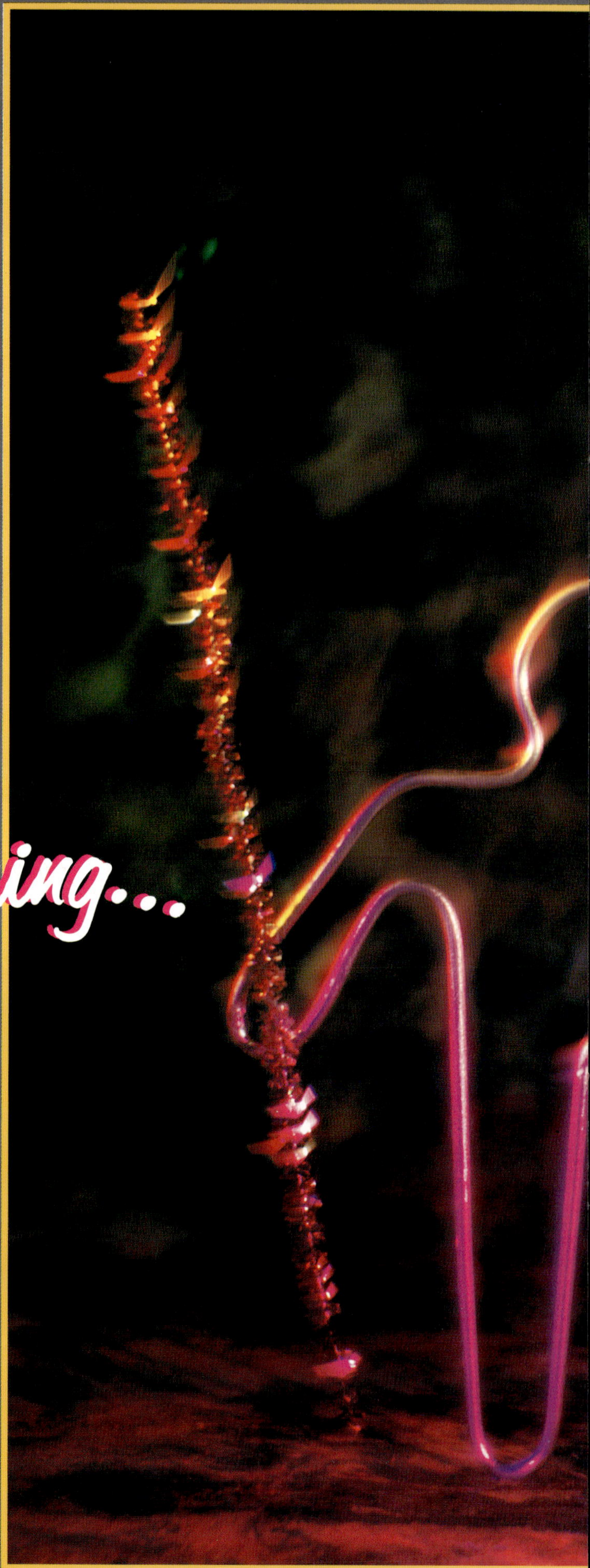

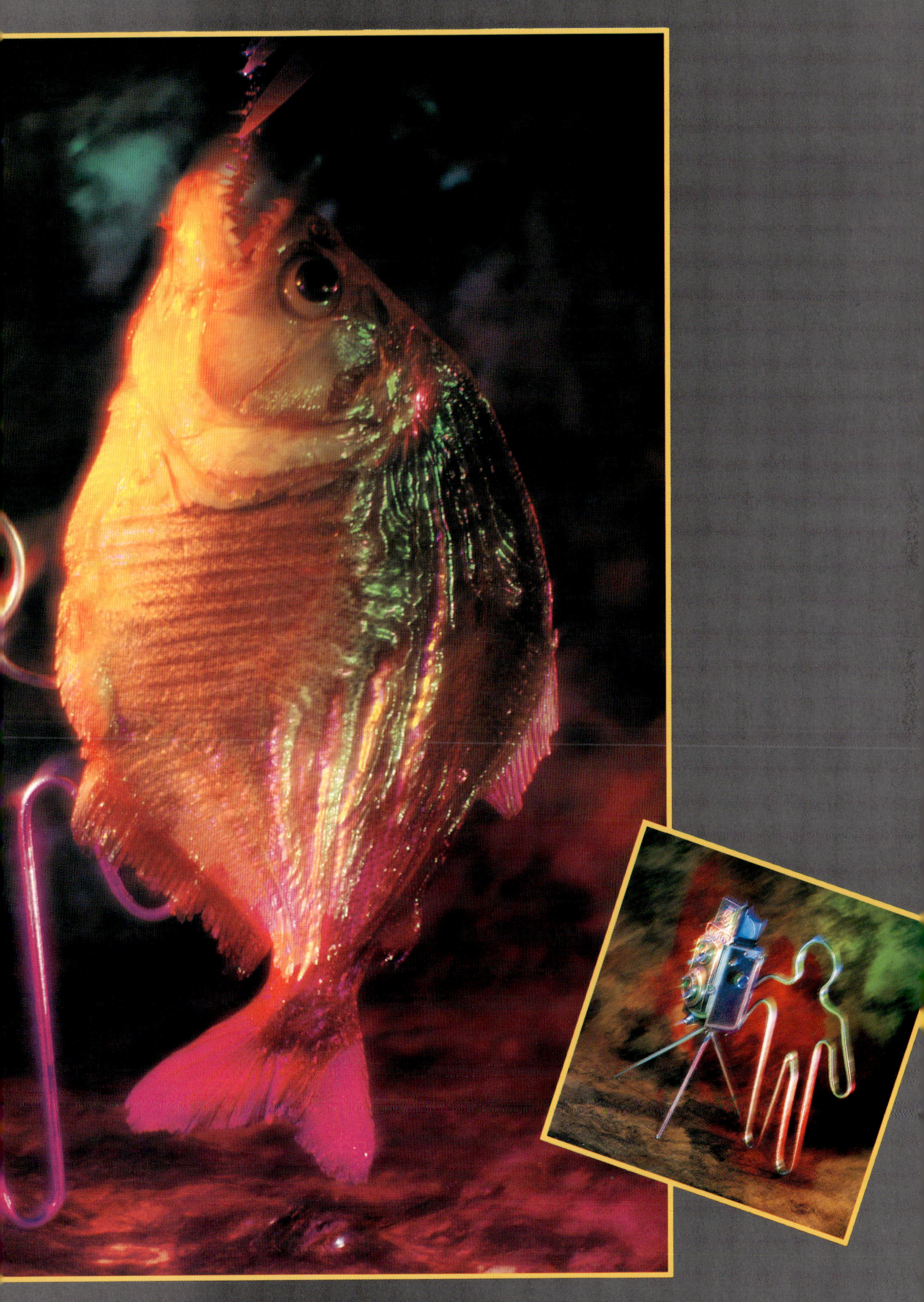

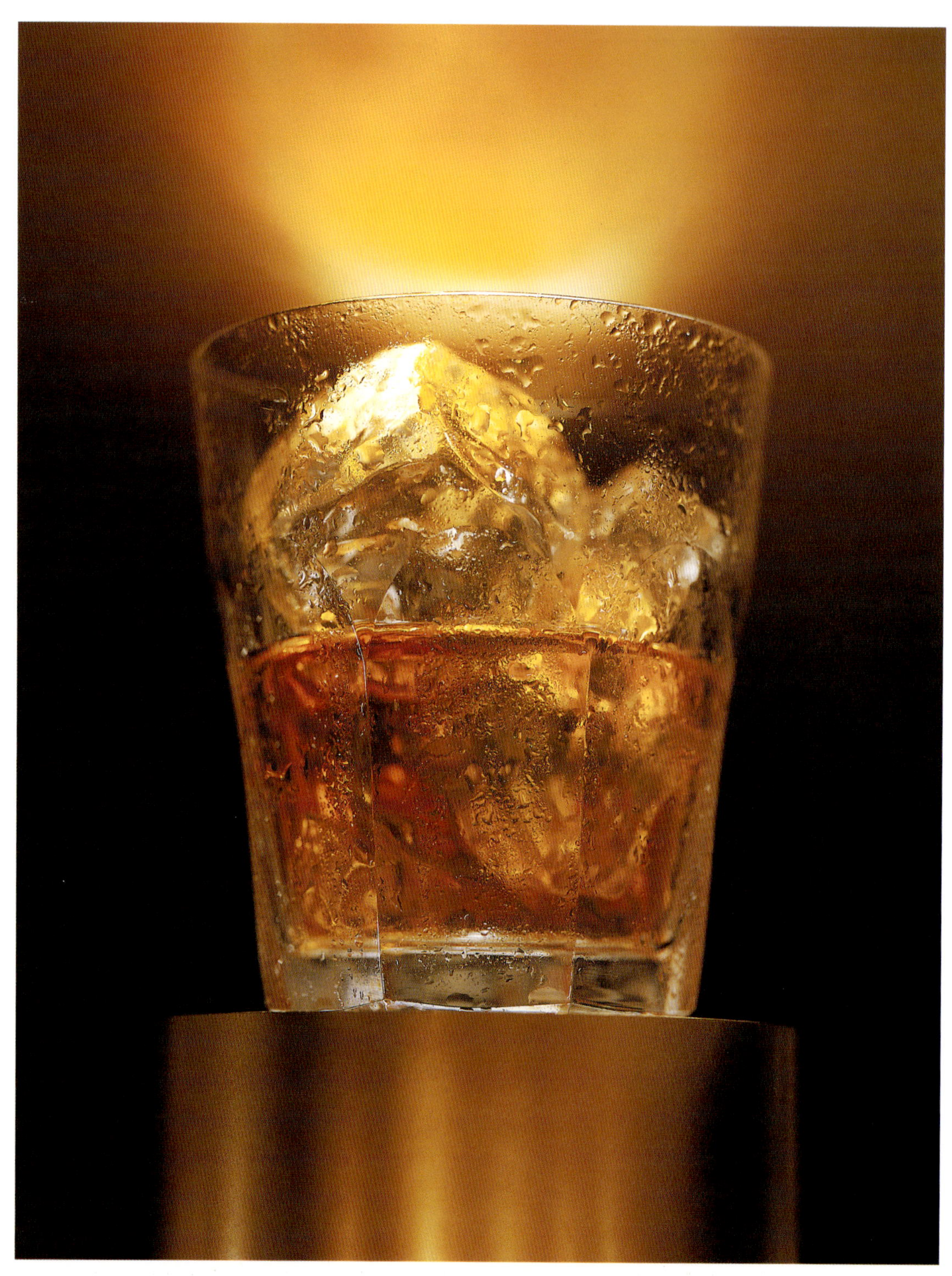

# C O U Z E N S

LARRY COUZENS PHOTOGRAPHY (212) 620 9790
16 EAST 17TH ST. NEW YORK N.Y. 10003

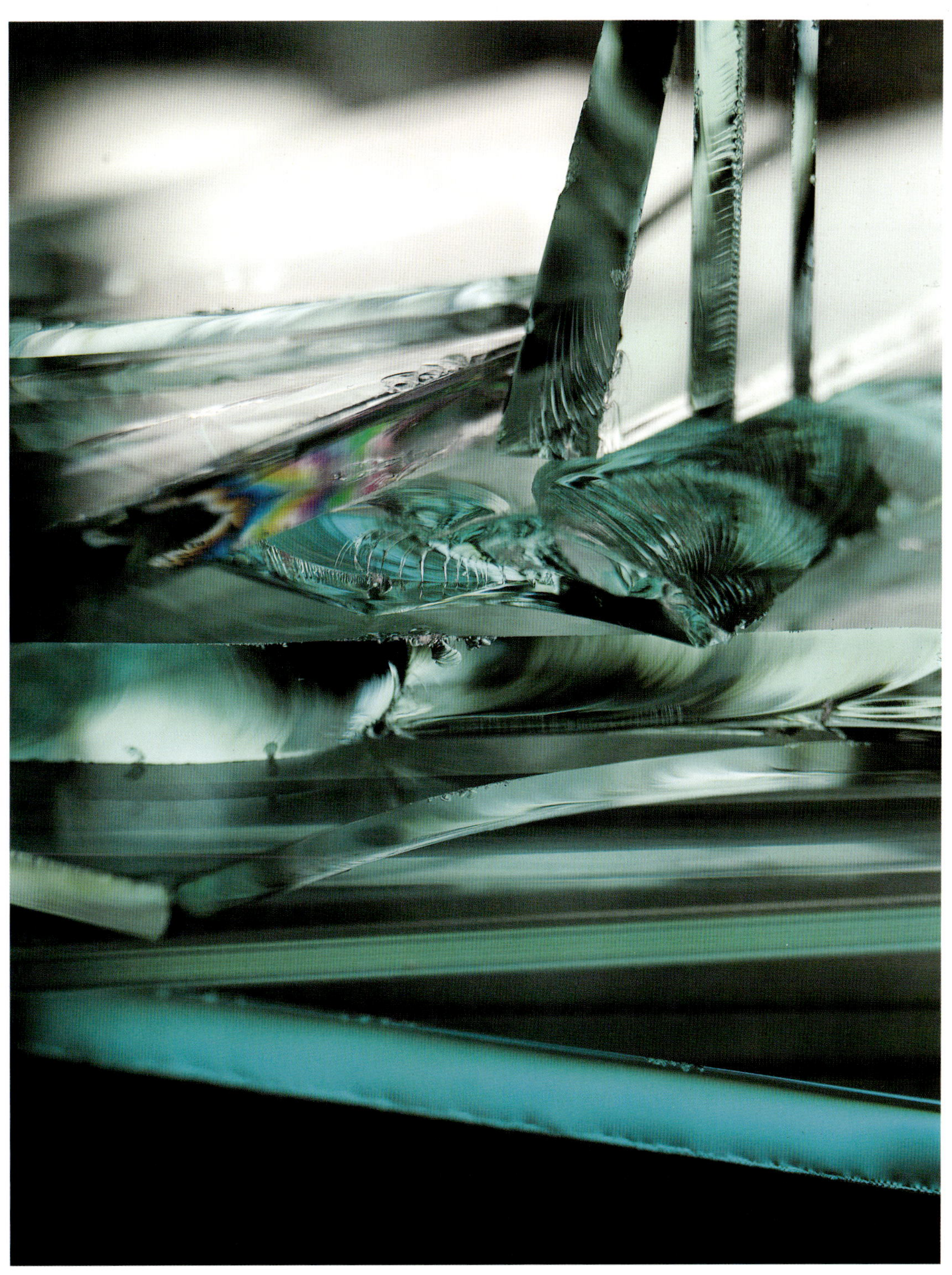

# C O U Z E N S

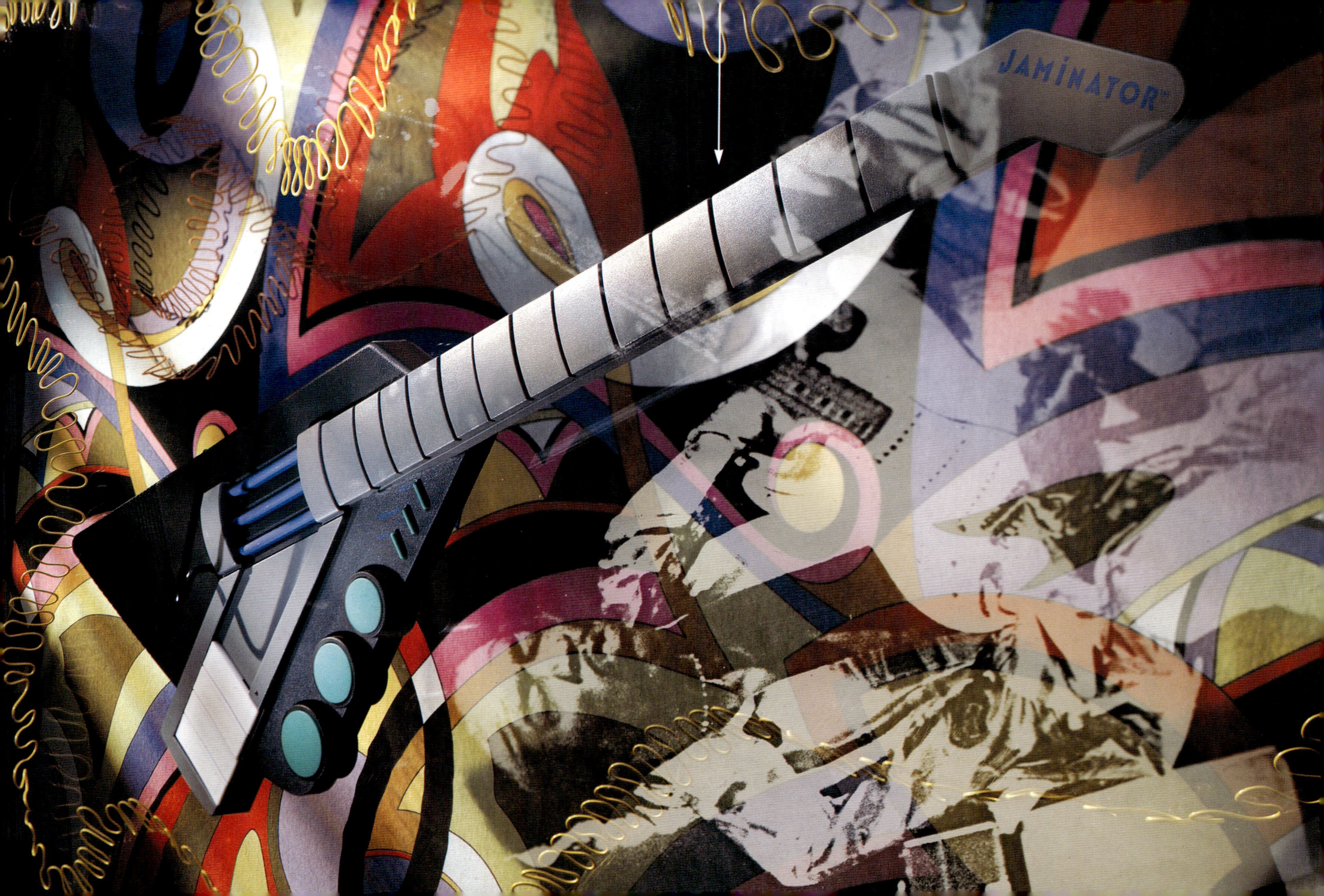
JAMINATOR™

# GALANTE

**DENNIS GALANTE** STUDIO: 133 WEST 22ND ST., N.Y.C. 10011  PHONE: **212-463-0938**   FAX: **212-463-0943**

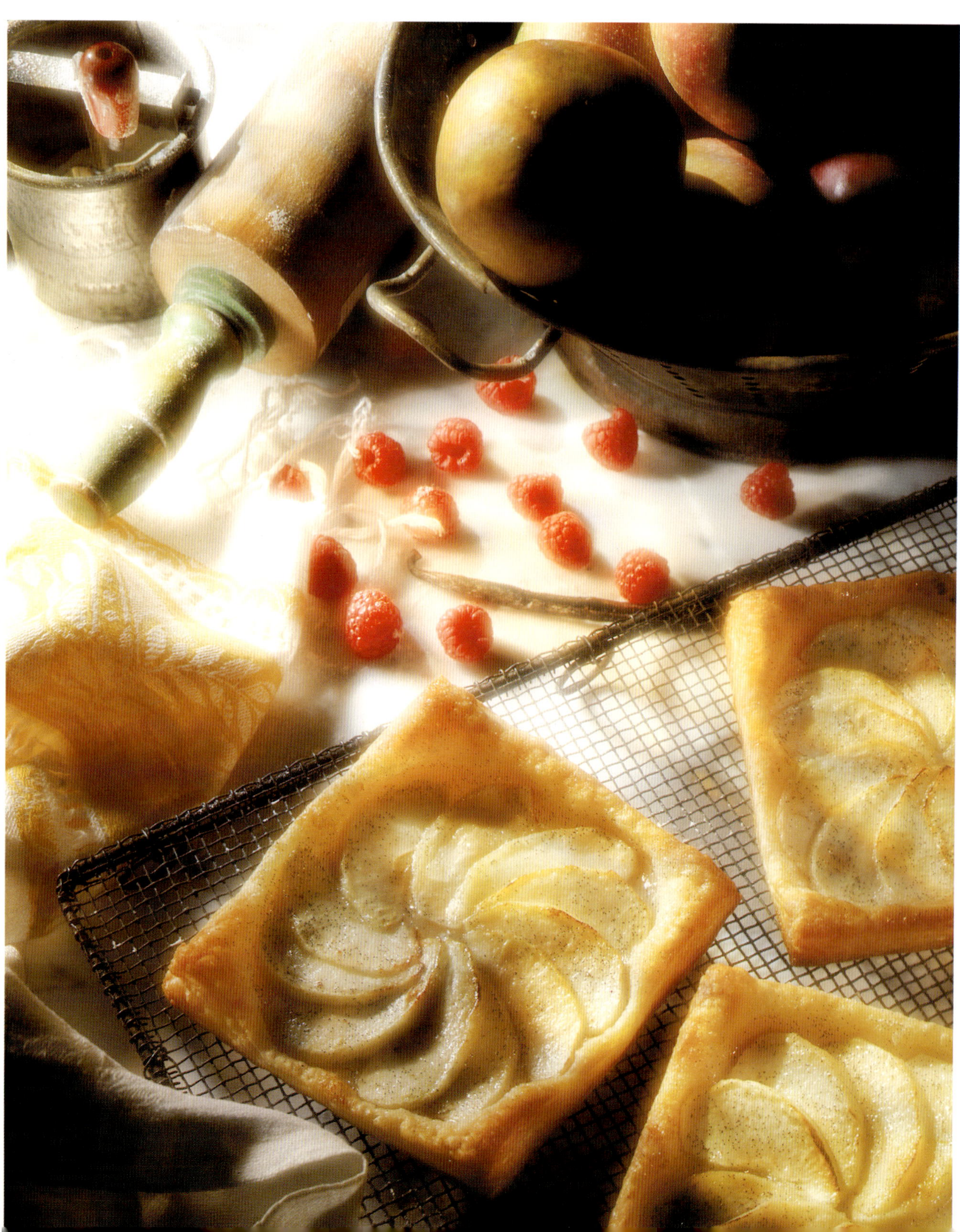

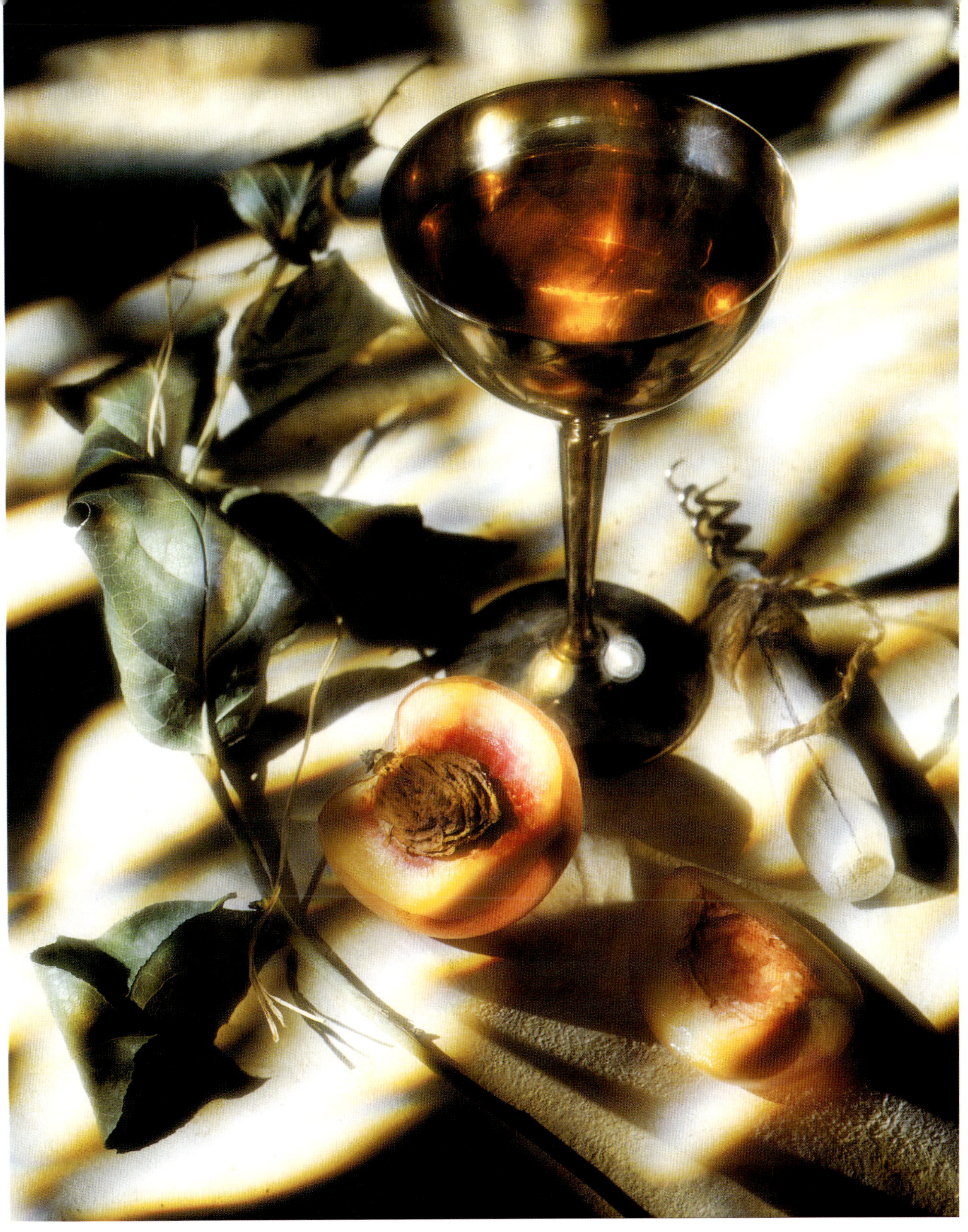


GALANTE

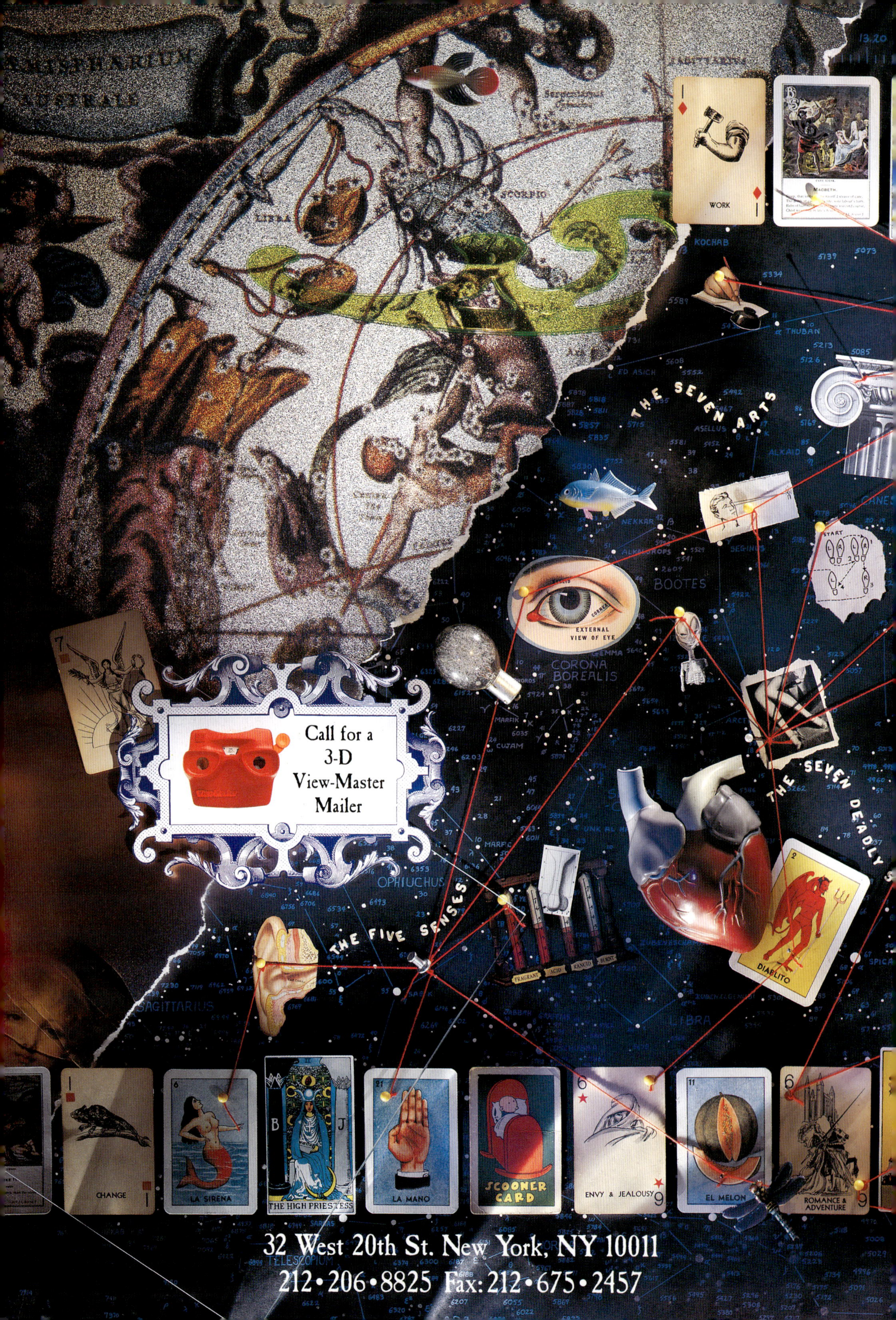
WORK
MACBETH
Call for a
3-D
View-Master
Mailer
THE SEVEN ARTS
THE SEVEN DEADLY S
THE FIVE SENSES
EXTERNAL
VIEW OF EYE
CORONA
BOREALIS
BOOTES
START
OPHIUCHUS
SCORPIO
LIBRA
SAGITTARIUS
DIABLITO
FRAGRANT ACID RANCID BURNT
CHANGE
LA SIRENA
THE HIGH PRIESTESS
LA MANO
SCOONER
CARD
ENVY & JEALOUSY
EL MELON
ROMANCE &
ADVENTURE
32 West 20th St. New York, NY 10011
212•206•8825 Fax:212•675•2457

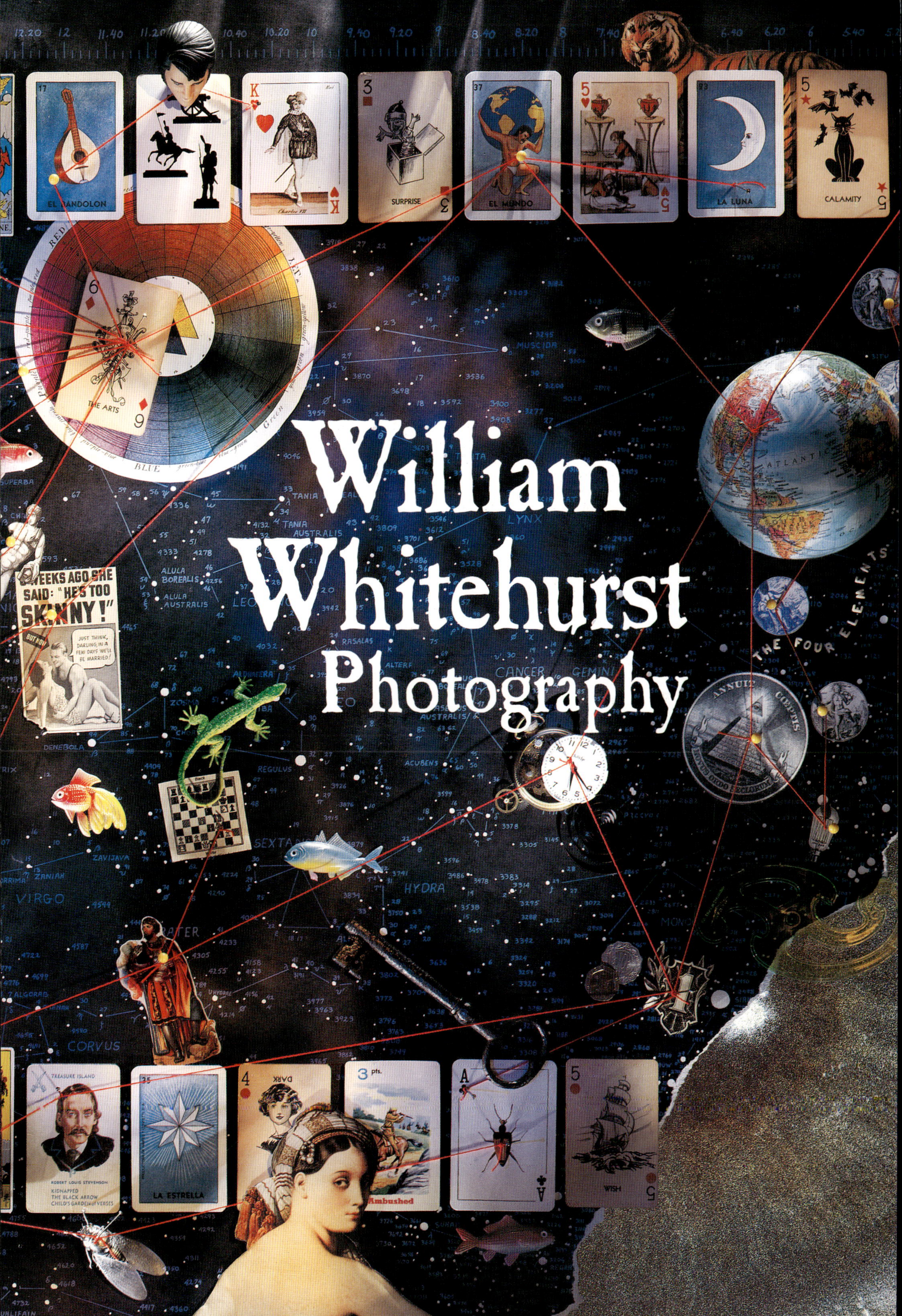

William
Whitehurst
Photography
THE FOUR ELEMENTS

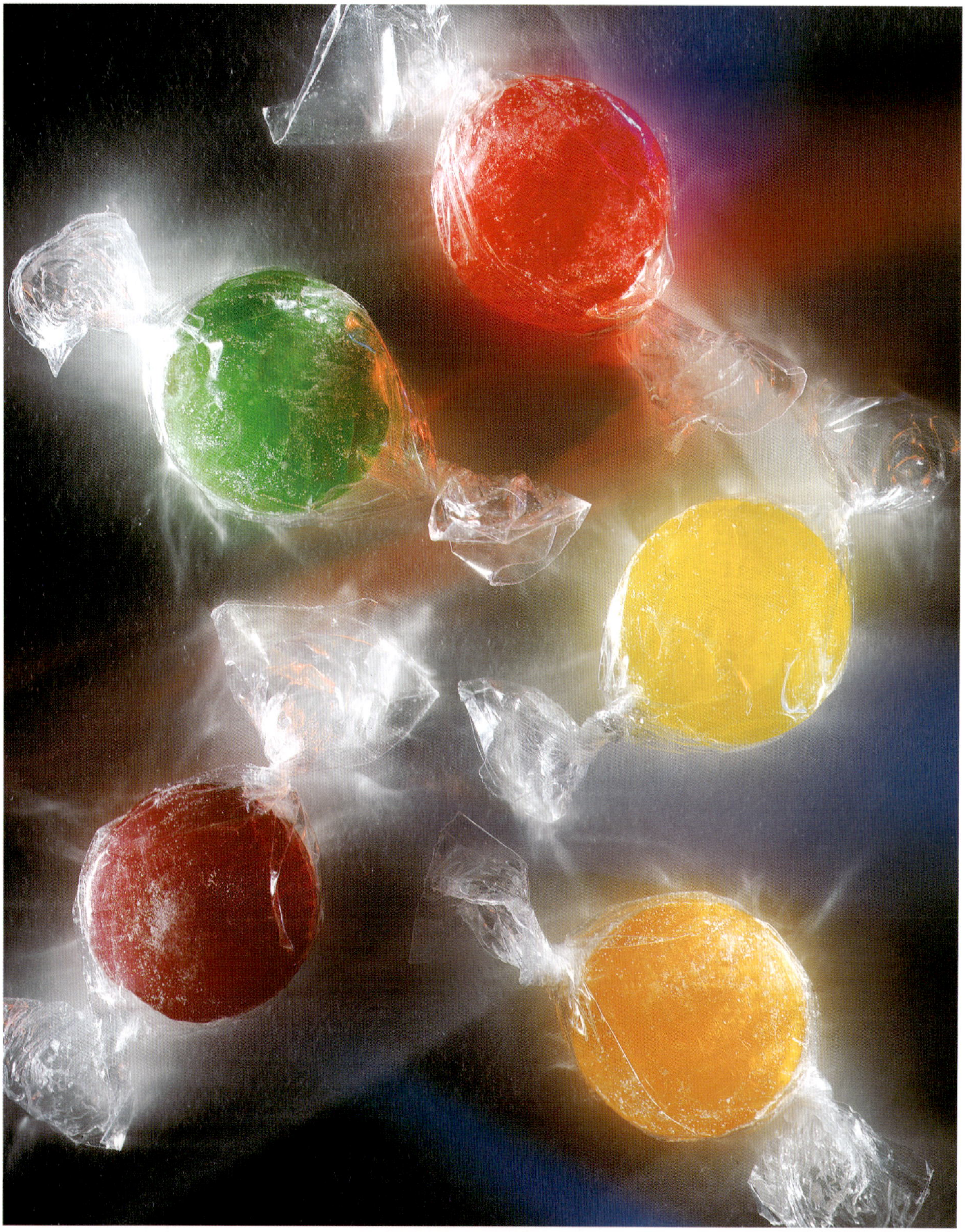

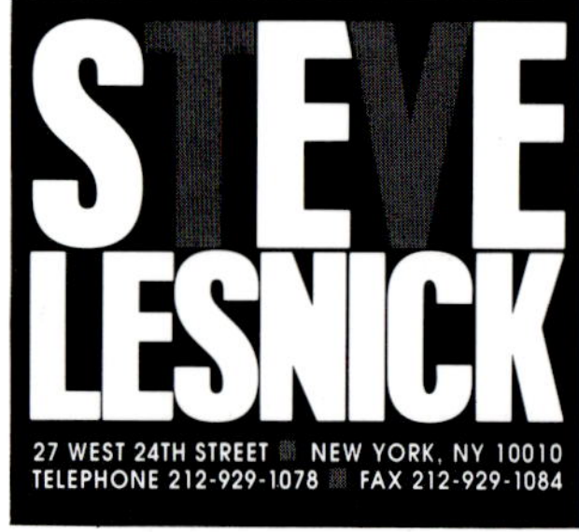

STEVE
LESNICK
27 WEST 24TH STREET ■ NEW YORK, NY 10010
TELEPHONE 212-929-1078 ■ FAX 212-929-1084

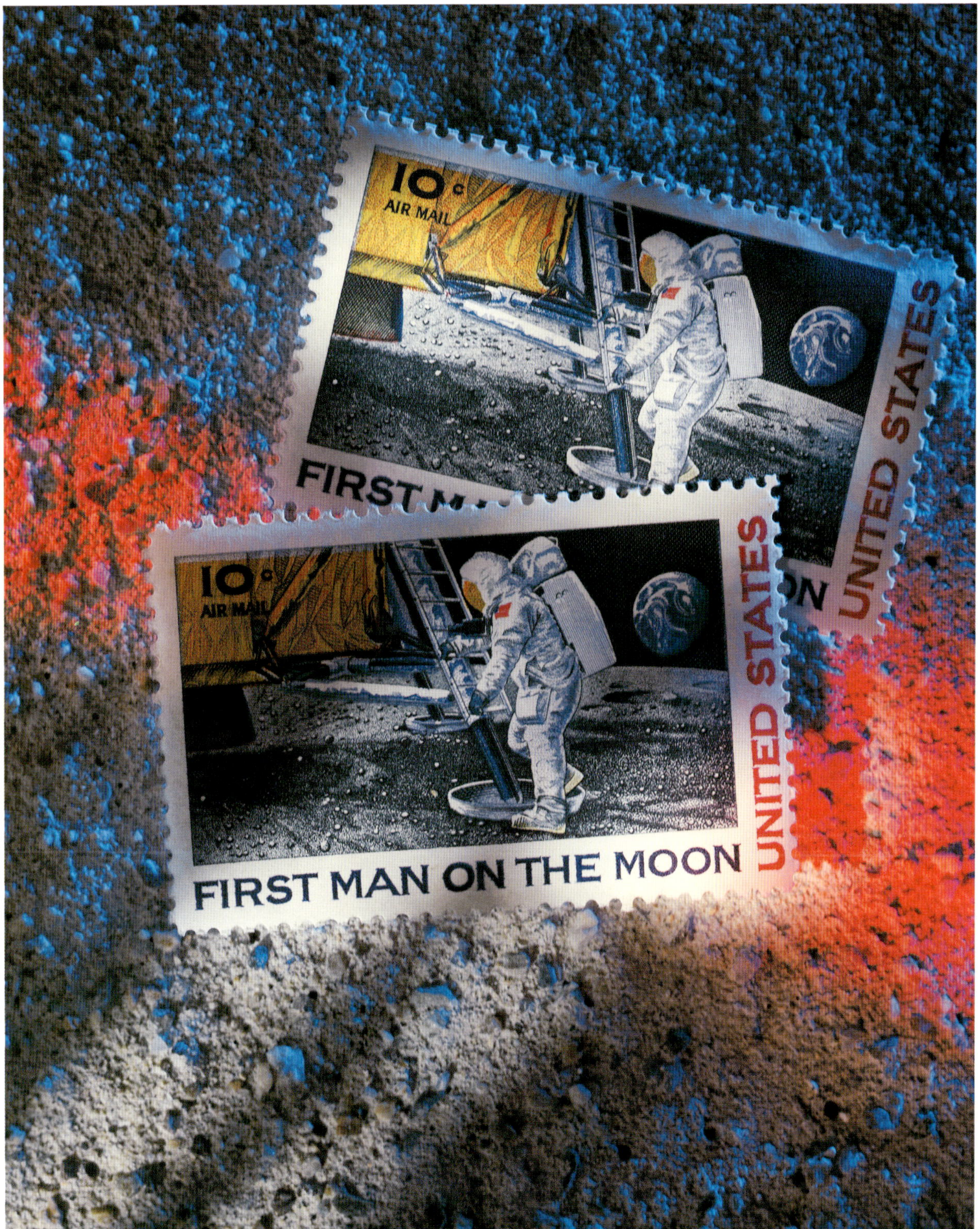

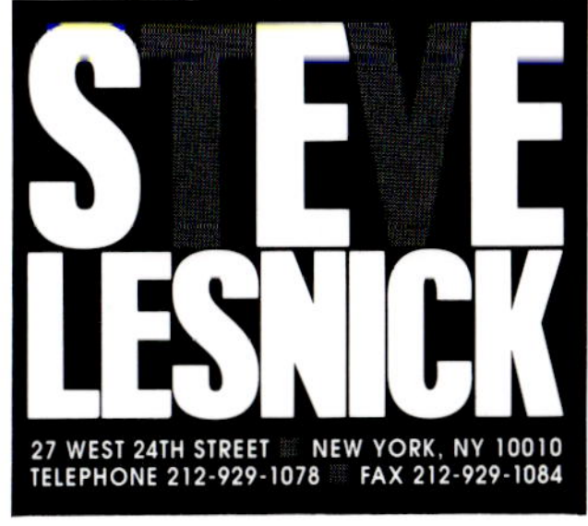
STEVE
LESNICK
27 WEST 24TH STREET   NEW YORK, NY 10010
TELEPHONE 212-929-1078   FAX 212-929-1084

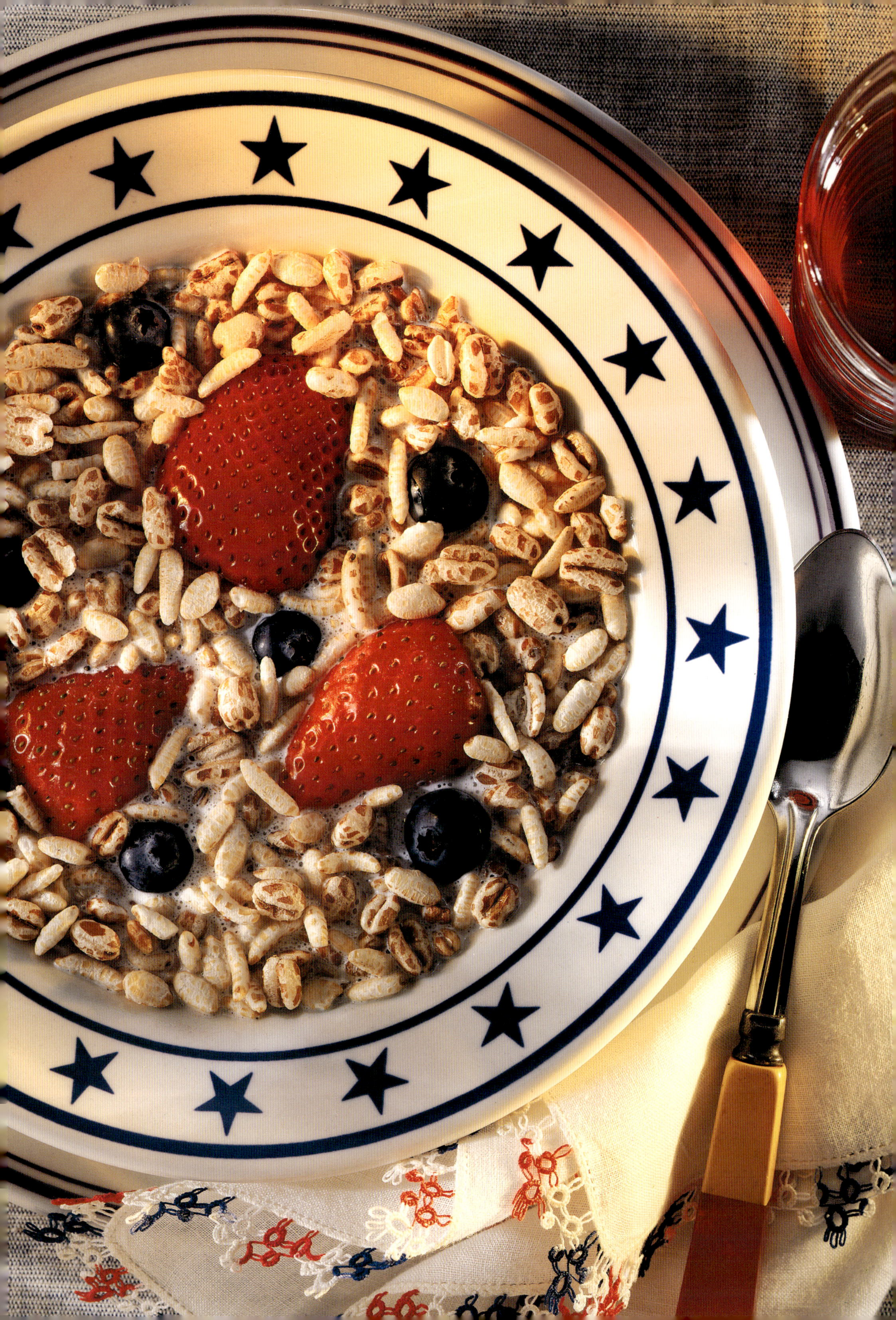

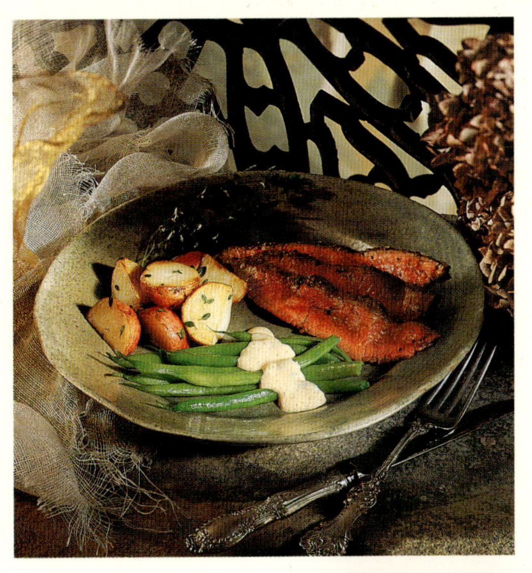

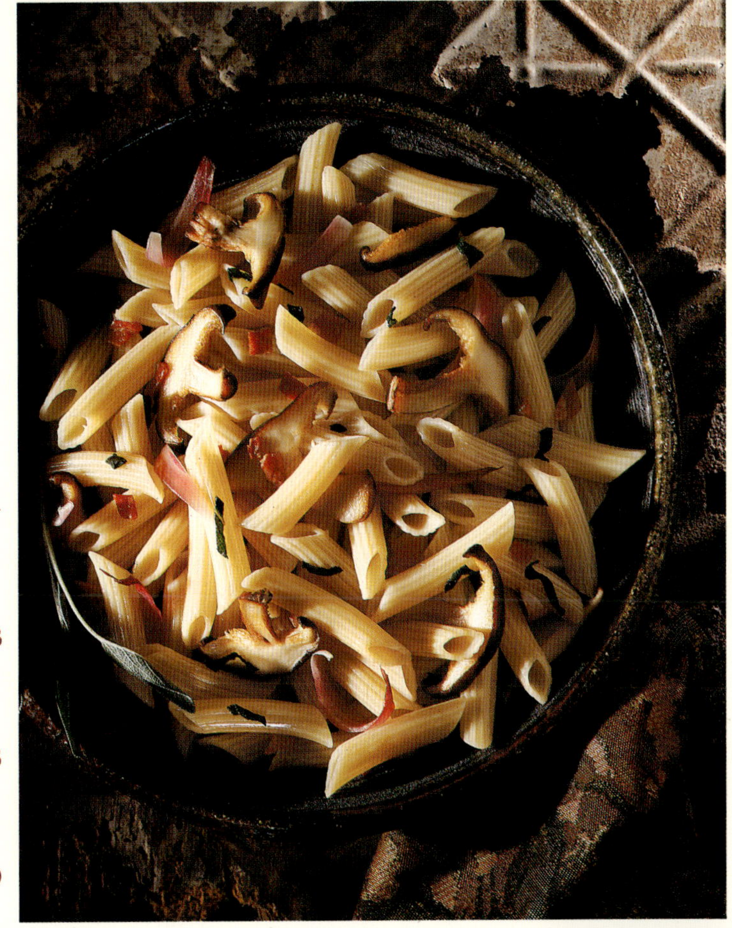

12 EAST 18TH STREET

NEW YORK, N.Y. 10003

TEL. 212·807·8028

FAX 212·366·9519

REPRESENTED BY

DARIO SACRAMONE

TEL. 212·929·0487

FAX 212·242·4429

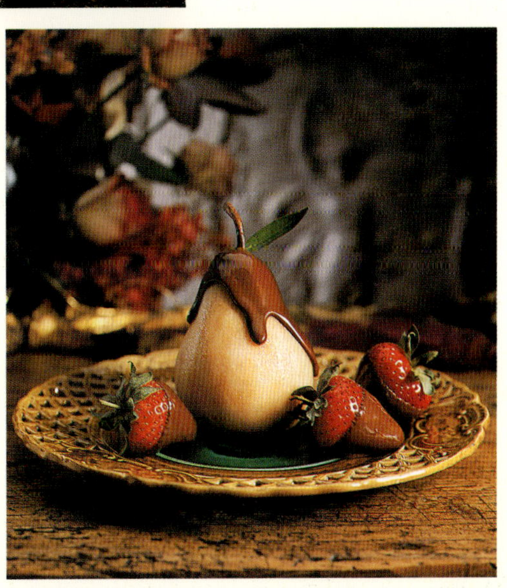

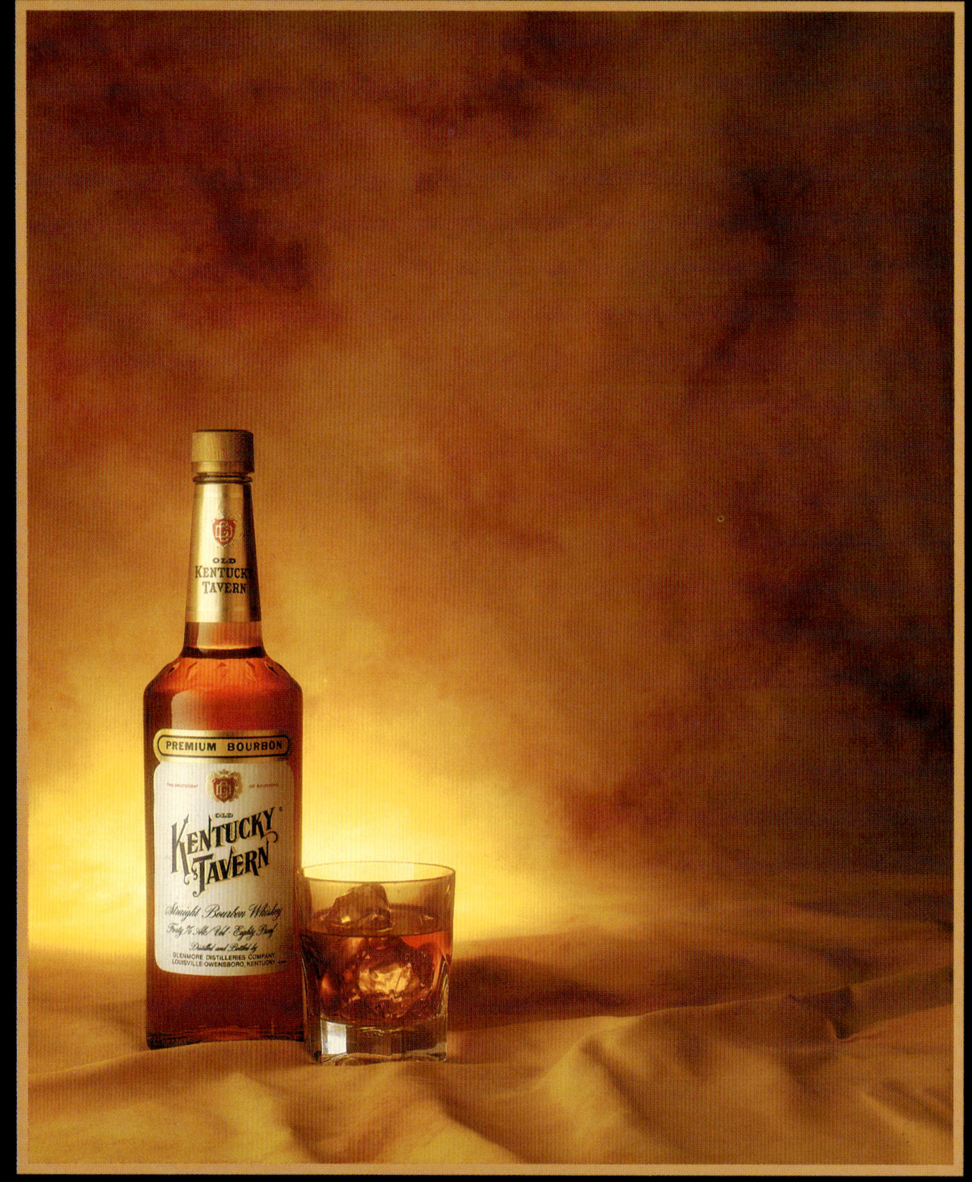


M b I i L N E

BILL MILNE PHOTOGRAPHY  140 WEST 22ND STREET, NEW YORK, NY 10011  TELEPHONE 212·255·0710

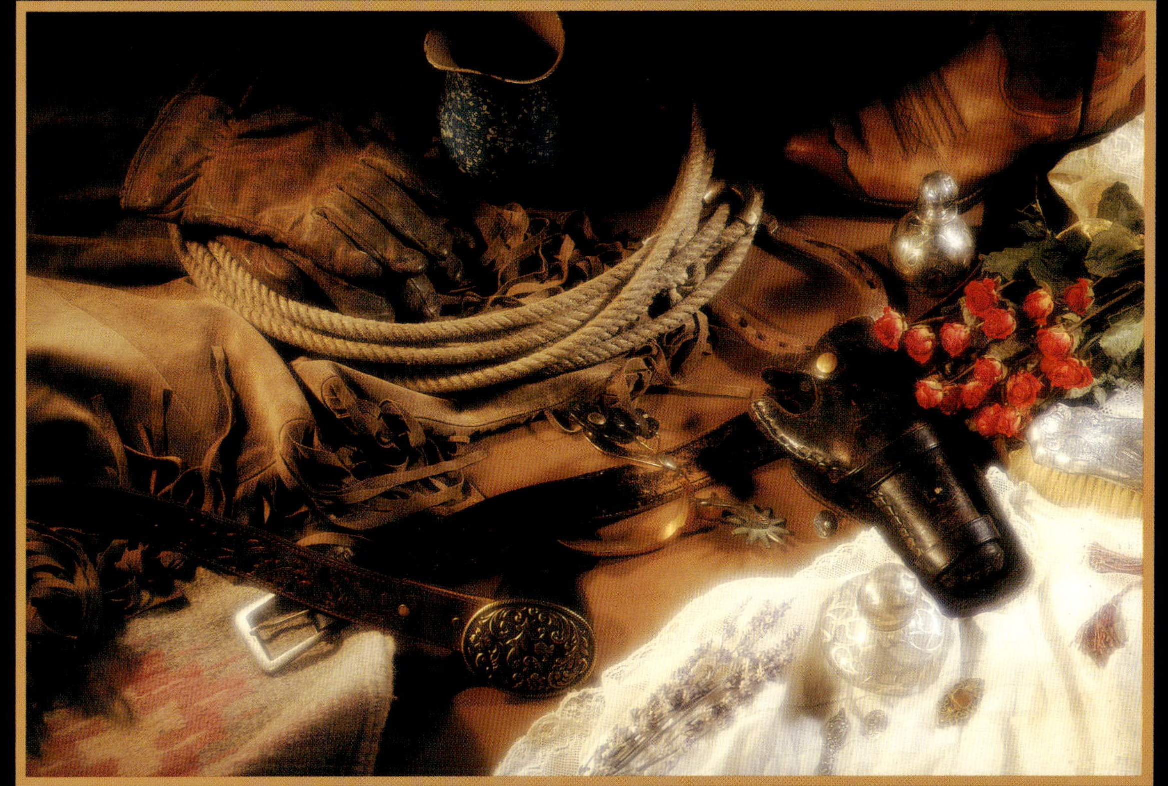

# M·b·I·L·I·N·E

BILL MILNE PHOTOGRAPHY  140 WEST 22ND STREET, NEW YORK, NY 10011  TELEPHONE 212·255·0710

REPRESENTATION LISA CICHOCKI

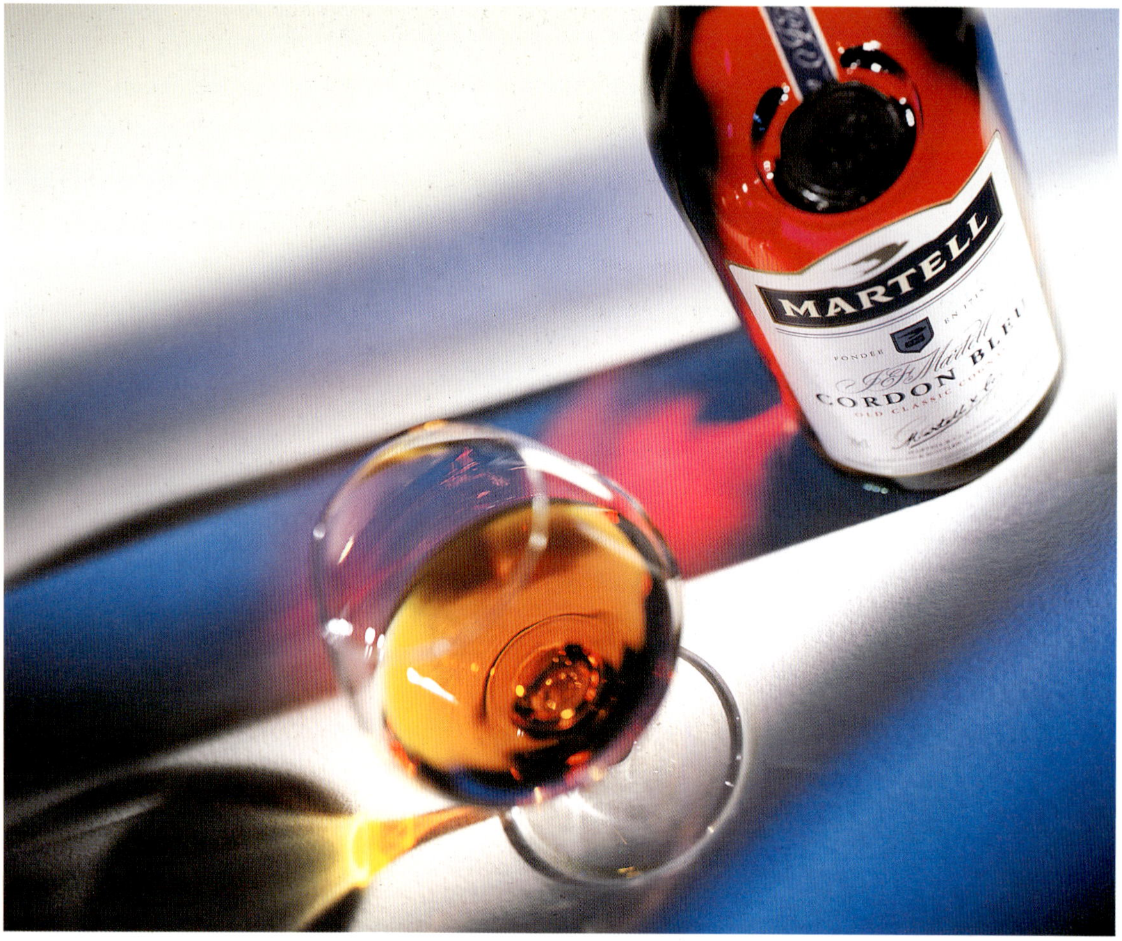

MARTELL
FONDEE EN 1715
J.&F. Martell
CORDON BLEU
OLD CLASSIC COGNAC

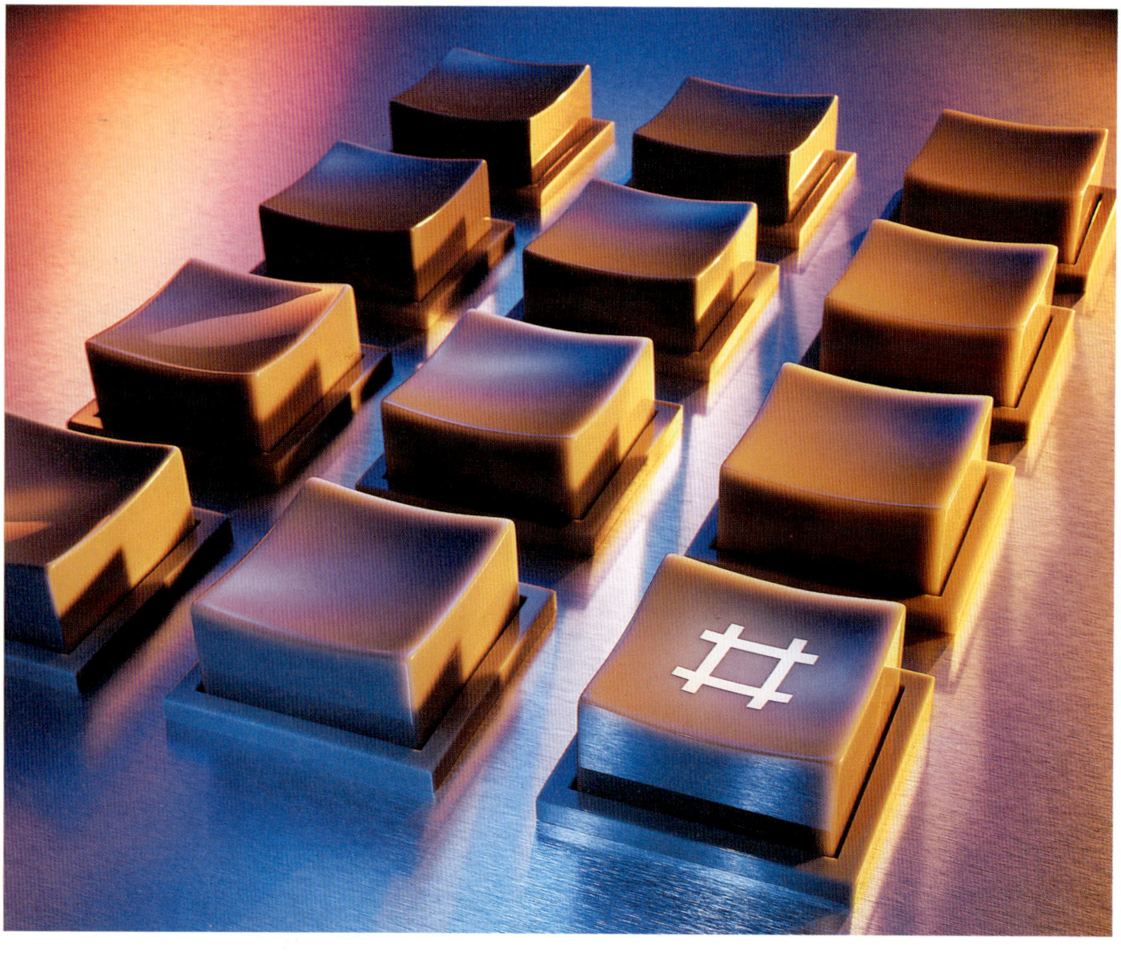

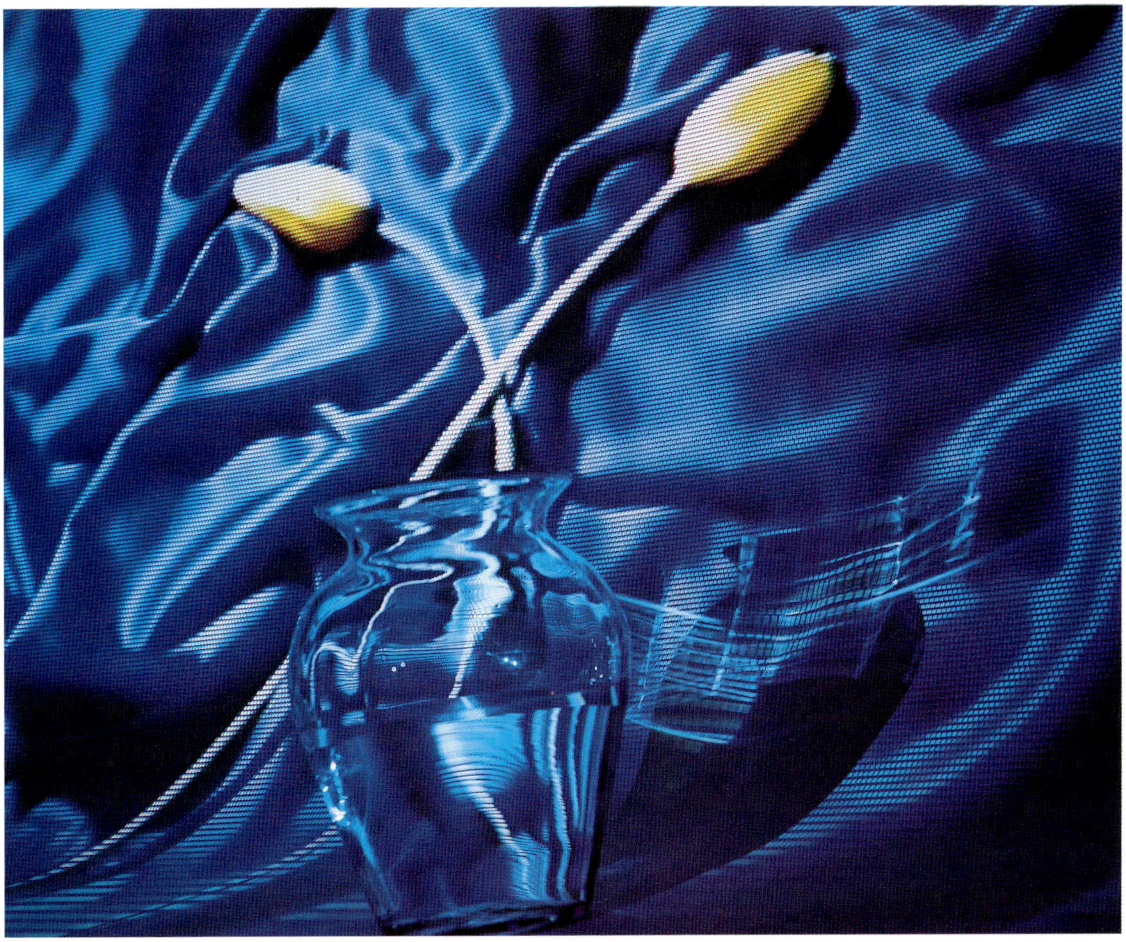

# CRAIG CUTLER STUDIO

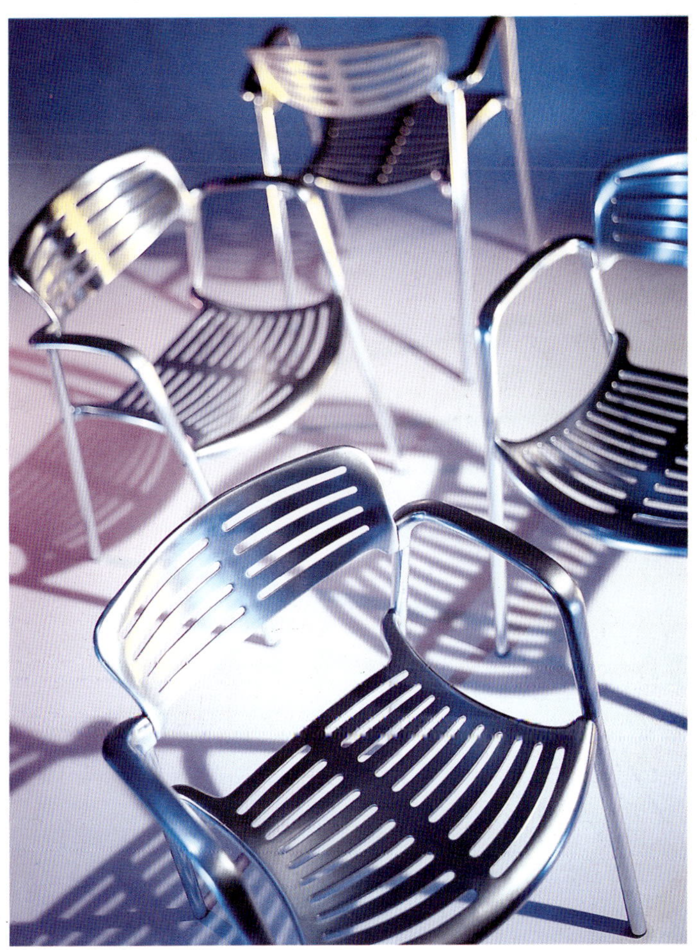

628-30 BROADWAY

NEW YORK, NY 10012

212·473·2892


REPRESENTED BY

MARZENA

212·772·2522

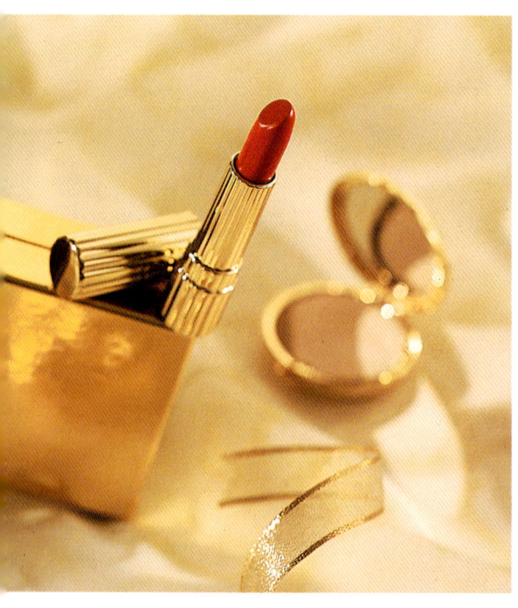



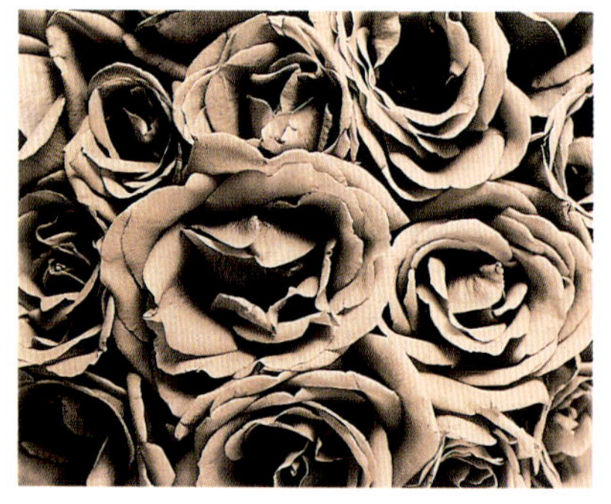

*22 west 21st street*

*212  929-8504*

*fax  212 645-4288*

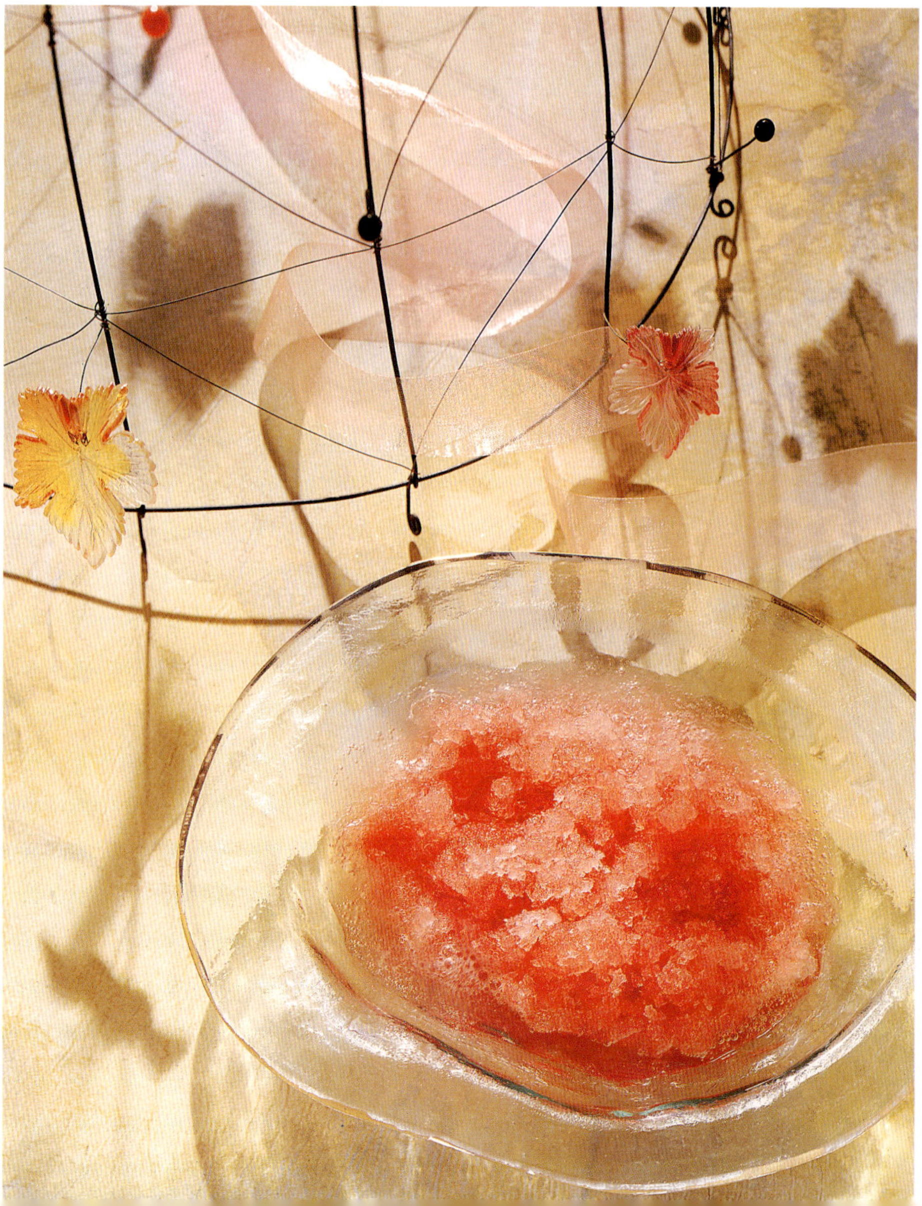

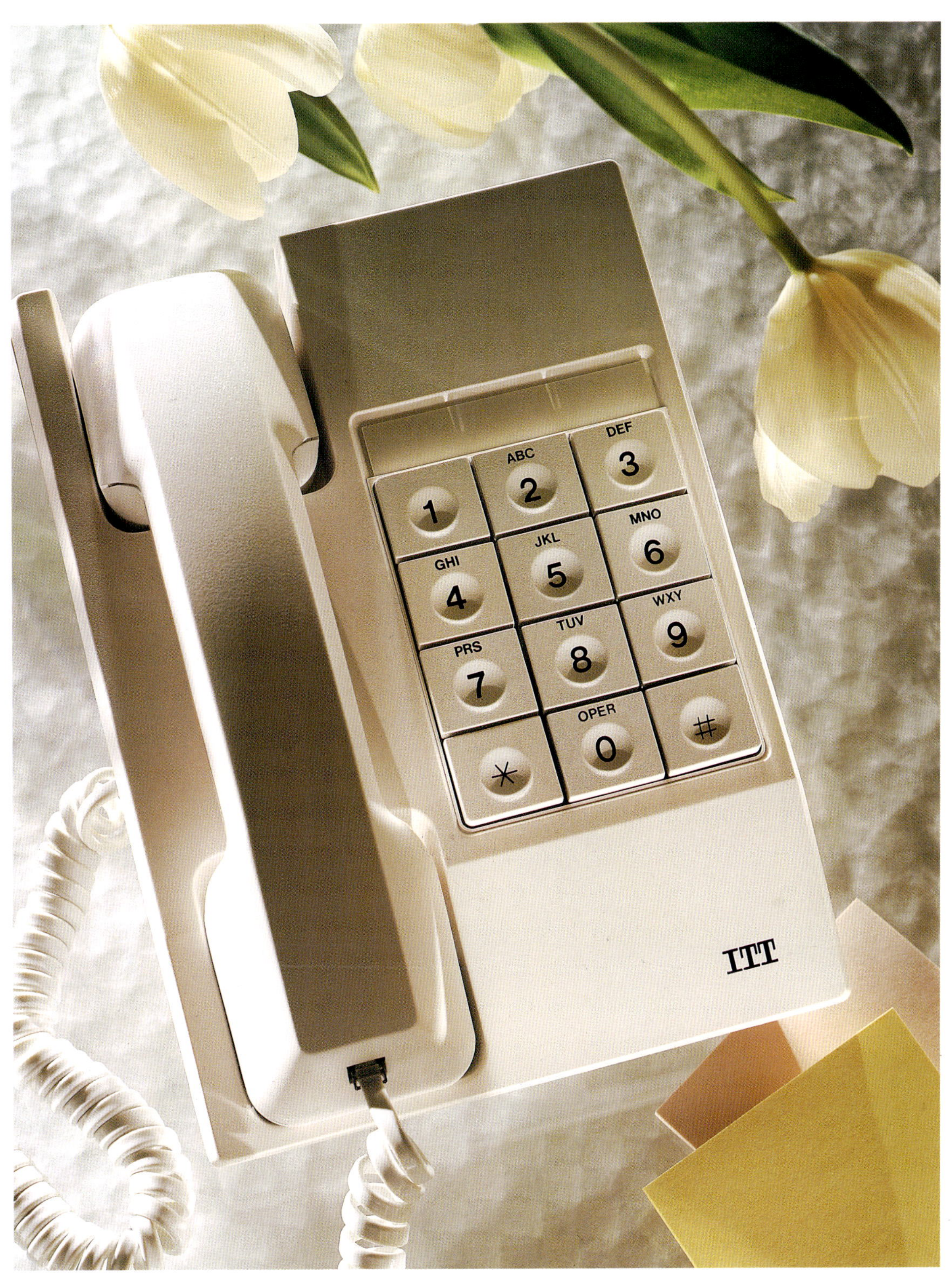

# E L I Z A B E T H   W A T T

PHOTOGRAPHY

212  929-8504  fax  212  645-4288

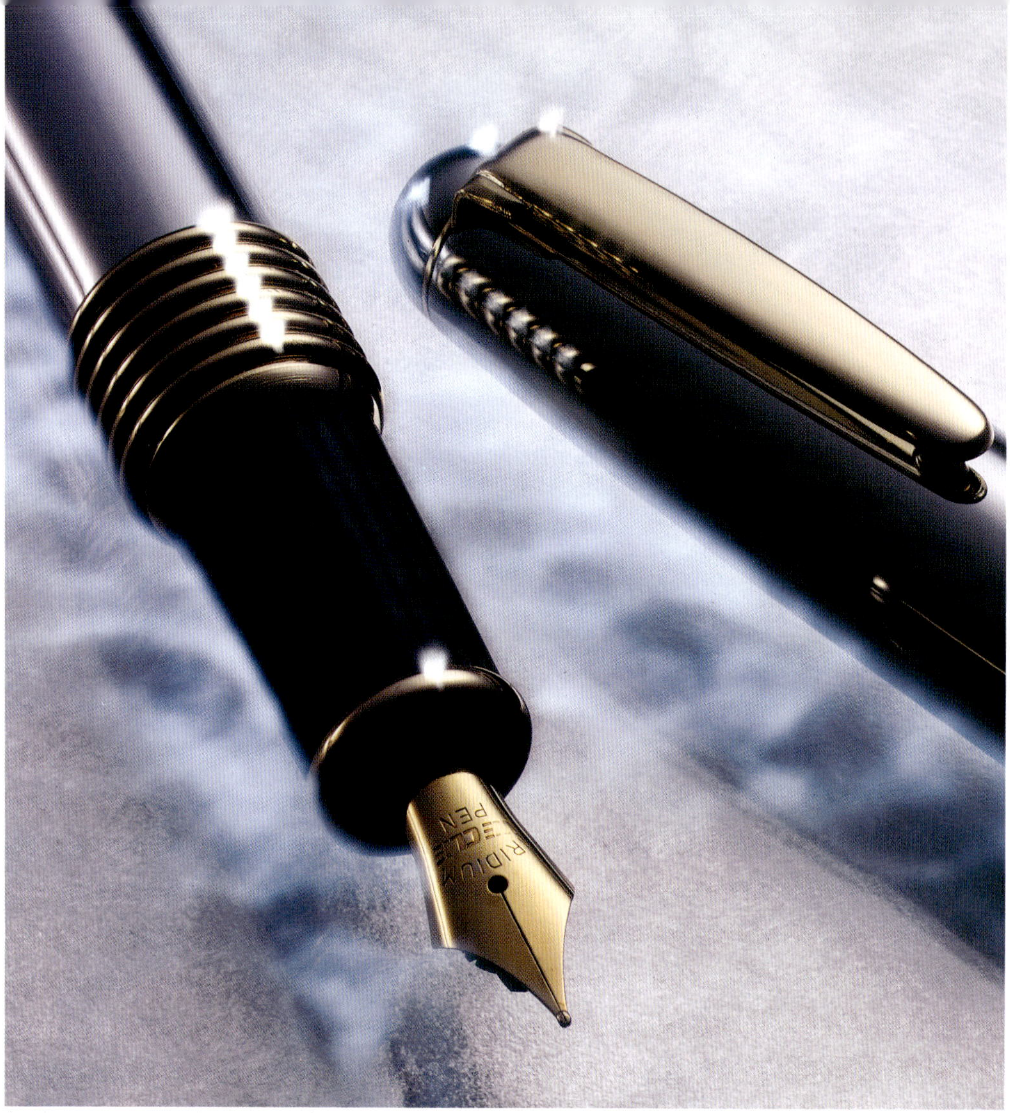

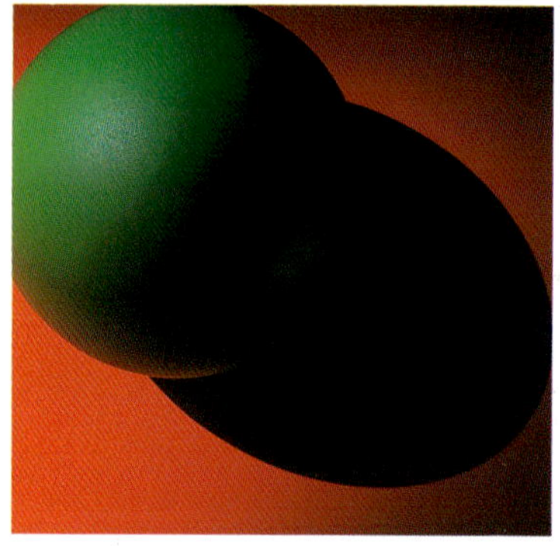

represented by

**Barbara Umlas**

212.534.4008

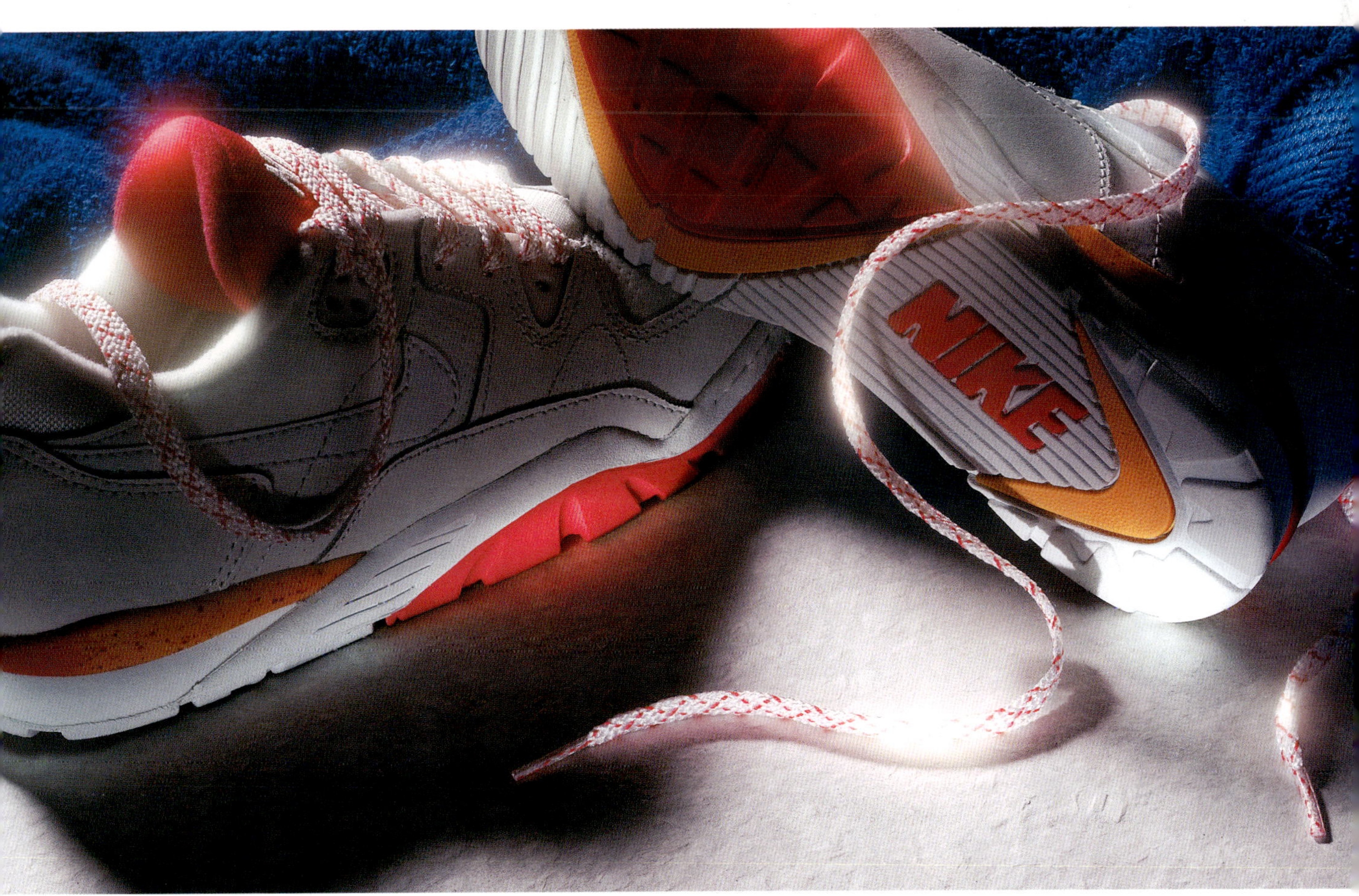
NIKE

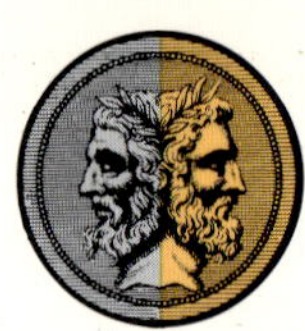

# MANNO

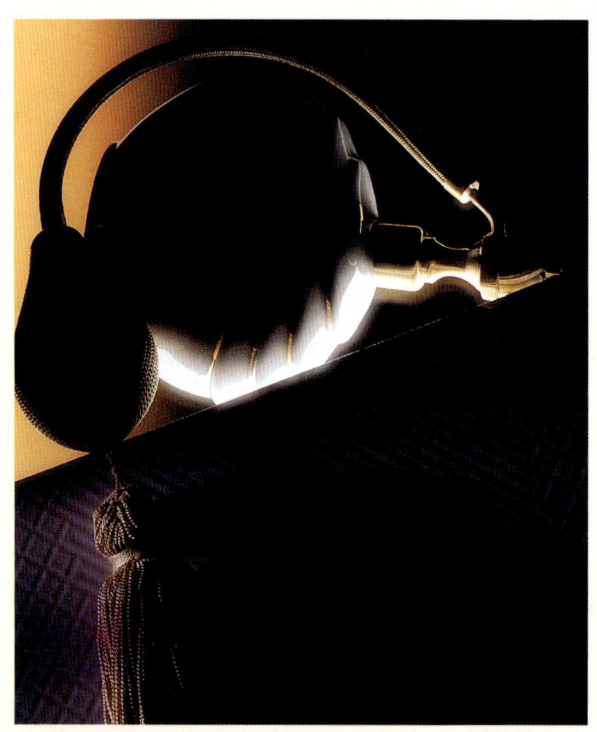

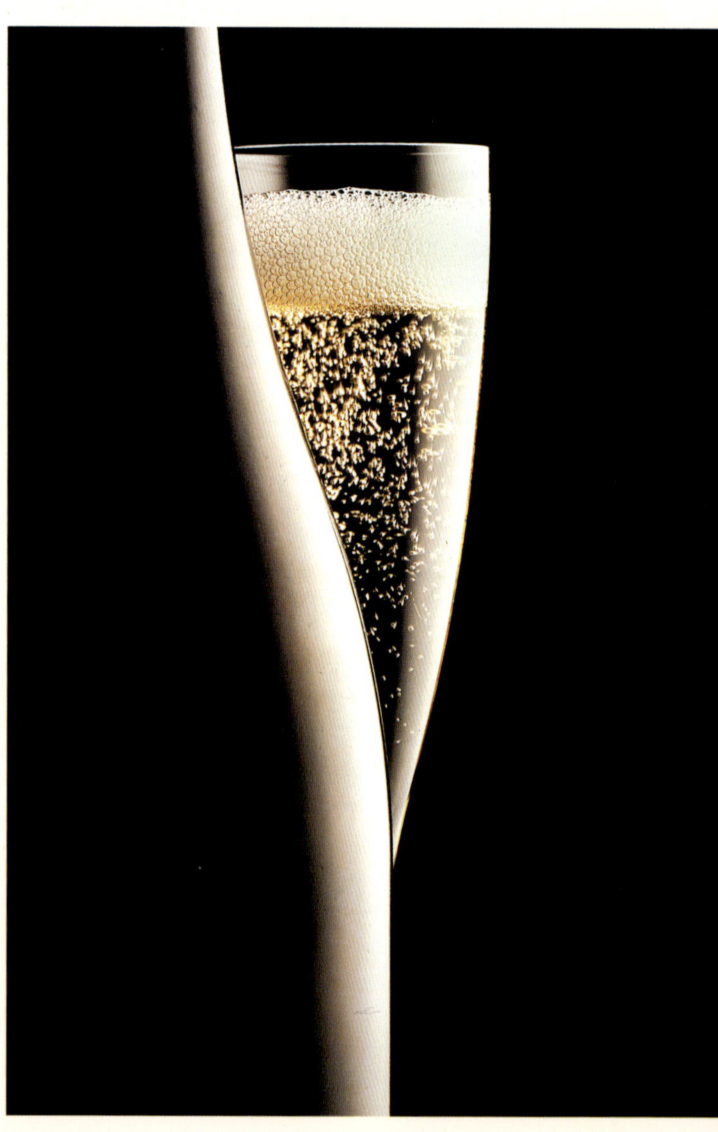

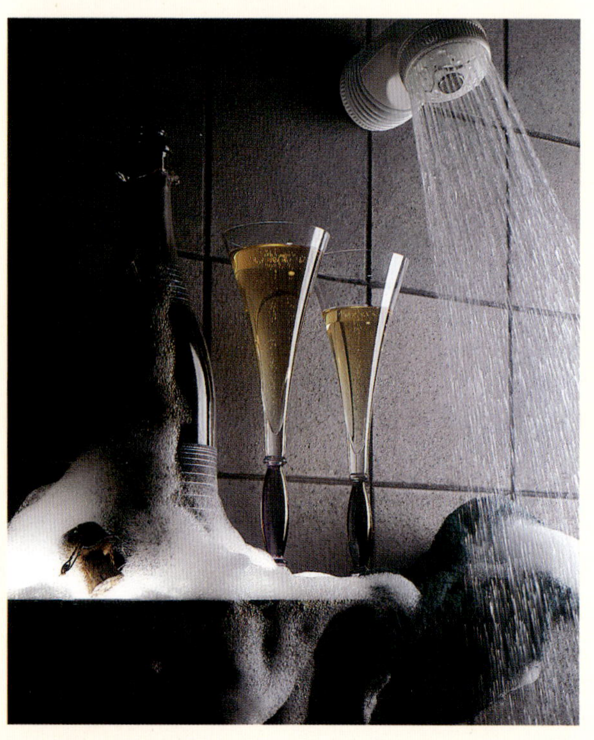

JOHN MANNO  20 W 22  NYC 10010  tel 212.243.7353  fax 212.243.7876

represented by Glenn Palmer-Smith  tel 212.769.3940

© 1992 JOHN MANNO

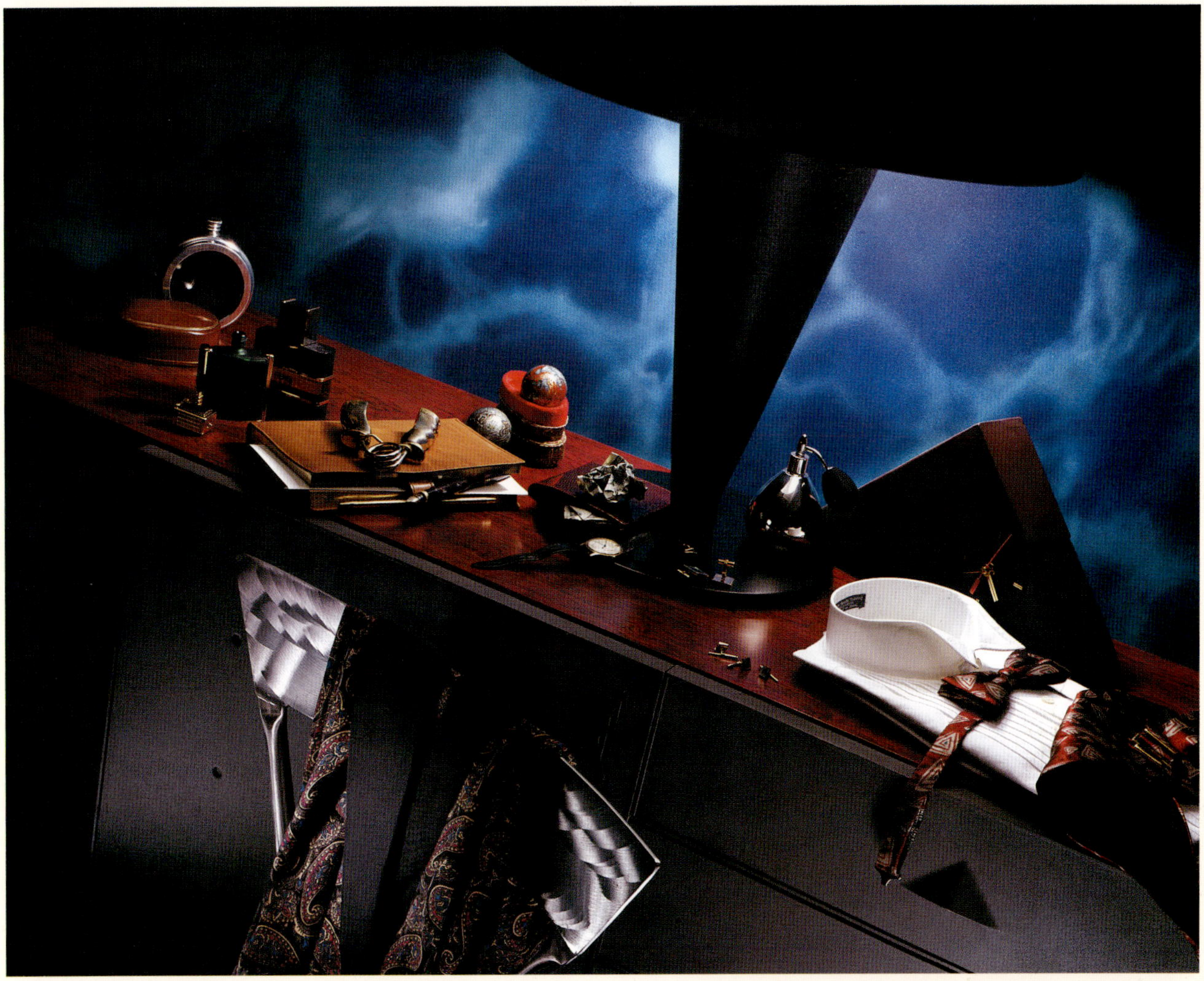

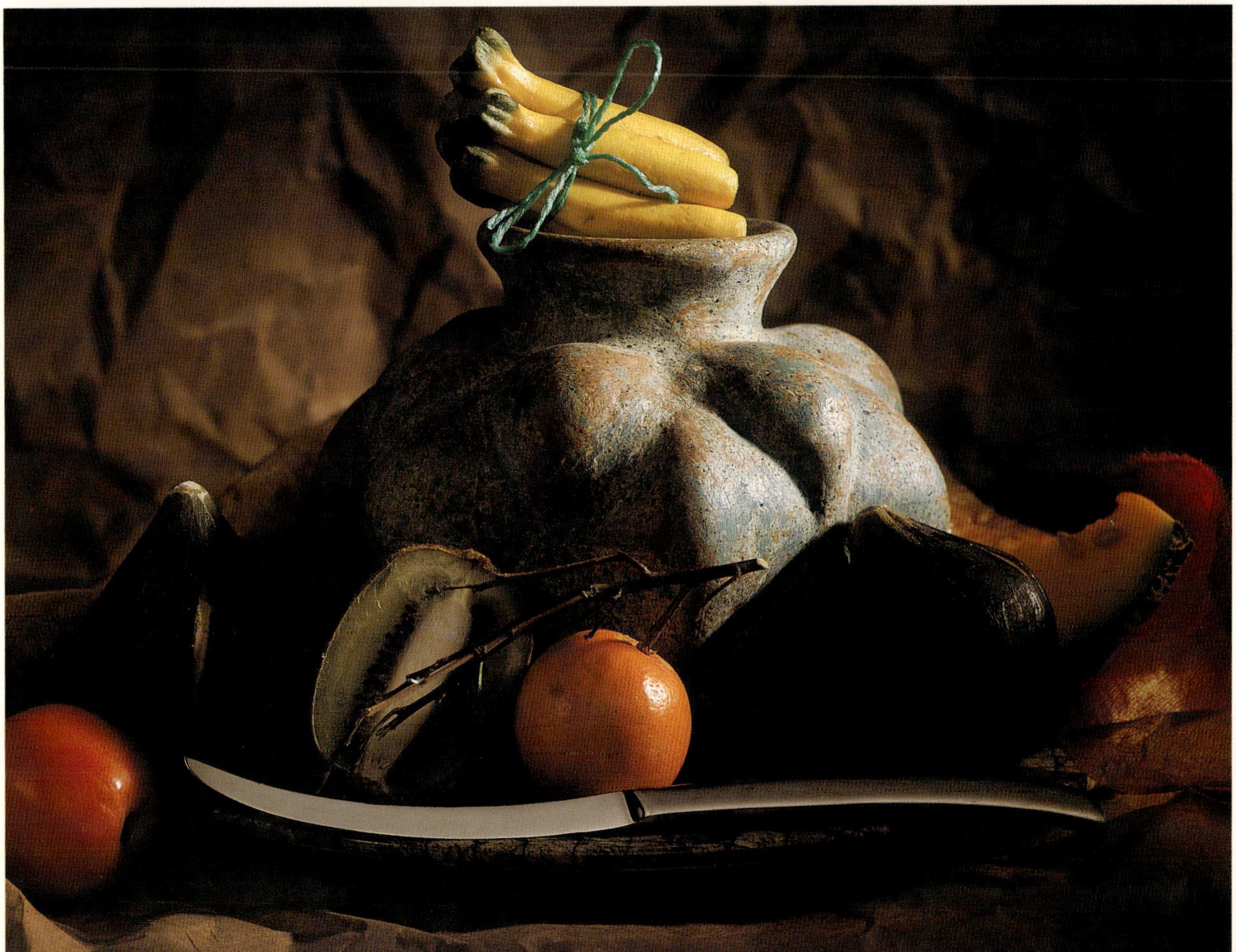

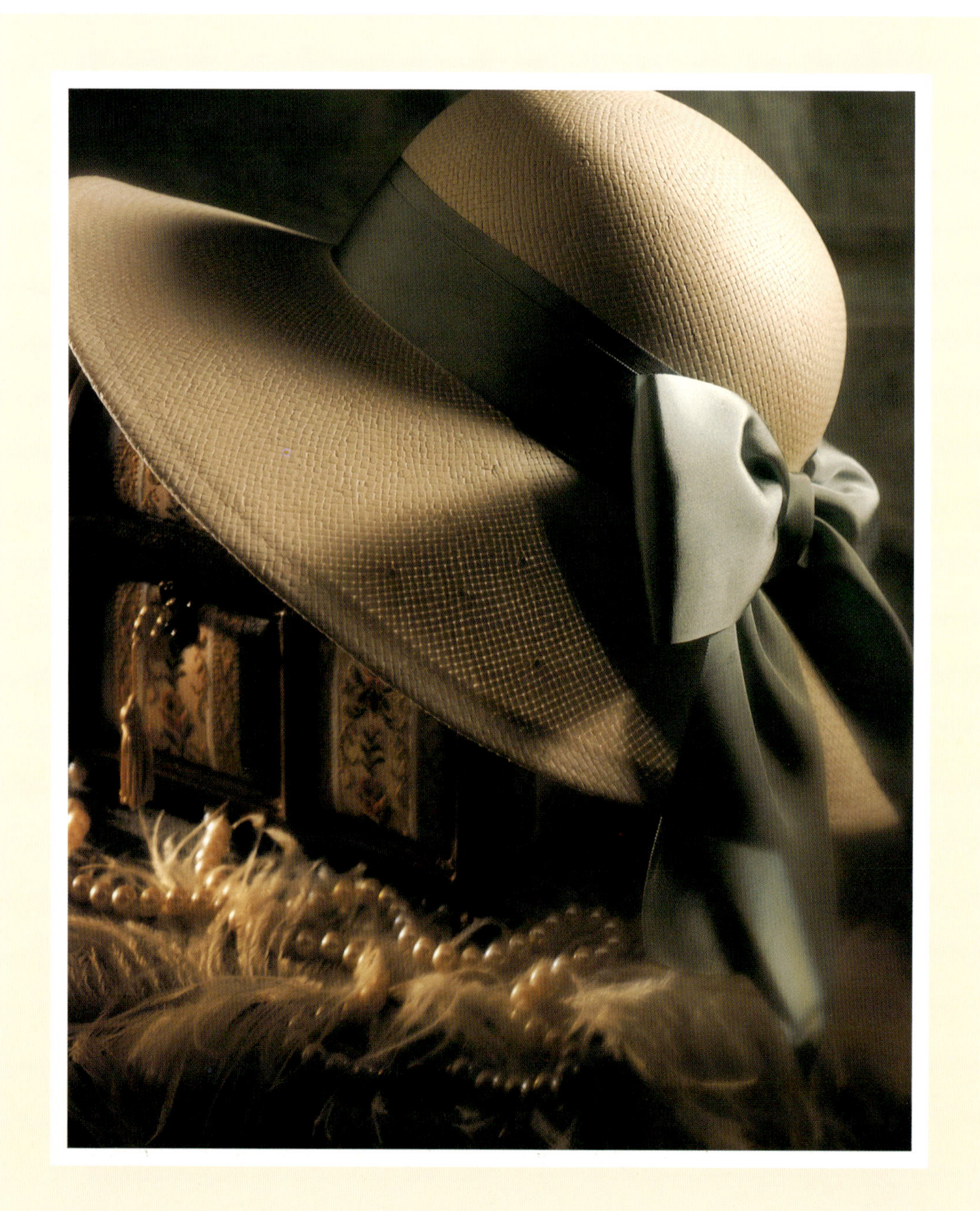

L · I · S · A
KOENIG
5 West 19th Street, New York, N.Y. 10011 (212) 929-5210

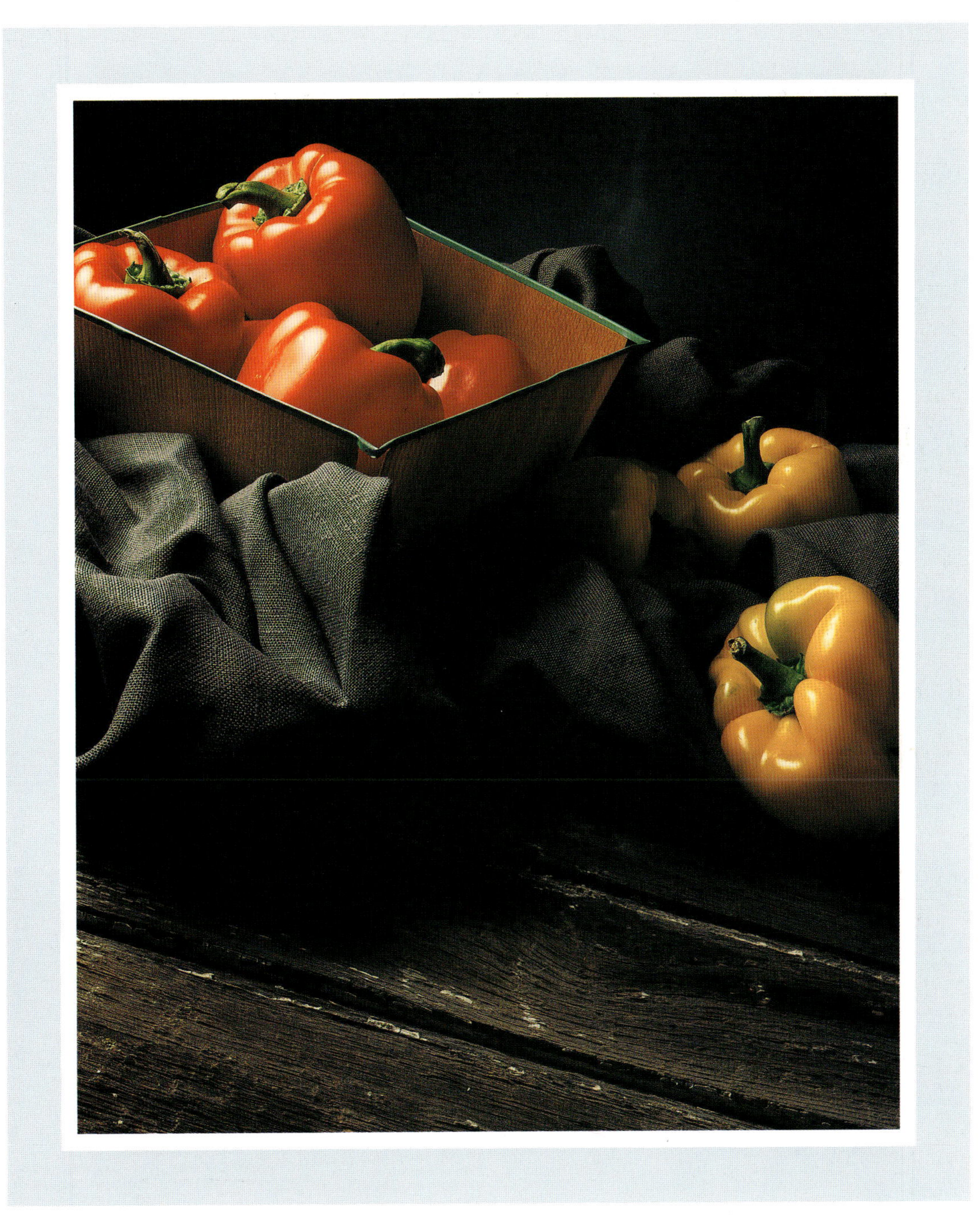

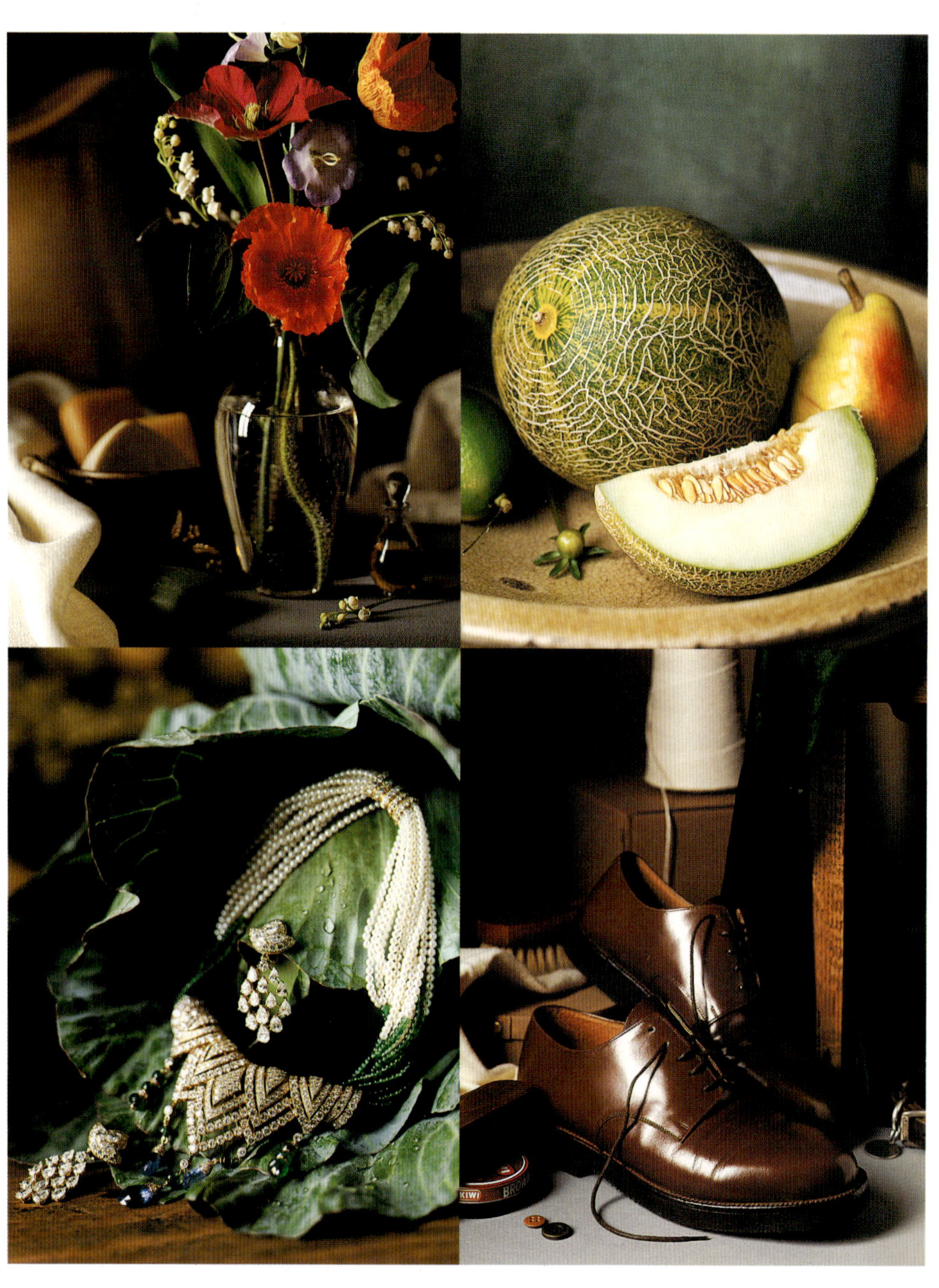

Brian **H**agiwara 212·674·6026 / *Agent: Robert Feldman 212·243·7319*

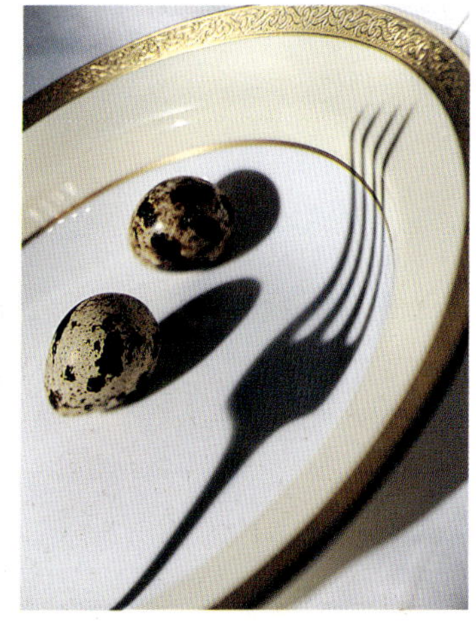

# OSKAR MARTINEZ STUDIO

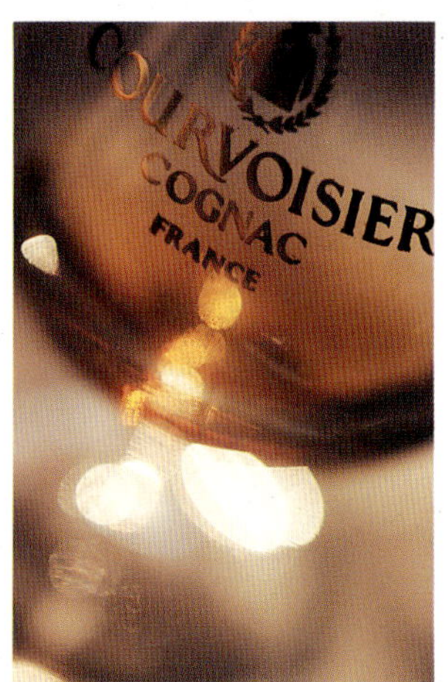

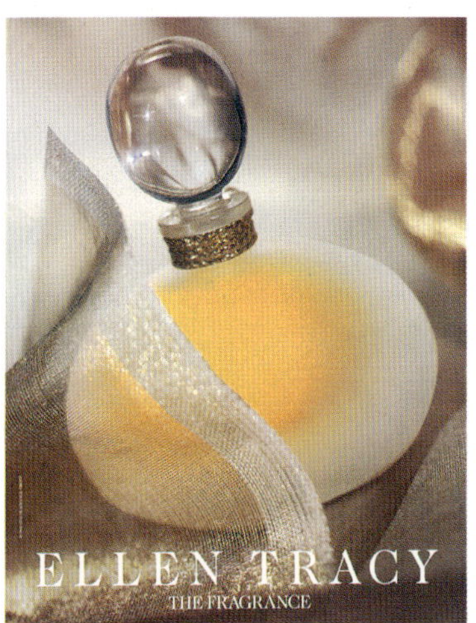



303 Park Avenue South, Suite 408, New York, New York 10010   212-673-0932

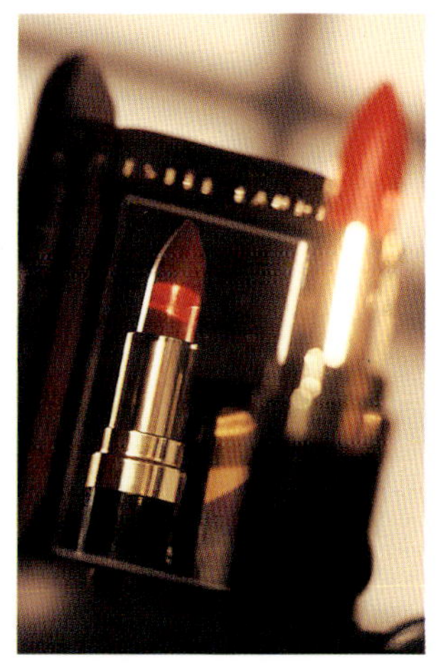

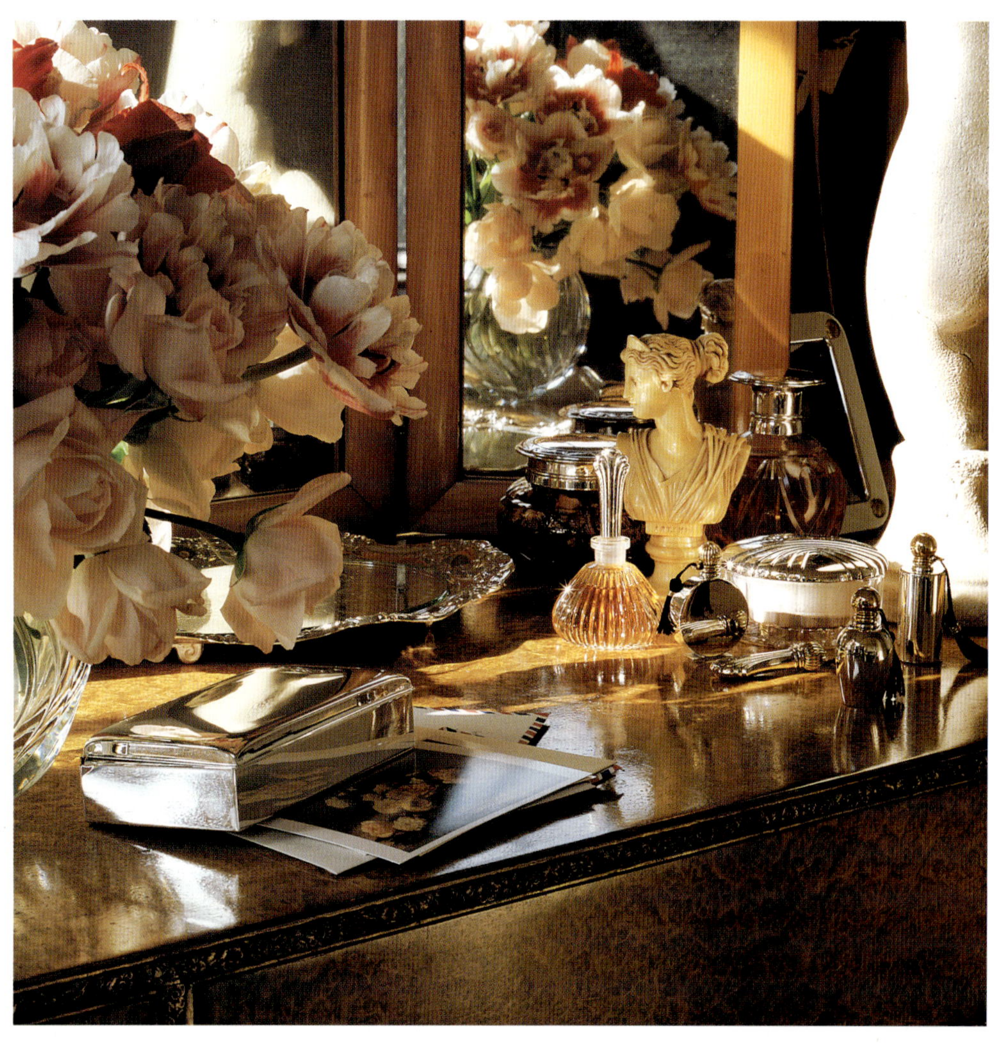

Represented by

Bernstein & Andriulli

212 682 1490

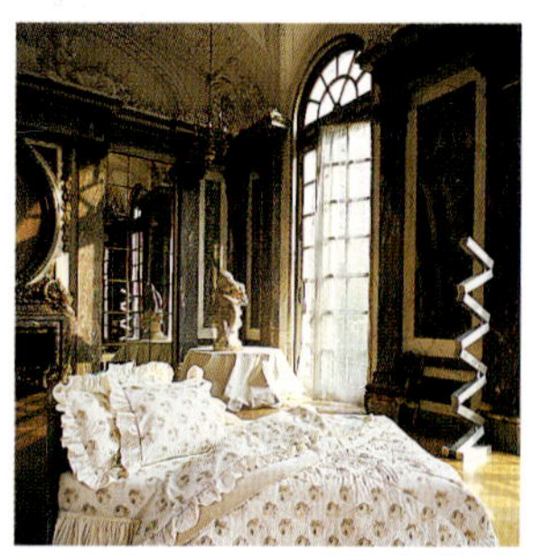

Studio  212 924 1074

# E L I Z A B E T H    H E Y E R T

# E L I Z A B E T H    H E Y E R T

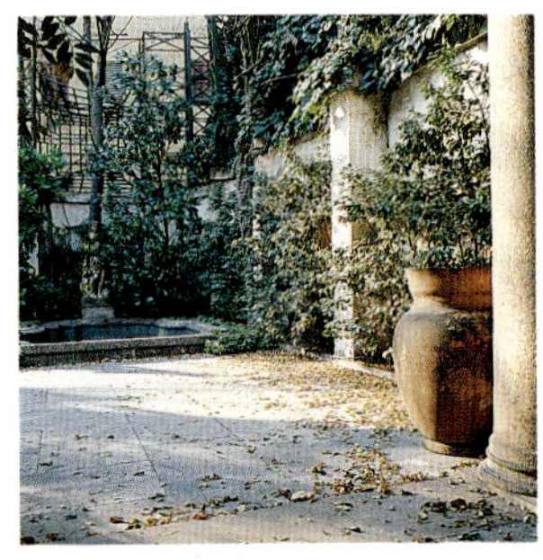

Represented by

Bernstein & Andriulli

212 682 1490


Studio  212 924 1074

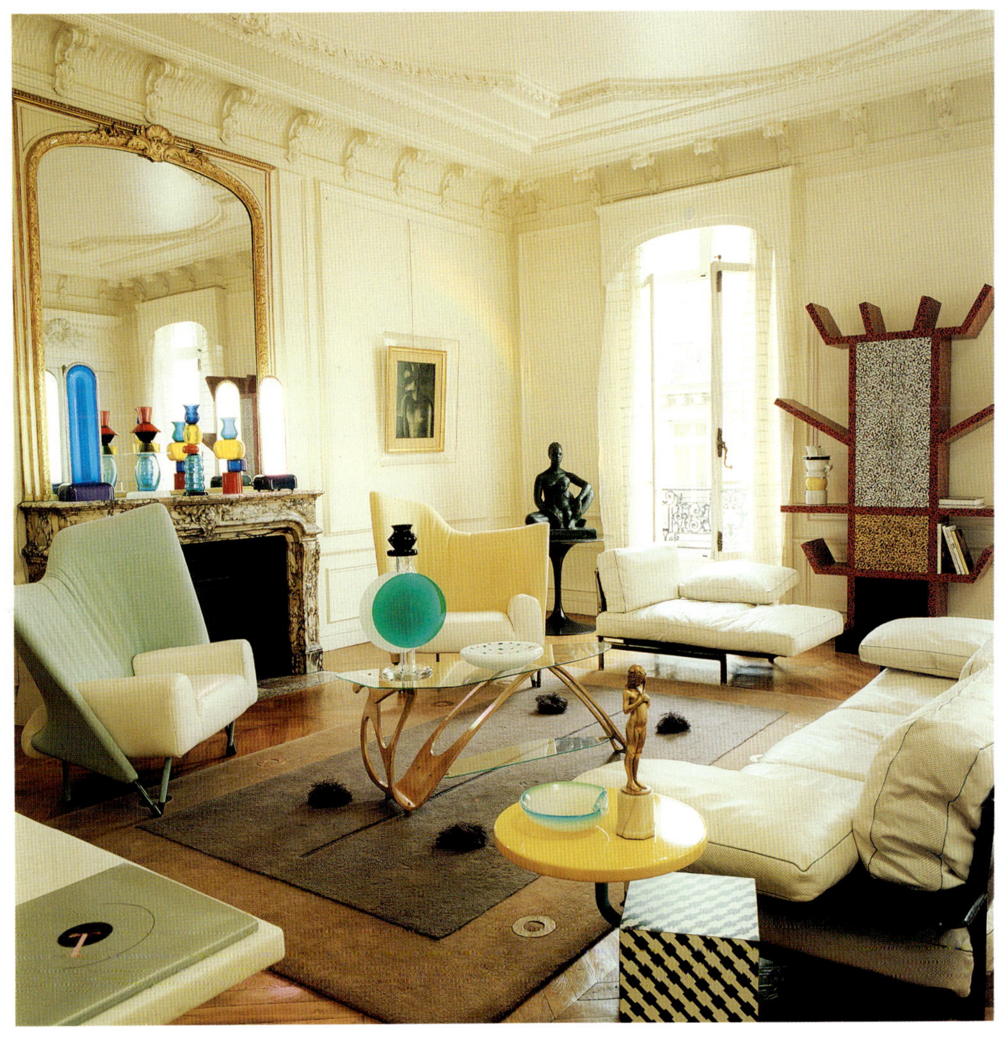

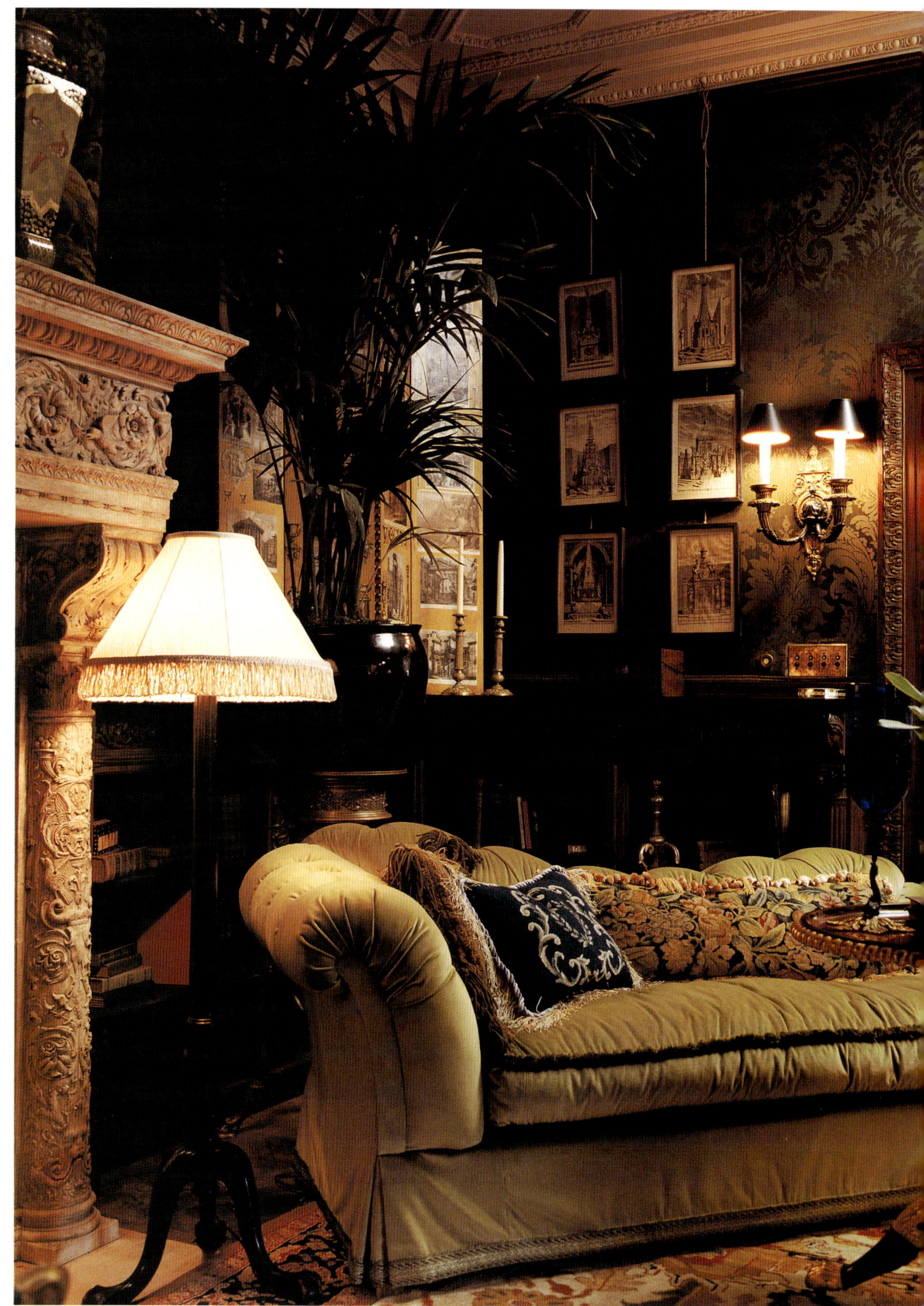
TOM M<sup>c</sup>CAVERA

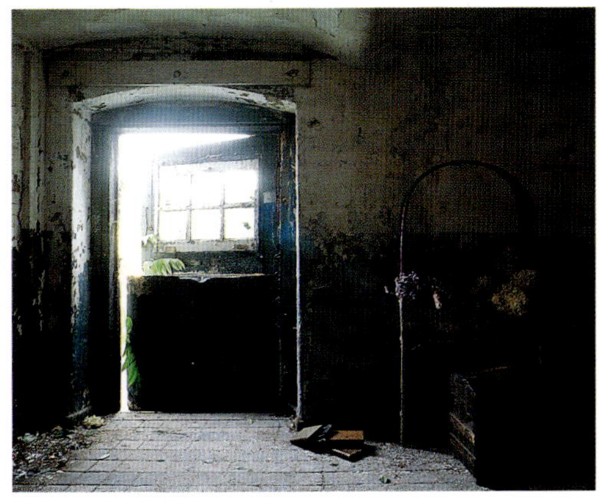

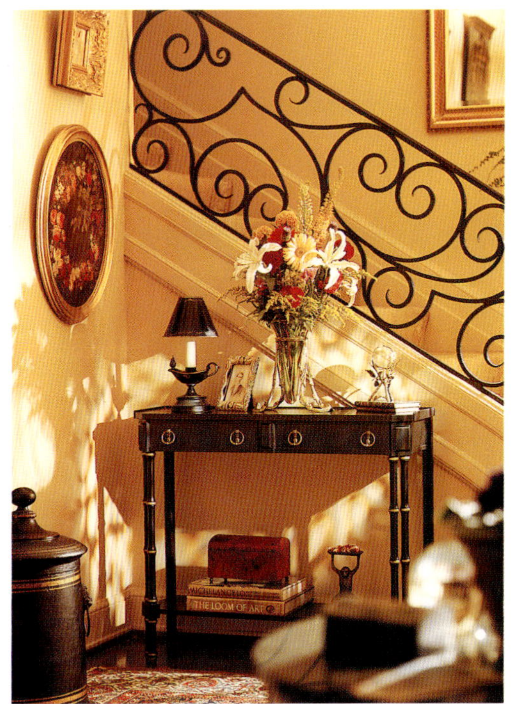

TOM M<sup>C</sup>CAVERA

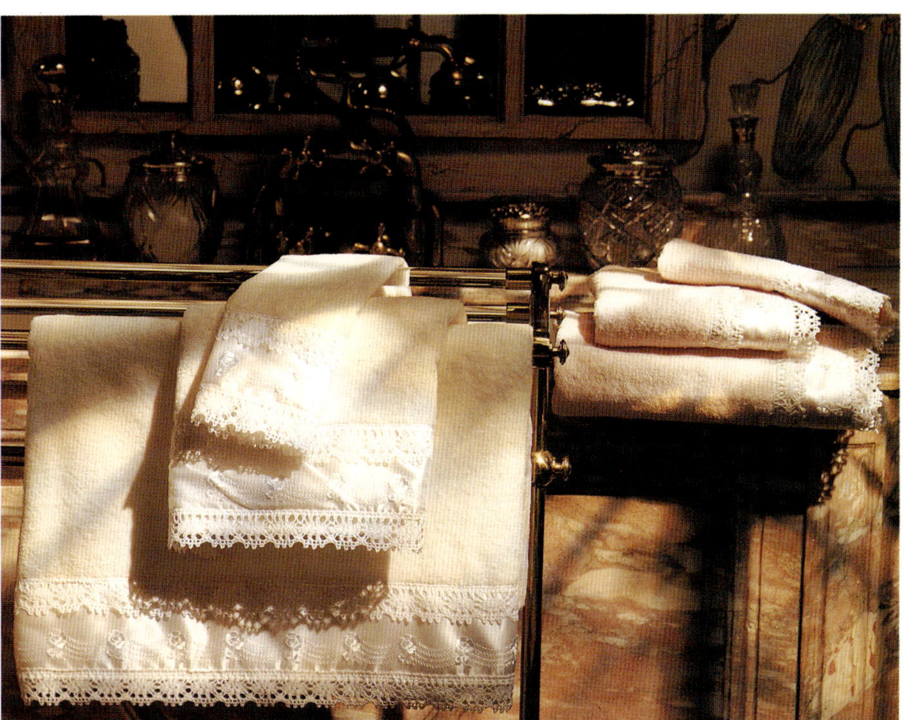

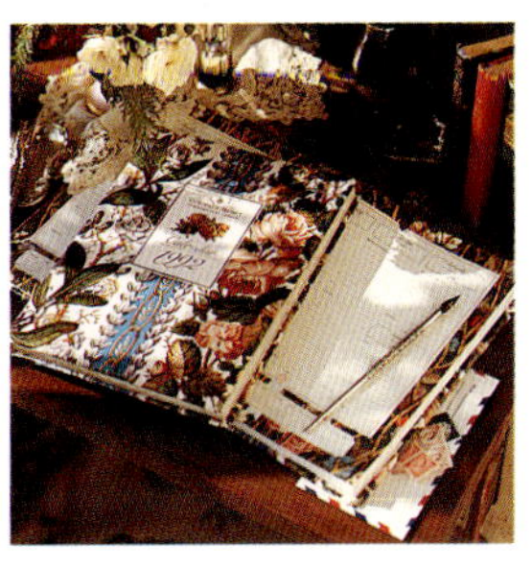

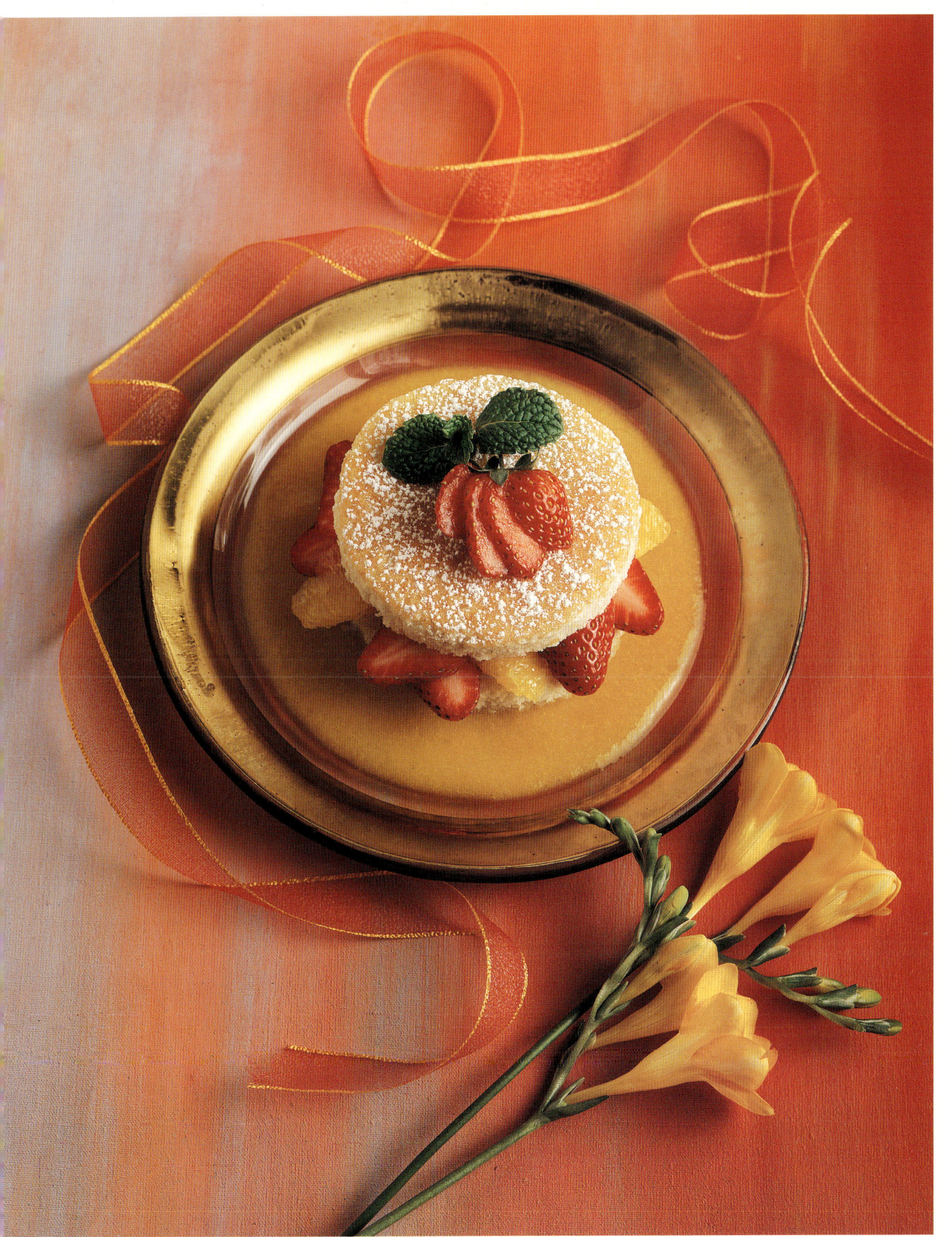

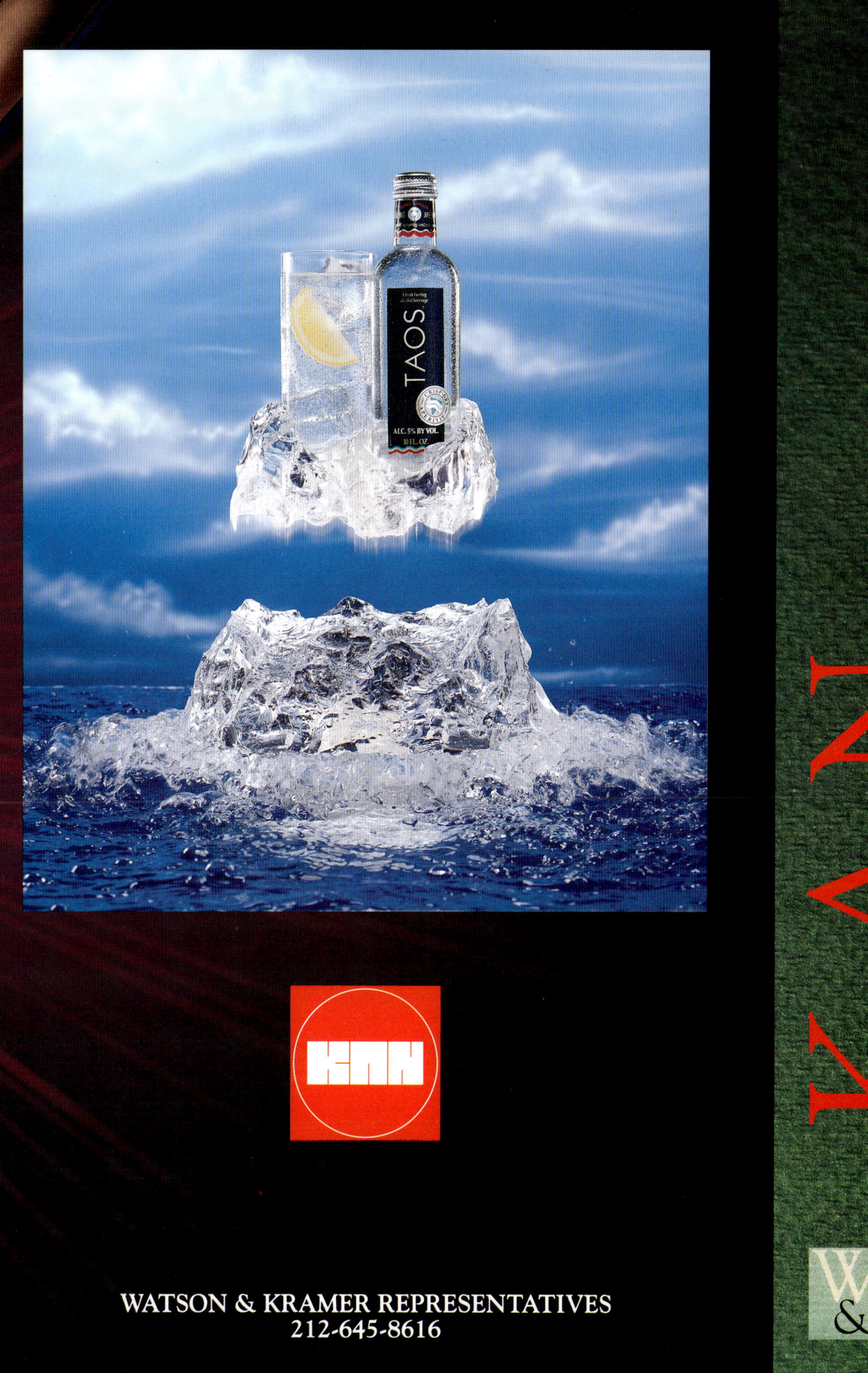

TAOS
ALC. 5% BY VOL.
10 FL. OZ.
KAN
KAN
WATSON & KRAMER REPRESENTATIVES
212-645-8616
W&K
© 1992 KAN

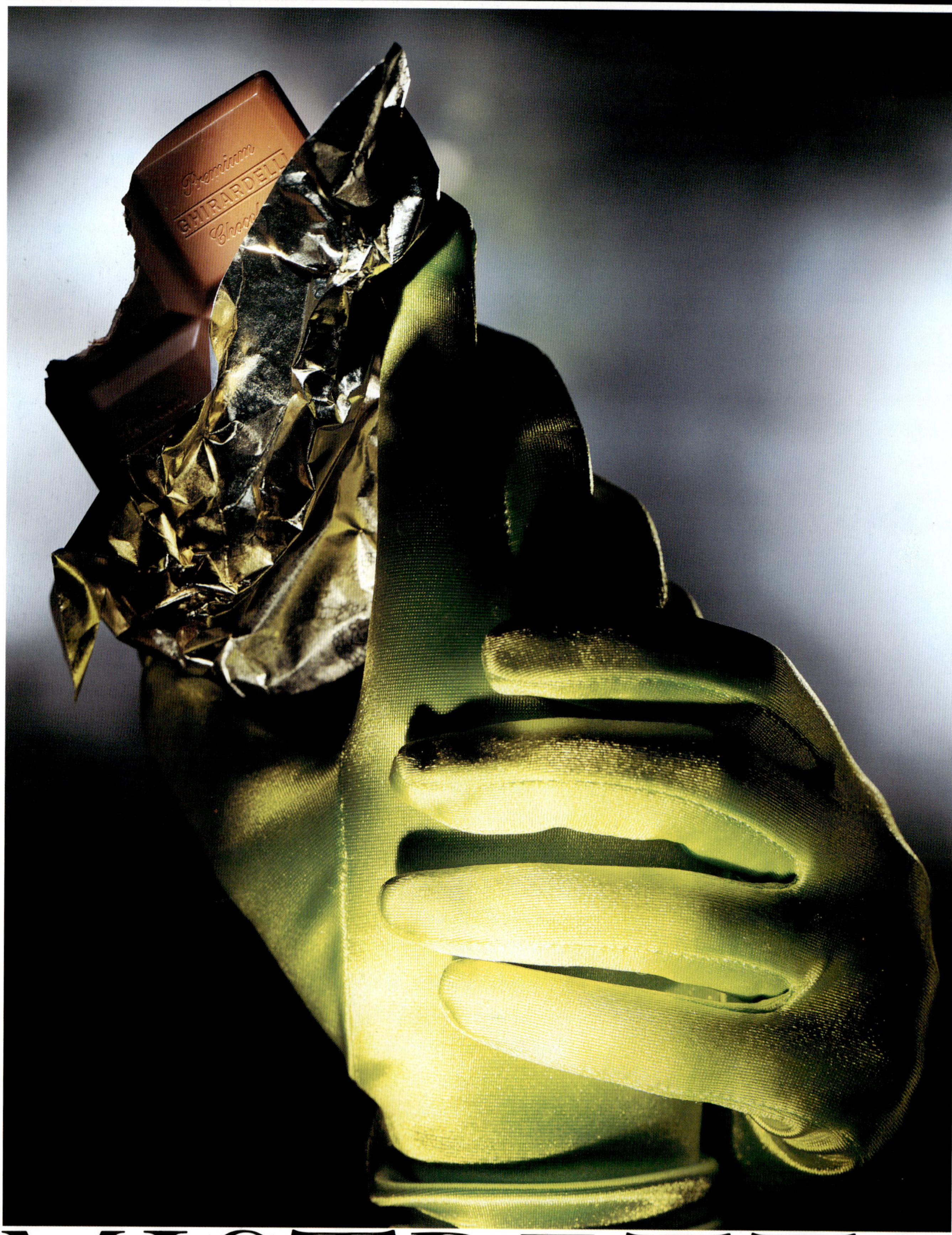

REPRESENTED BY LIZ LI 212-889-7067
Premium
GHIRARDELLI
Chocolate
MISTRETTA

# MISTRETTA

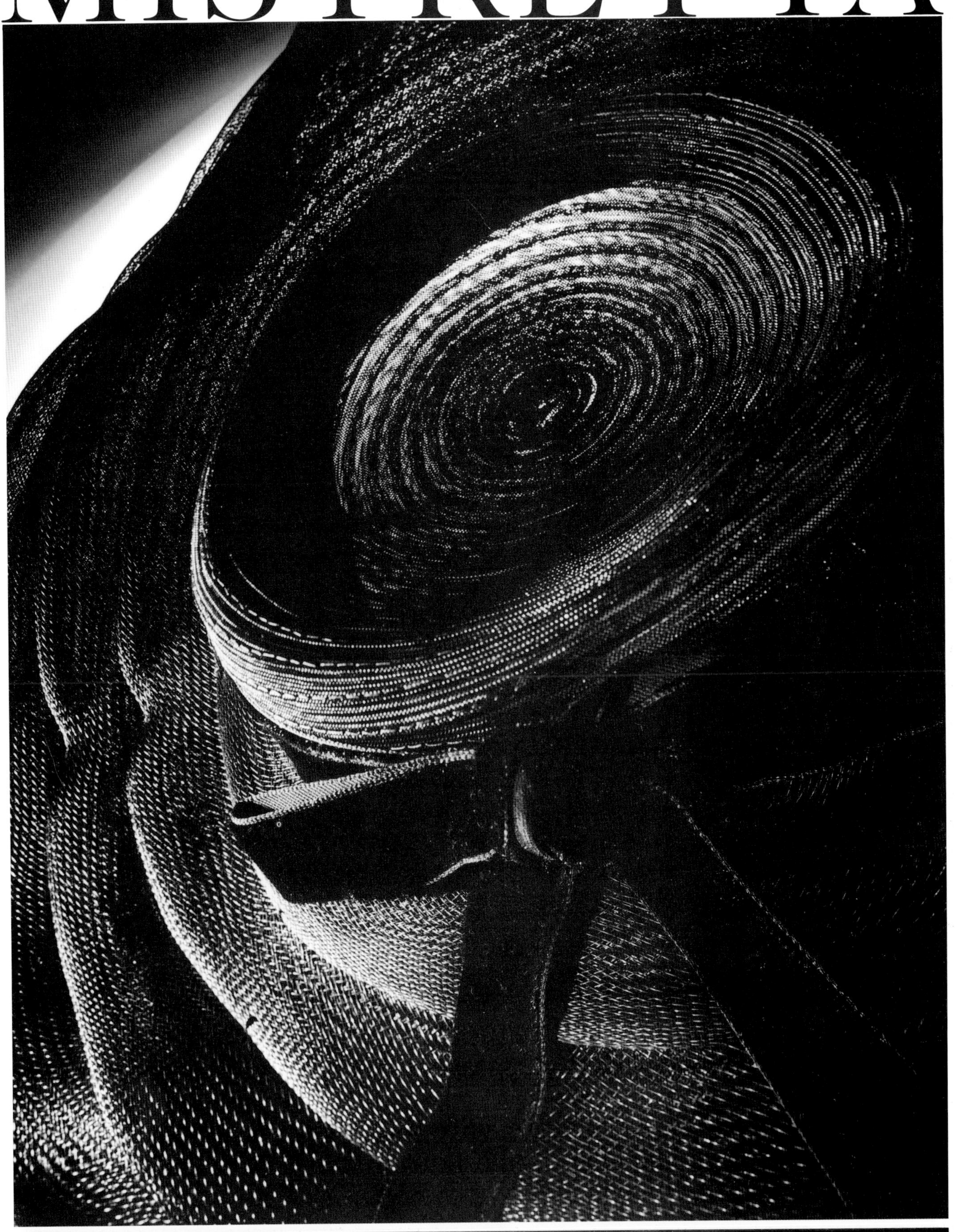

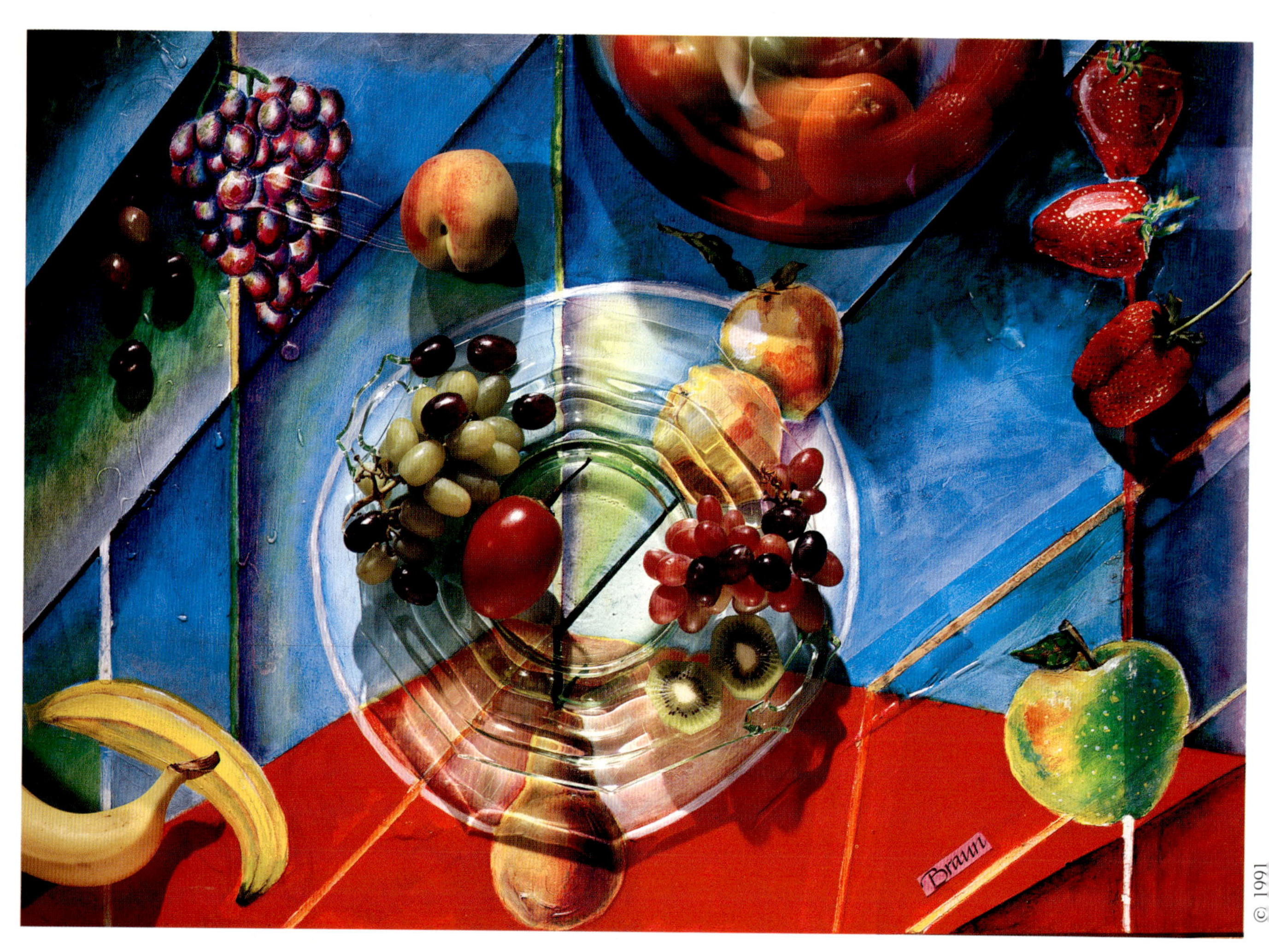


# W E N D Y   B R A U N

## PHOTO ILLUSTRATION

212.274.1582

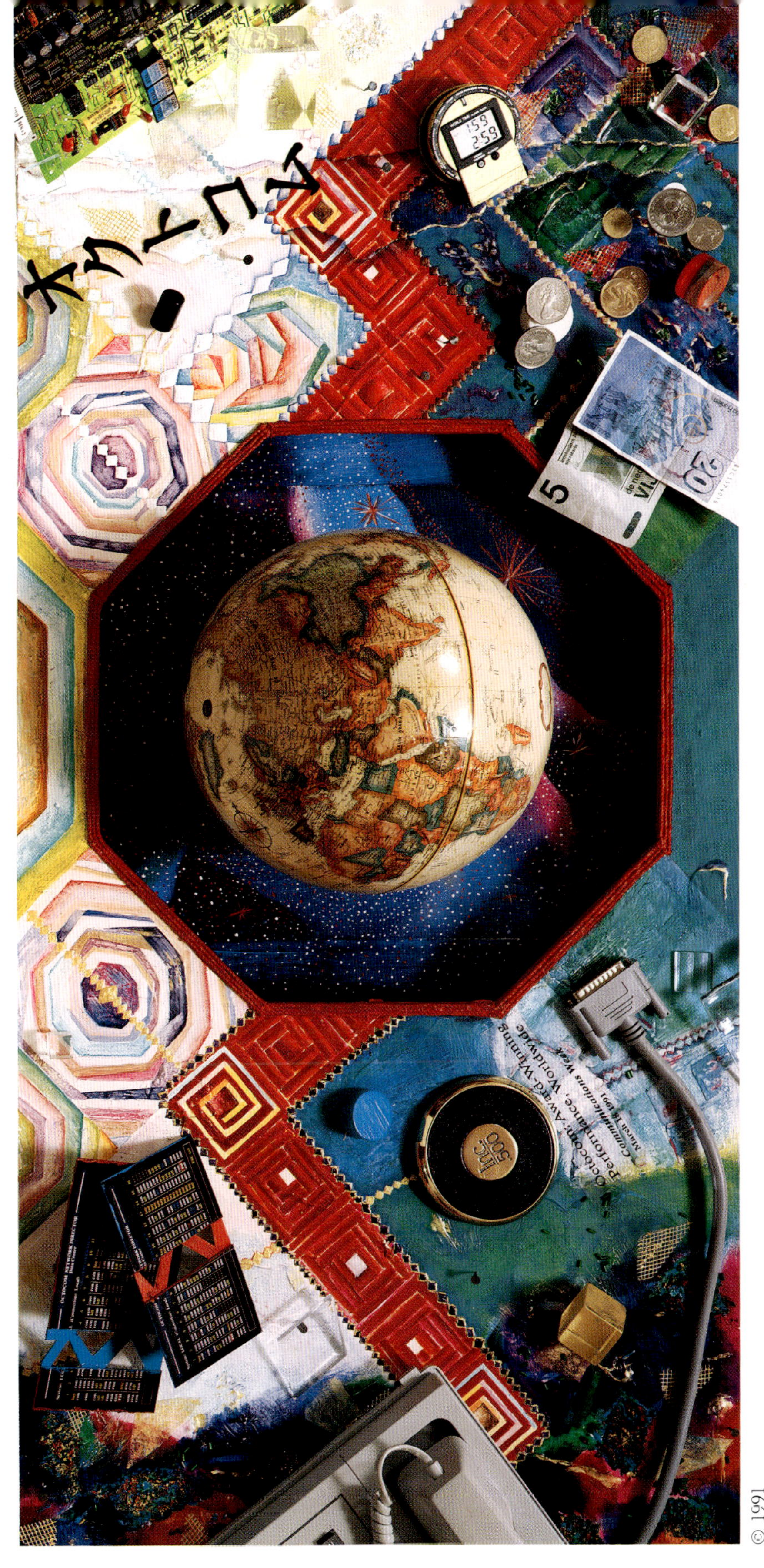

# WENDY BRAUN

PHOTO ILLUSTRATION

212.274.1582

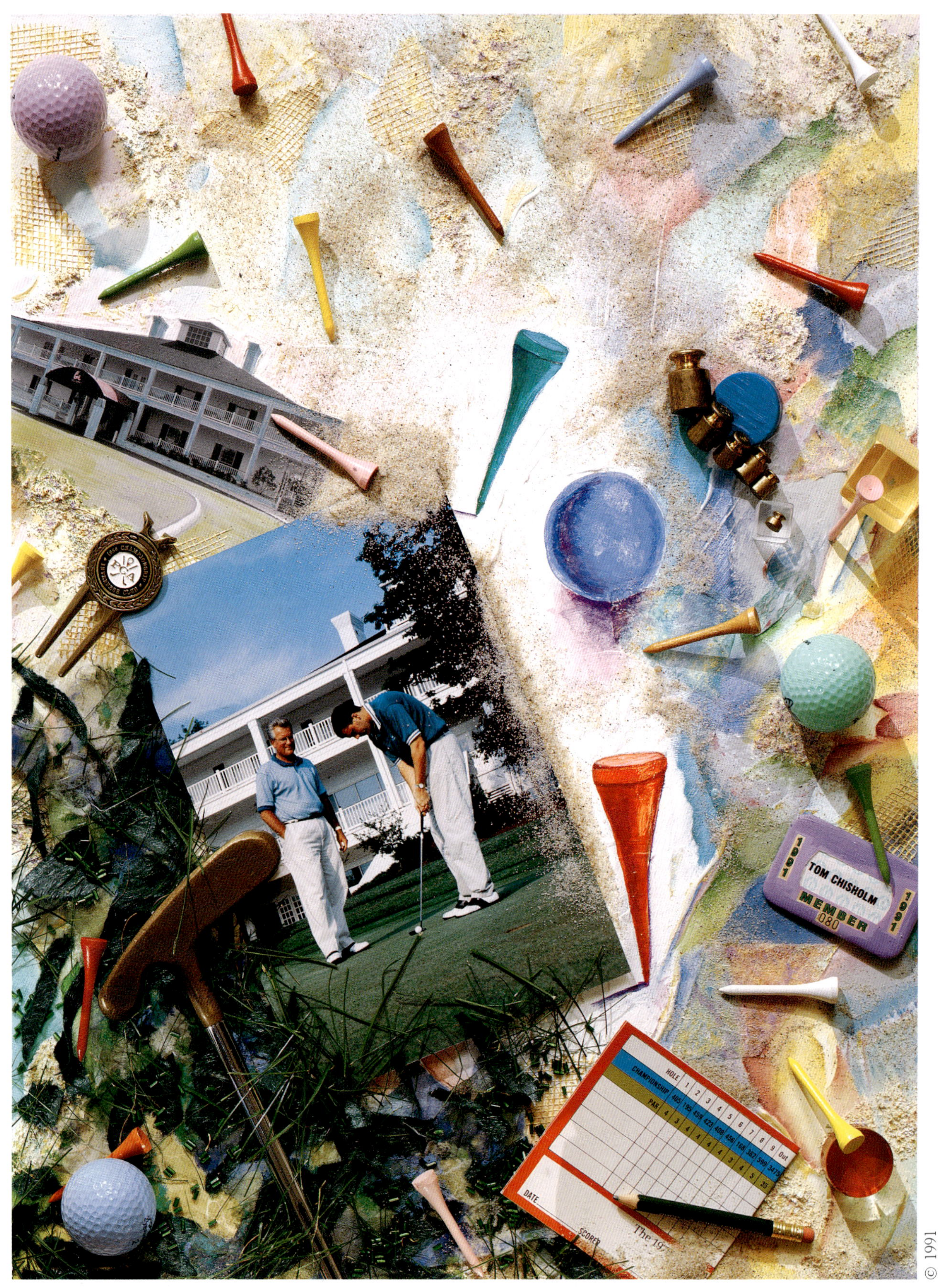

# WENDY BRAUN

PHOTO ILLUSTRATION

212.274.1582

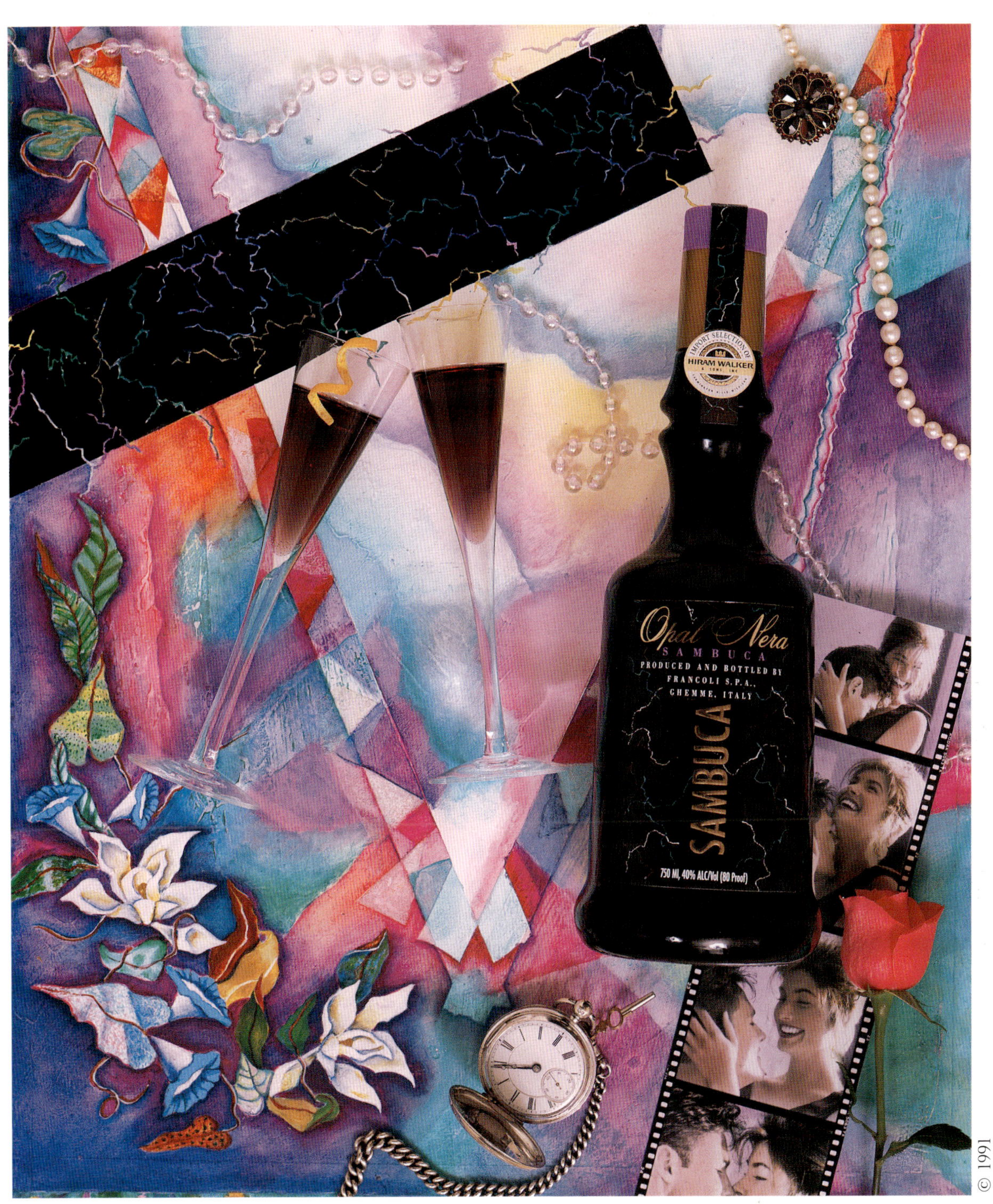


# WENDY BRAUN

PHOTO ILLUSTRATION

212.274.1582

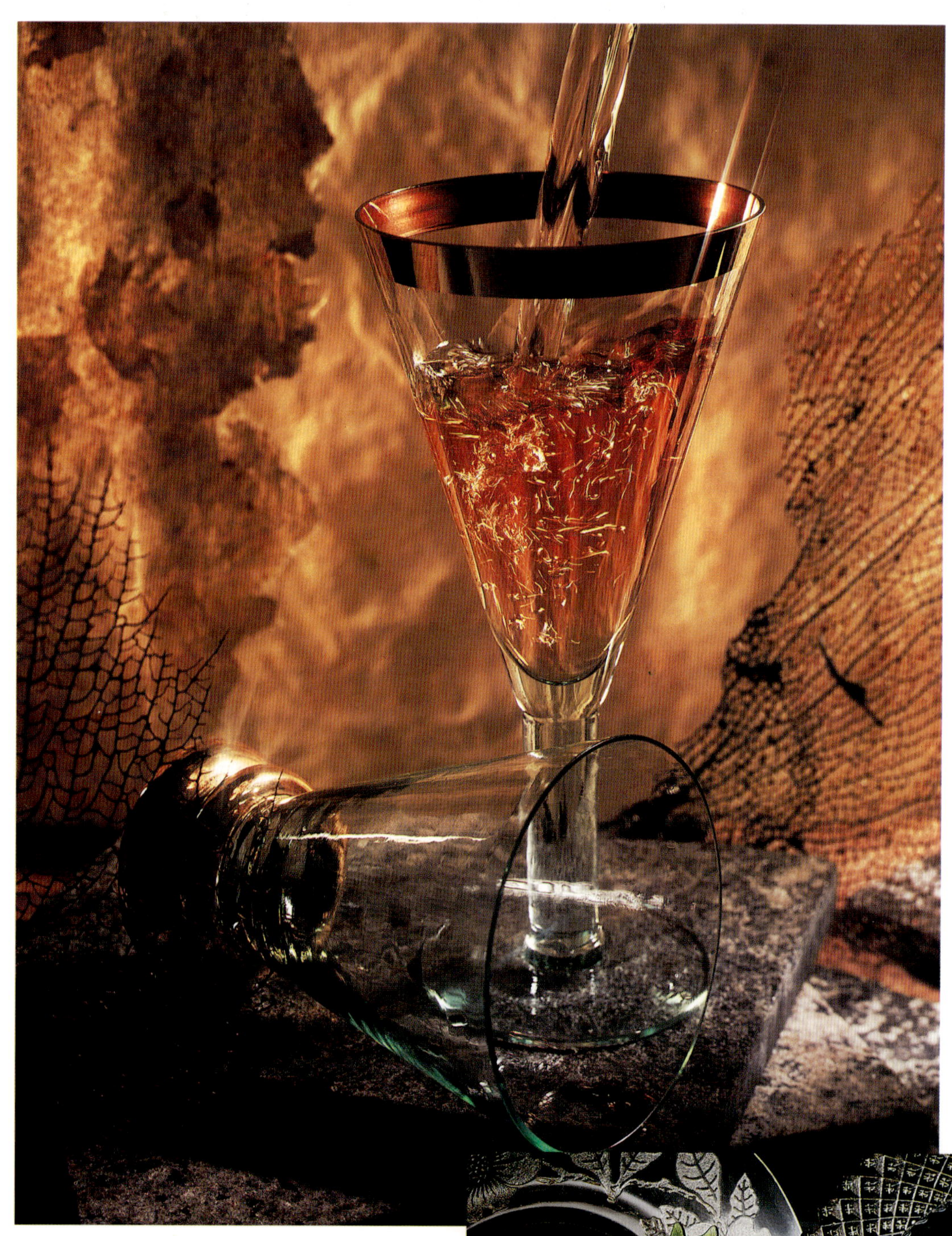



PAUL LACHENAUER

876 BROADWAY

NEW YORK, NY 10003

(212) 529-7059

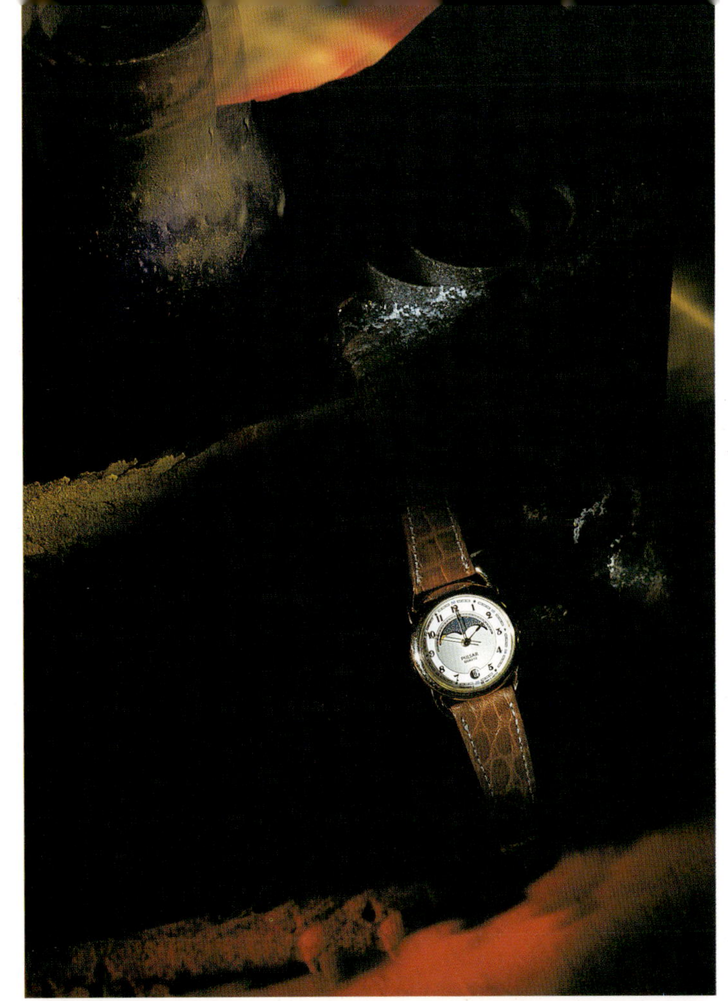

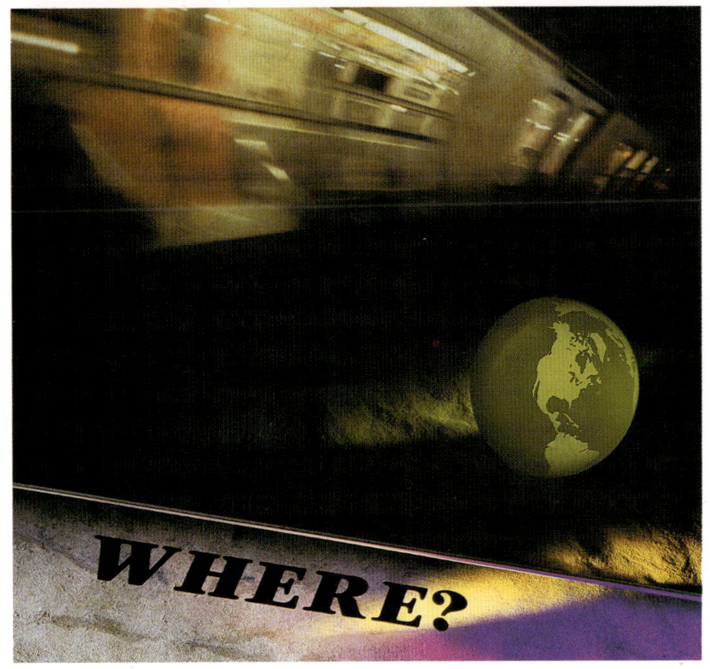



E A R L   R I P L I N G

3 3   W E S T   S E V E N T E E N T H   S T R E E T
N E W   Y O R K   C I T Y   N Y   1 0 0 1 1
2 1 2   7 2 7   2 4 9 3

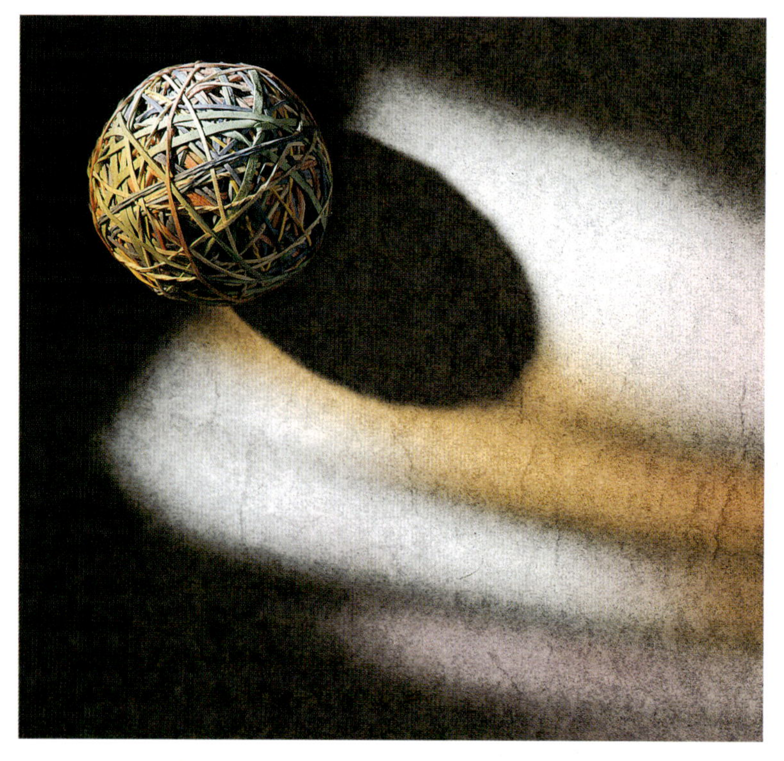

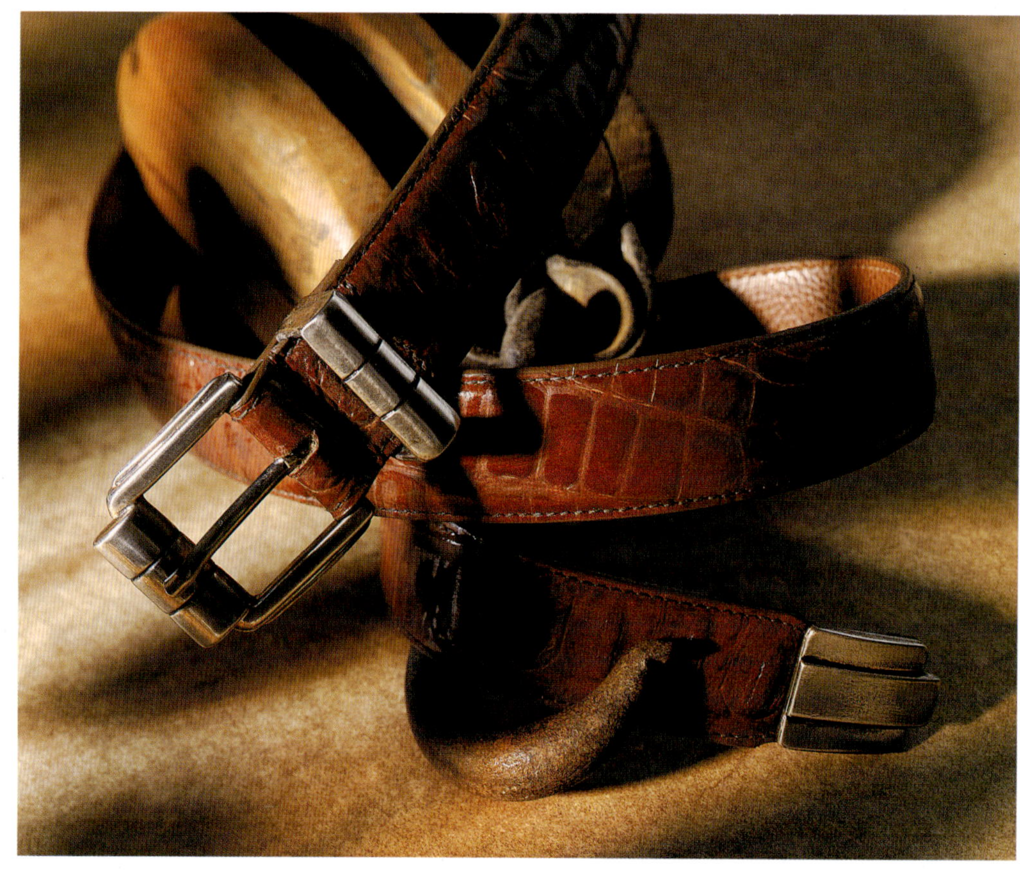

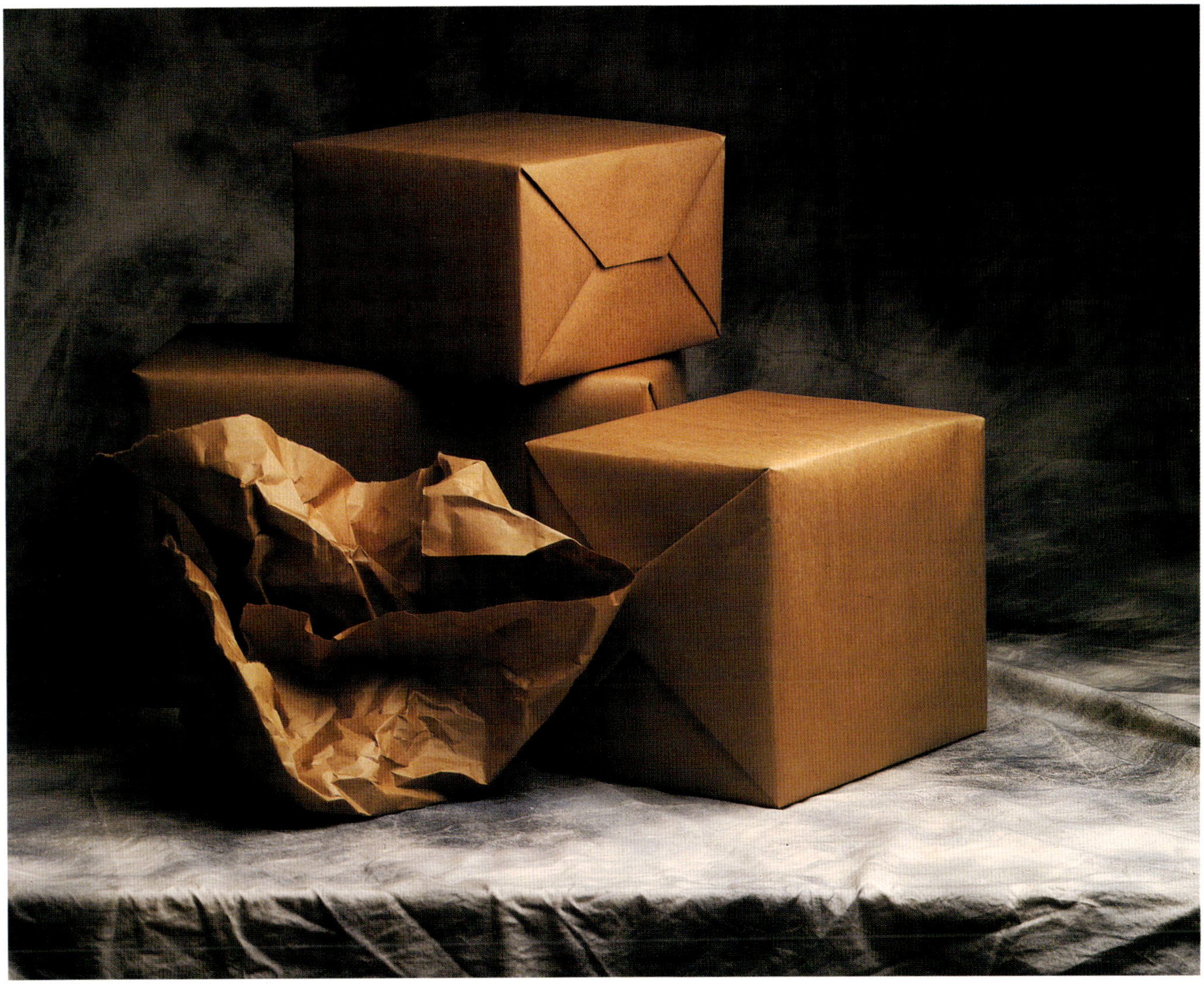

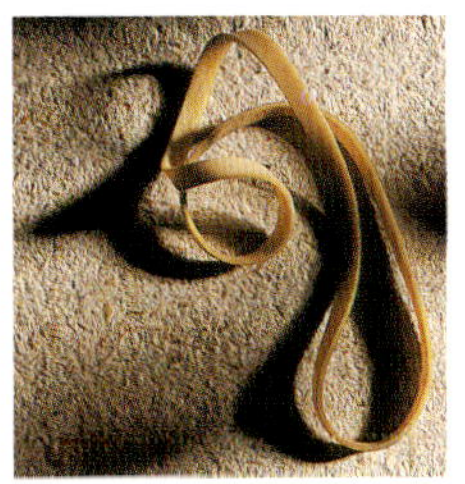

**GEORGE BRENNER**
P H O T O G R A P H Y

31 W 31  N Y C  10001
2 1 2    2 4 4    0 0 2 5

REPRESENTED  BY  JESSICA  SPEART  212  673  2289

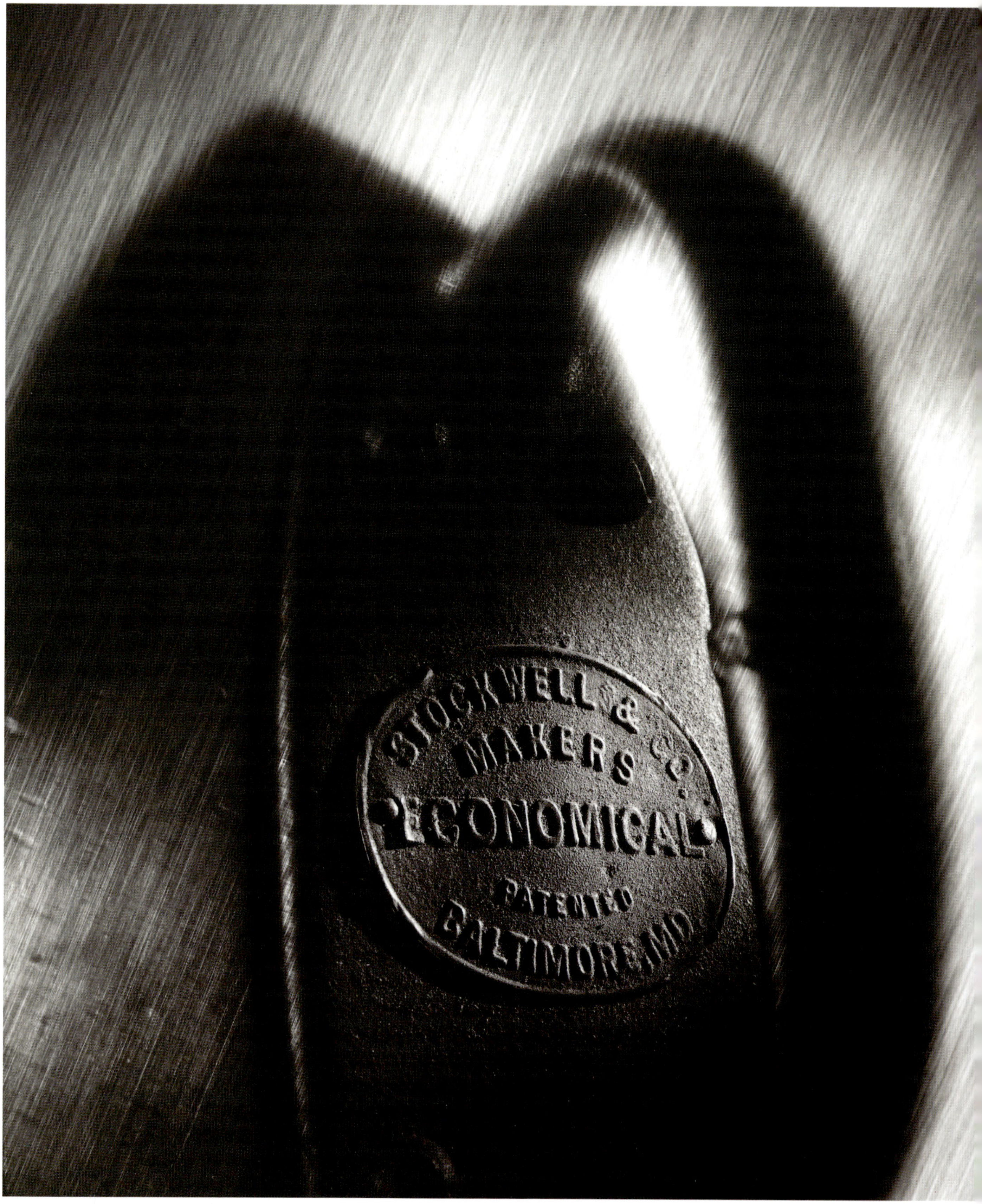

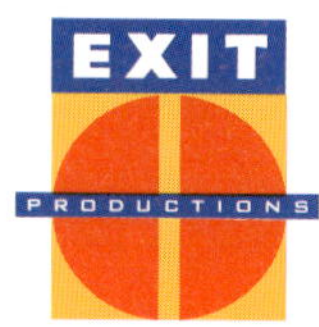

Exit Productions Inc., 180 Franklin Street, New York, NY 10013 Anne-Marie Turbitt Phone: 212-925-8750 Fax: 212-925-8810

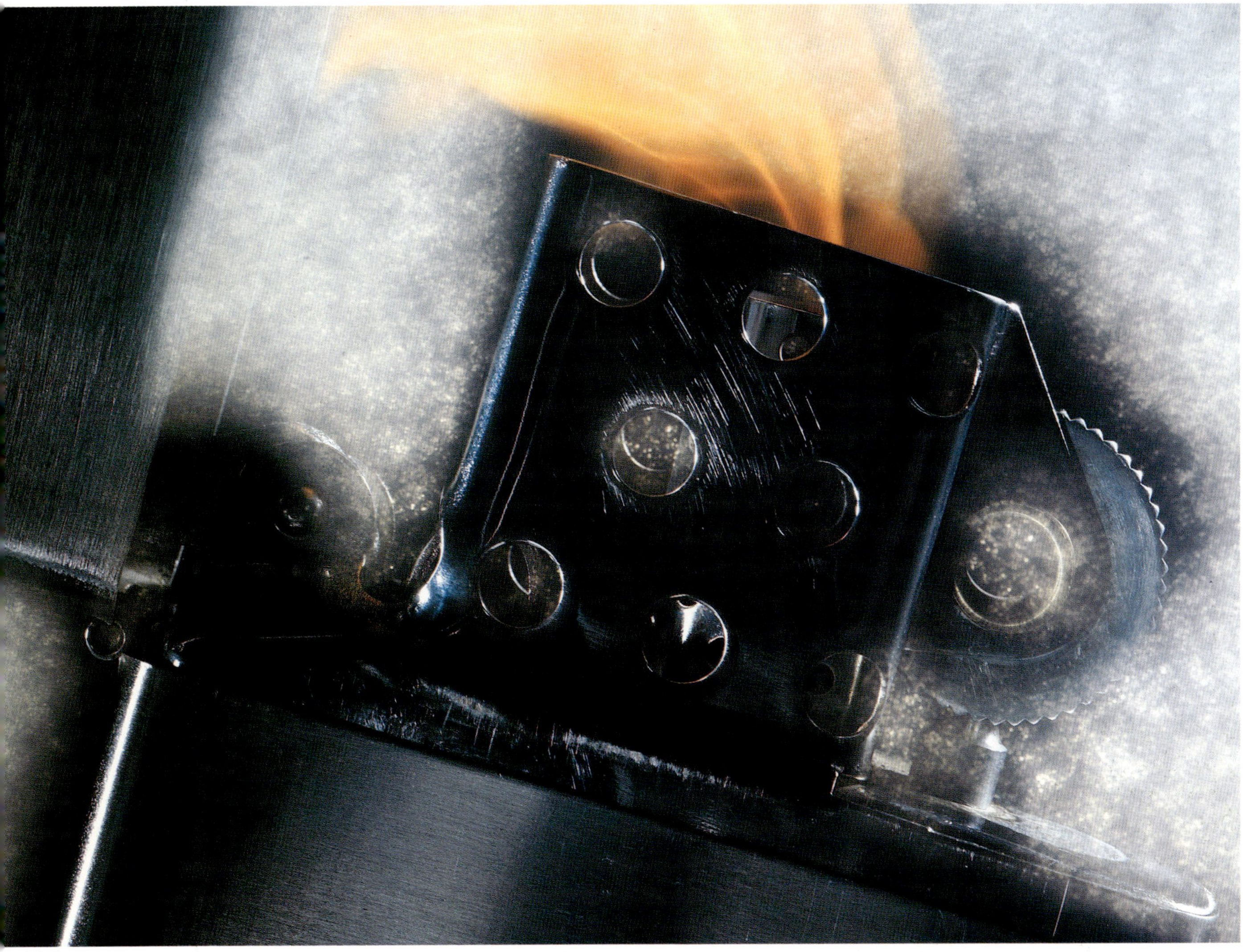

69

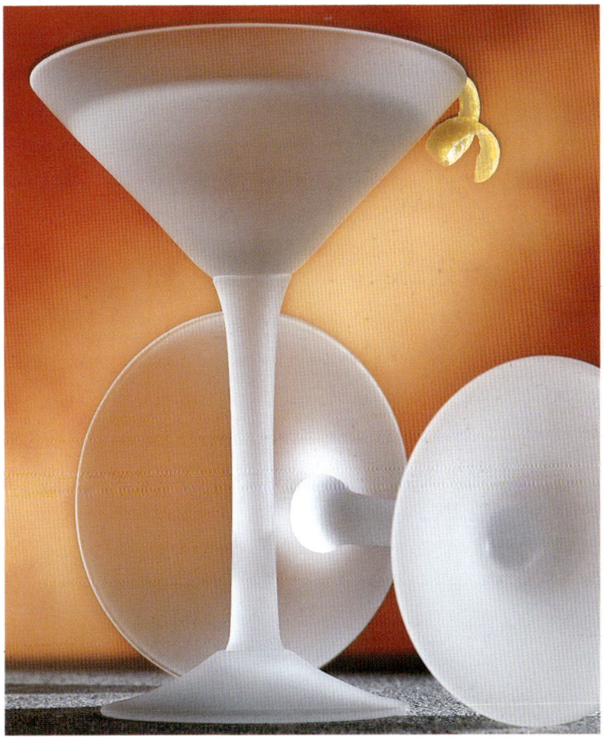

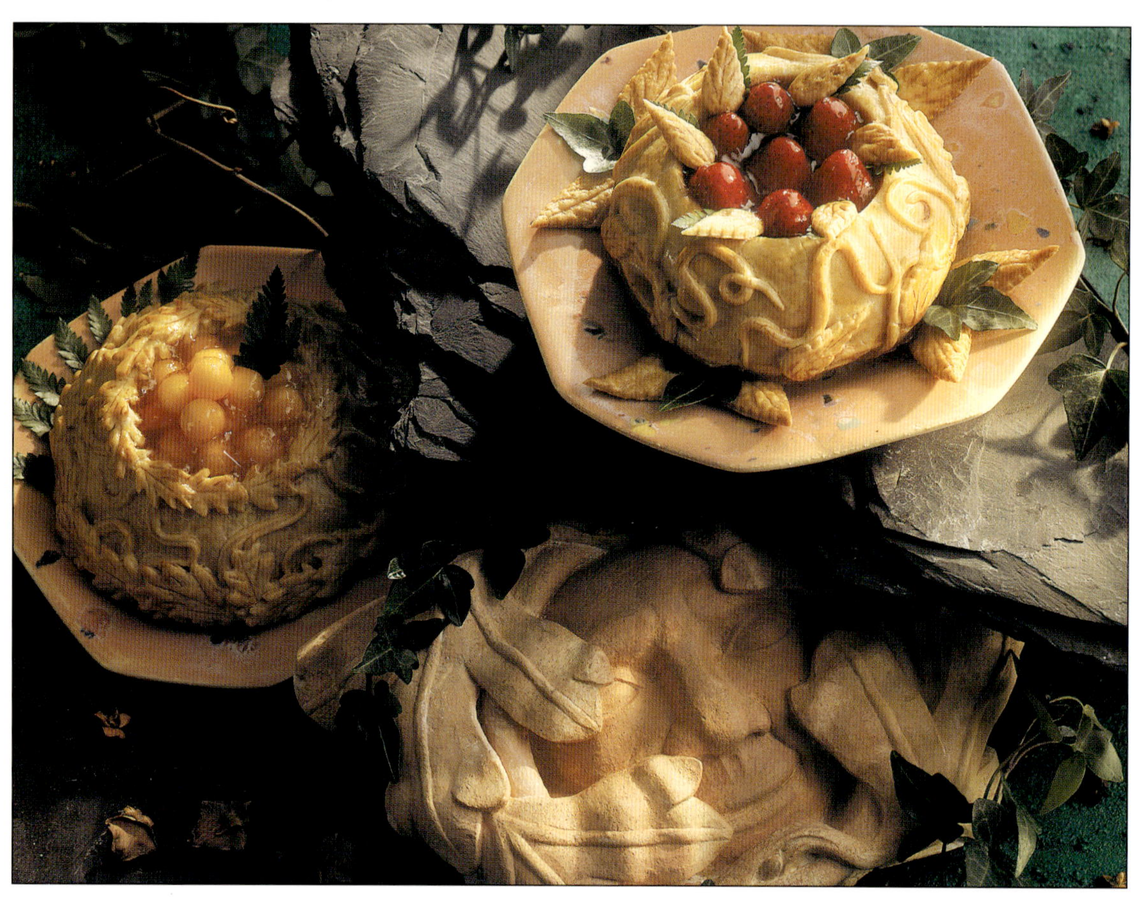

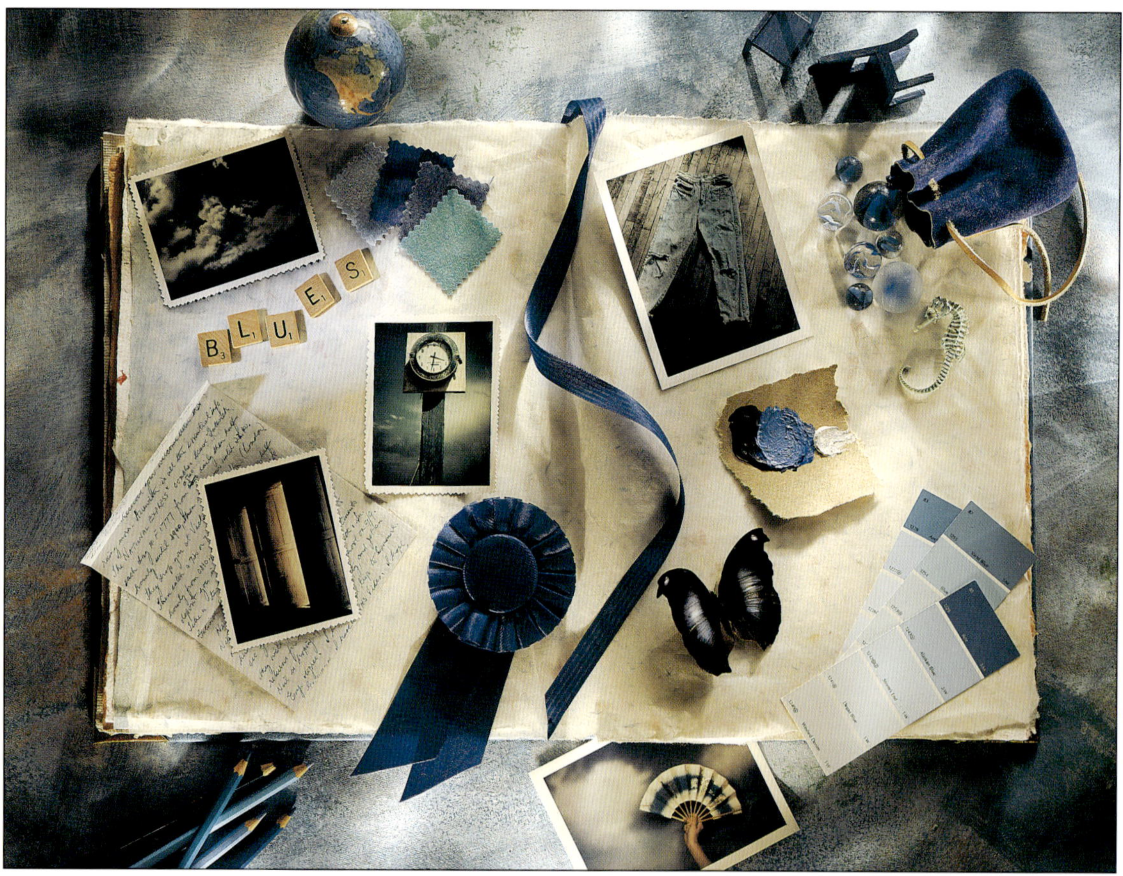
BLUES

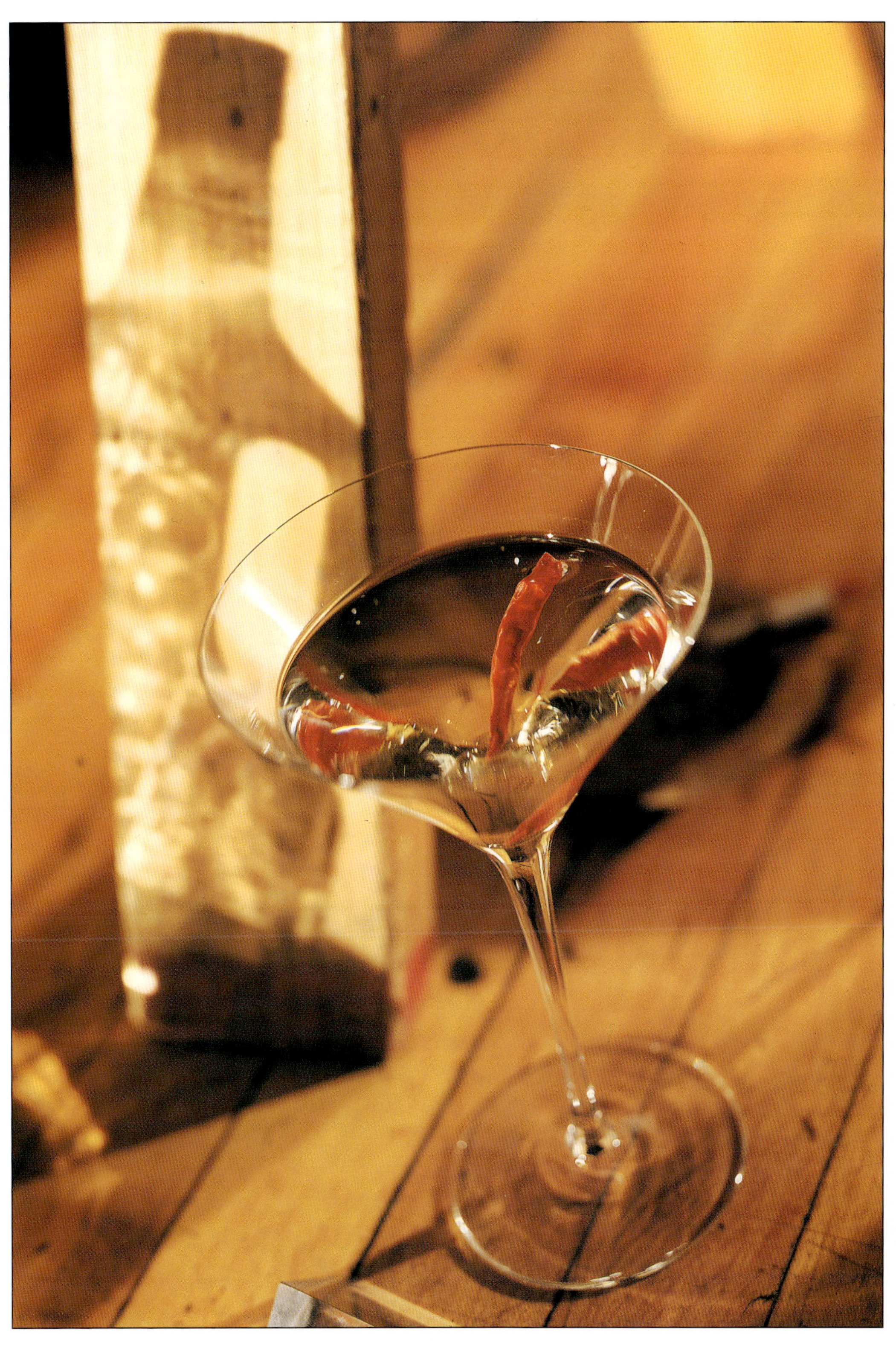

# Colin Cooke

380 Lafayette Street, NYC 10003-6923
212-254-5090
Telefax 212-979-9524
•
Represented by Robert Bacall   212-254-5725

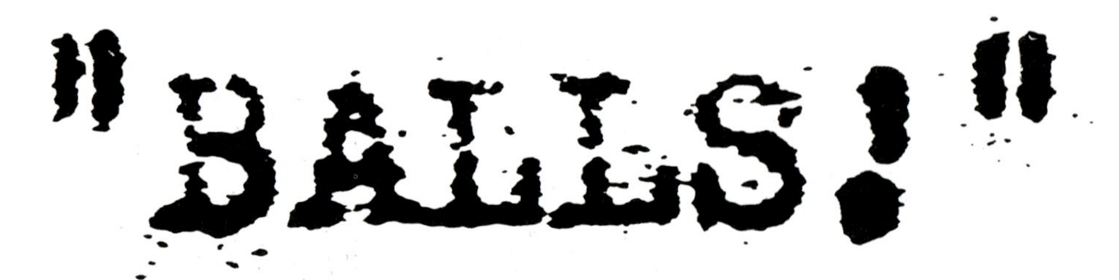


said the queen.

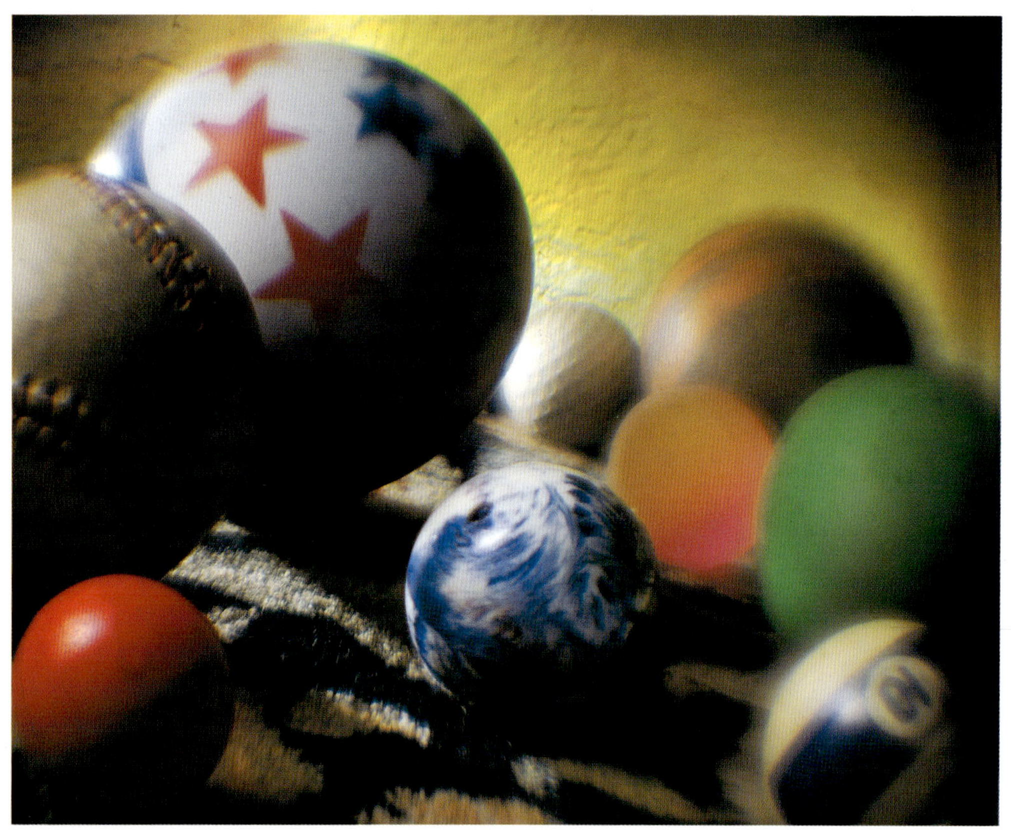

"if I had them, I would
be king."

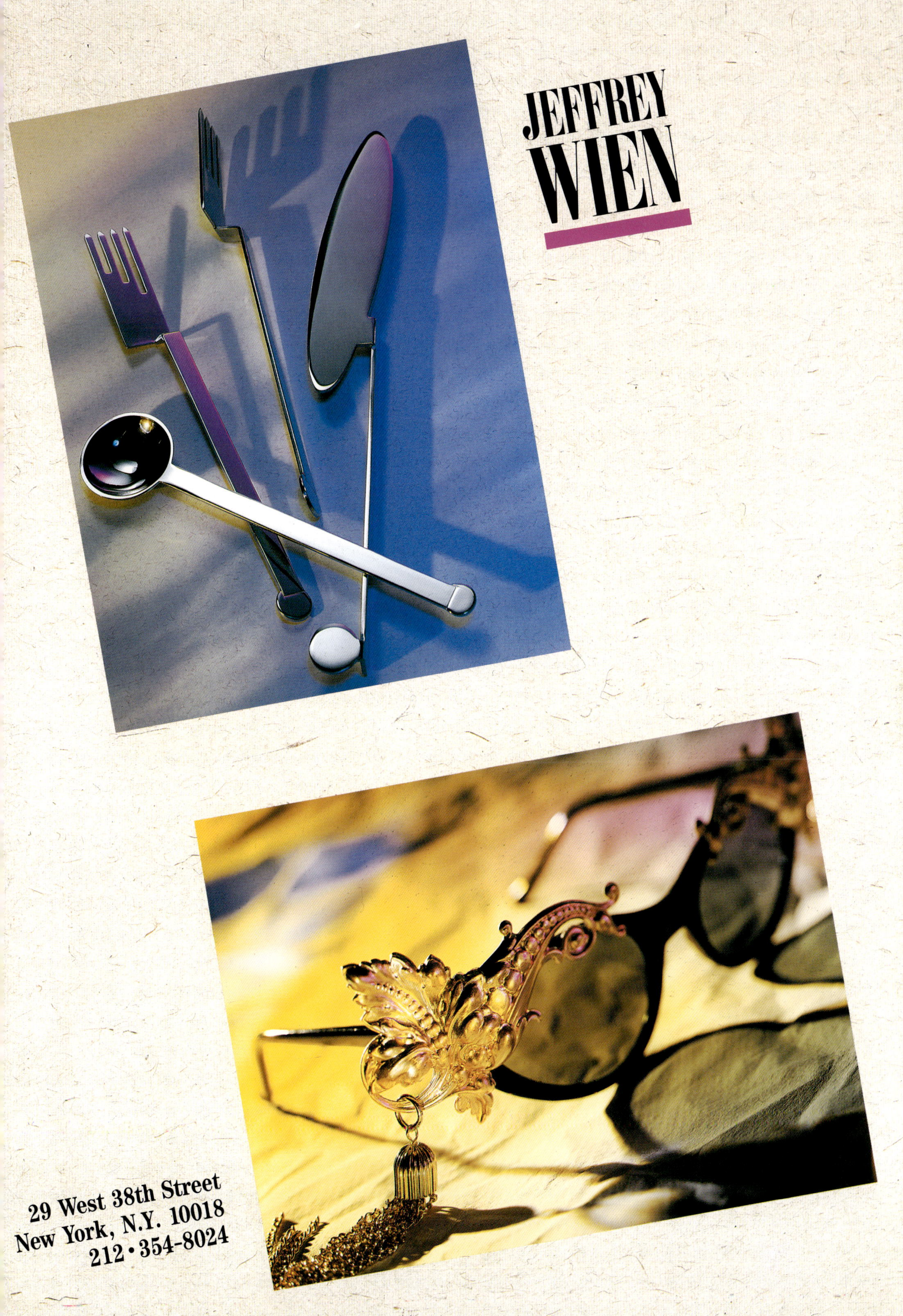

JEFFREY
WIEN

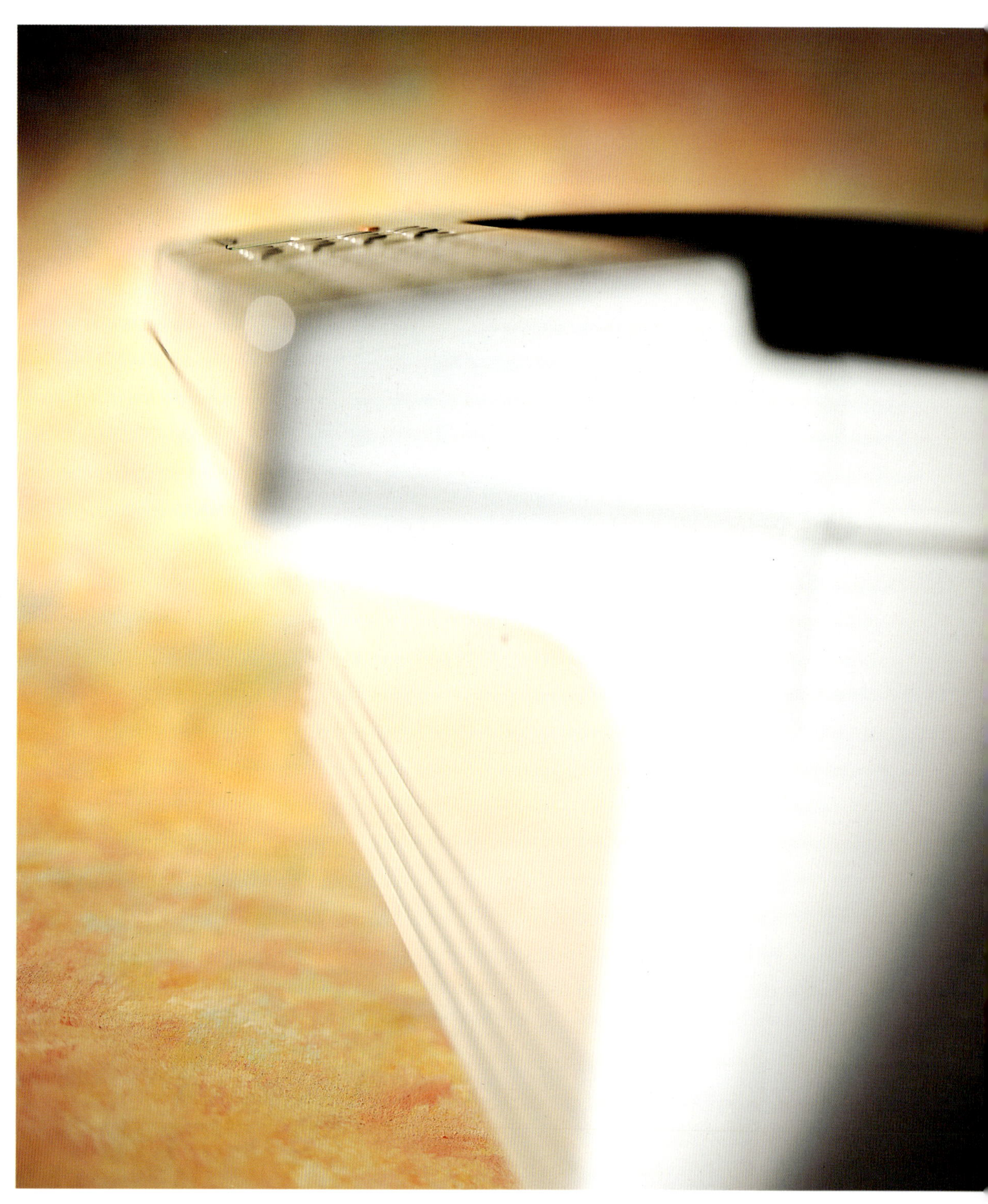

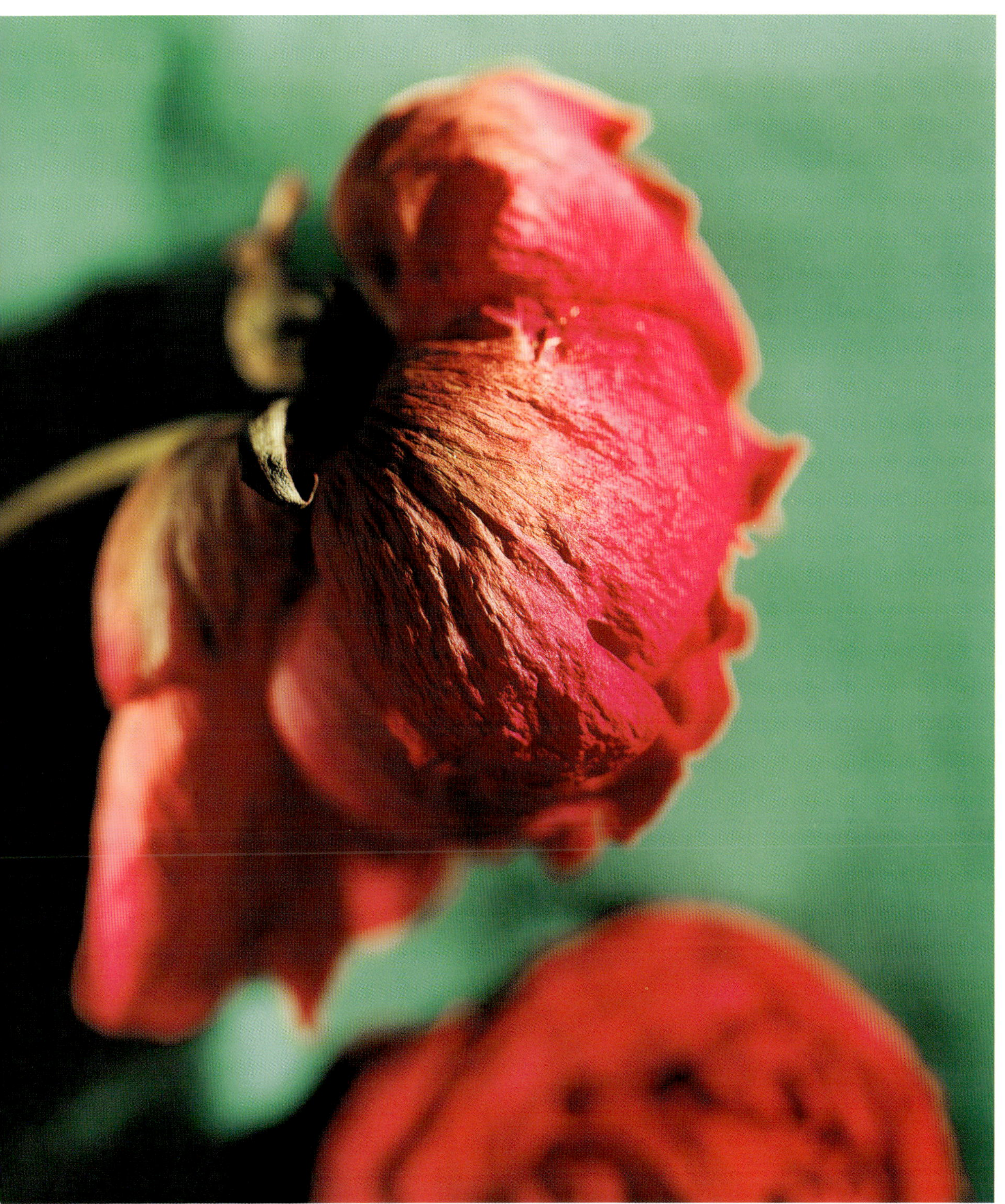

NORA SCARLETT

37 WEST
TWENTIETH ST.
NEW YORK
NEW YORK
10011
212
741-2620

CONTACT
GERALD &
CULLEN RAPP, INC
212
889-3337

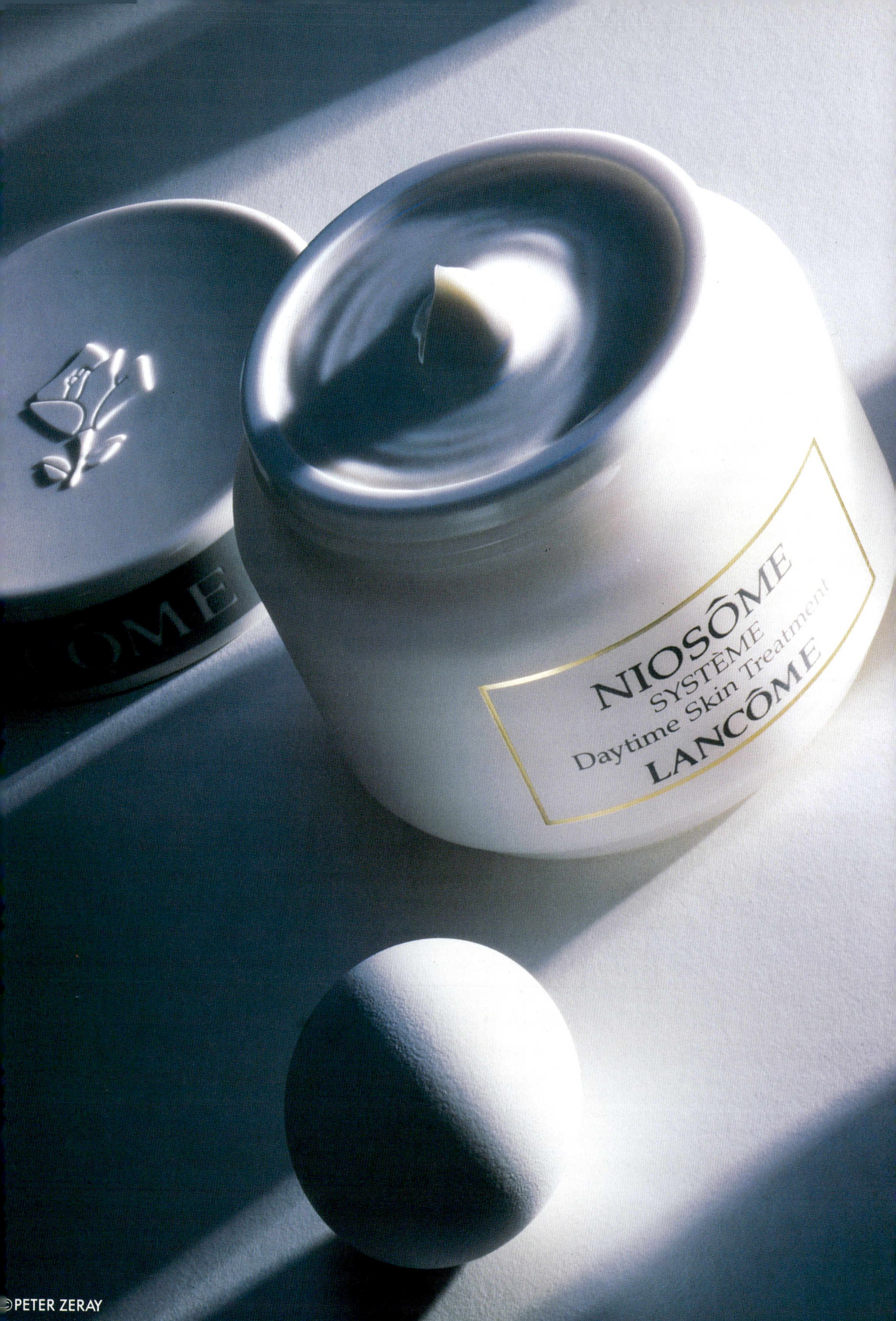
NIOSÔME
SYSTÈME
Daytime Skin Treatment
LANCÔME

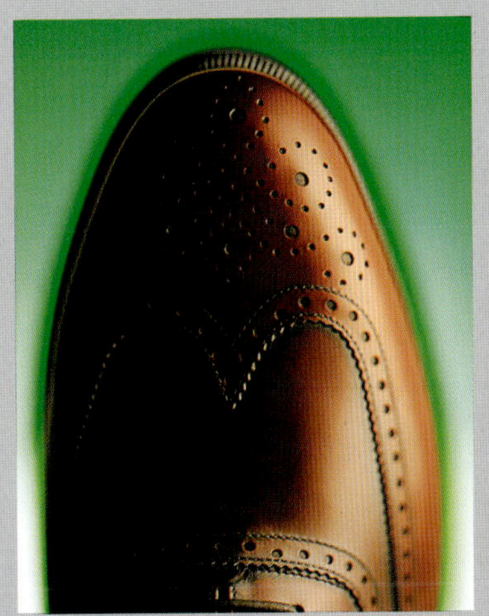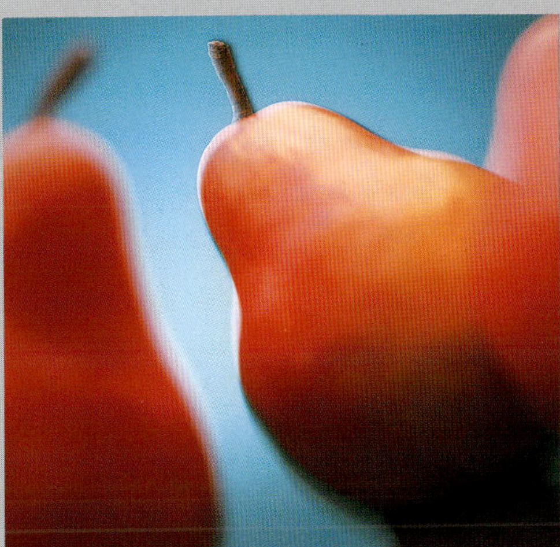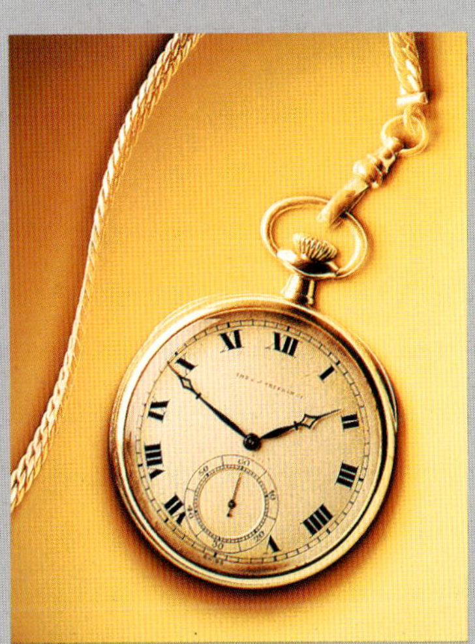

# PETER ZERAY

113 EAST 12TH STREET   NEW YORK 10003   674 0332

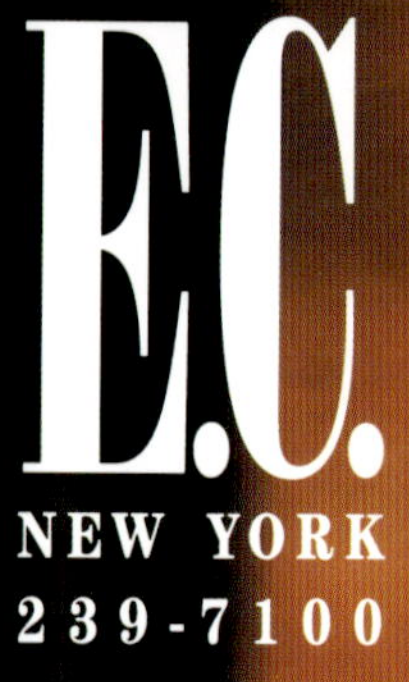


EARL CULBERSON IS REPRESENTED BY LINDA GLASS AND DIANE HENNING • 732-6694

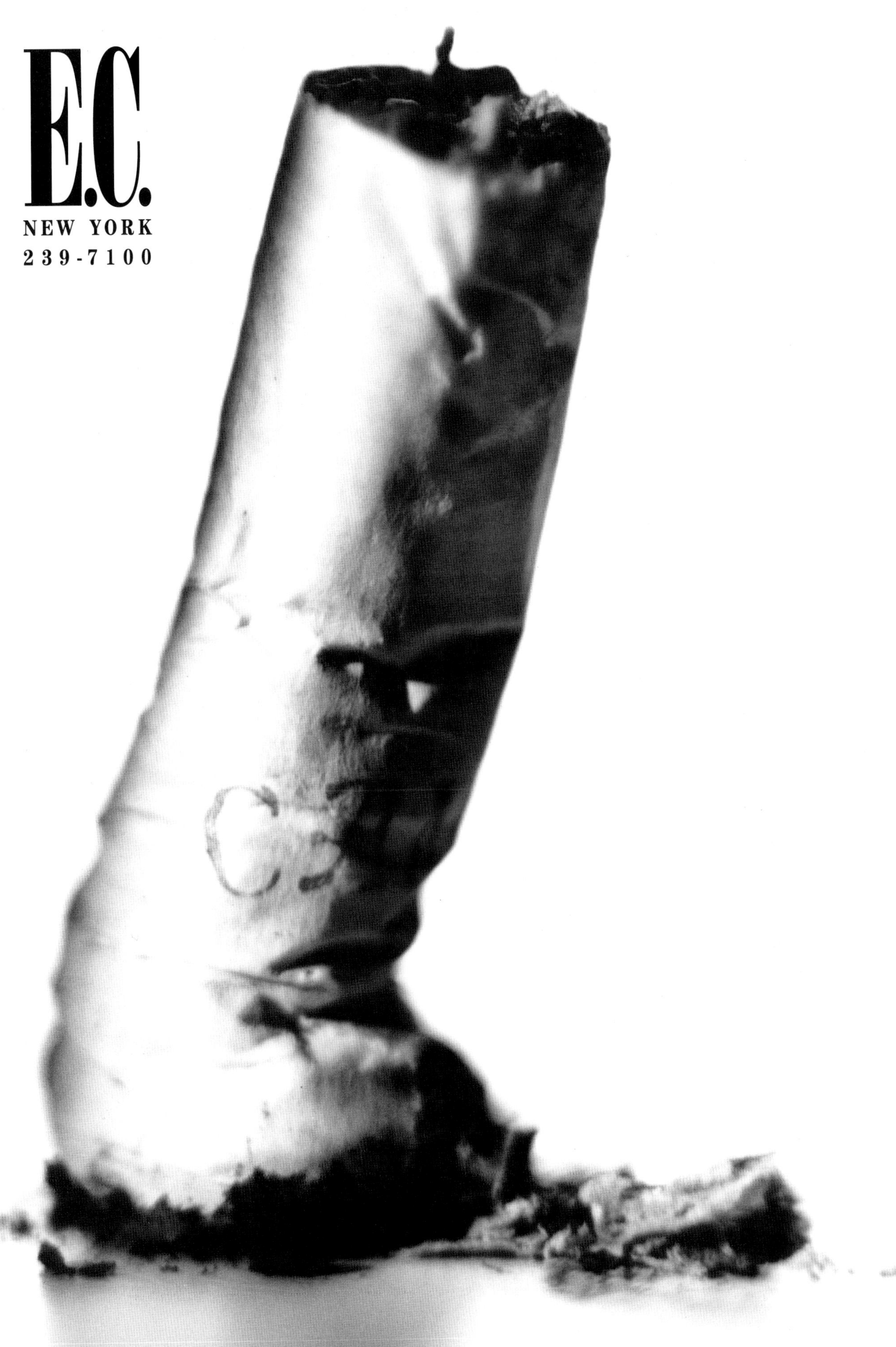
E.C.
NEW YORK
239-7100
EARL CULBERSON IS REPRESENTED BY LINDA GLASS AND DIANE HENNING • 732-6694

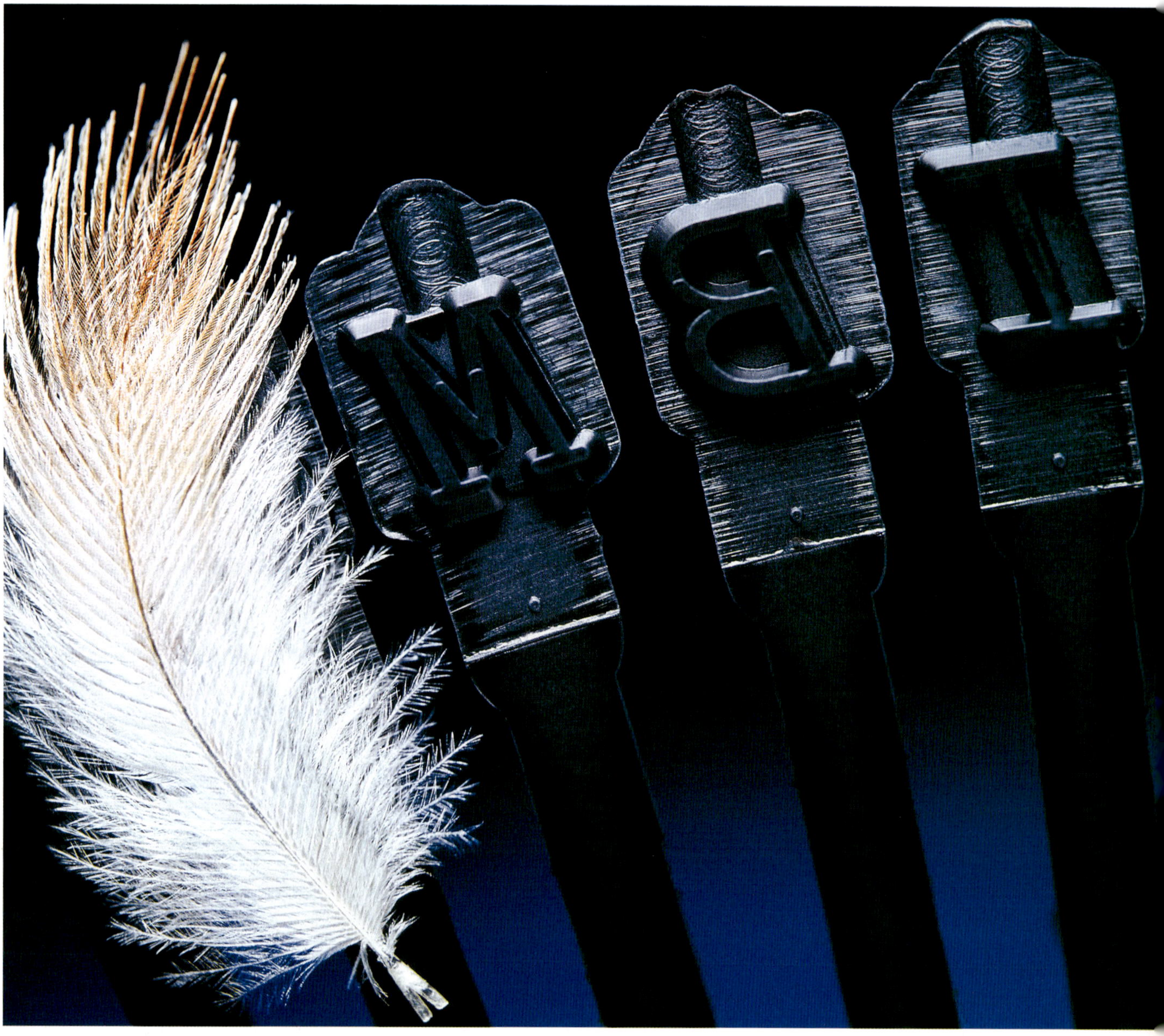

# CLOSE UP, MACRO AND MICRO

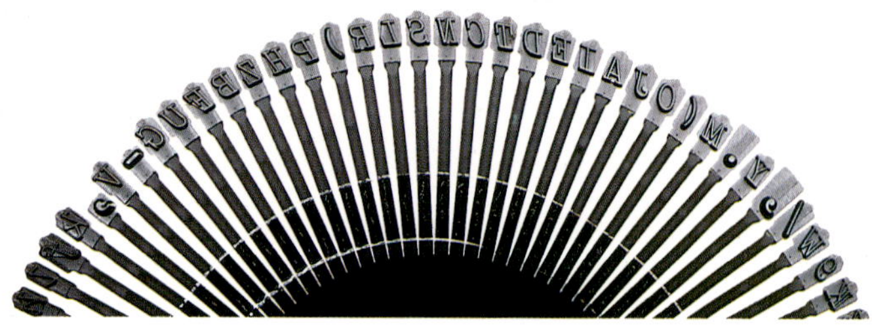

## LASZLO STERN

11 WEST 30TH STREET, NEW YORK 10001
212-239-6600

# EUGENE WEISBERG

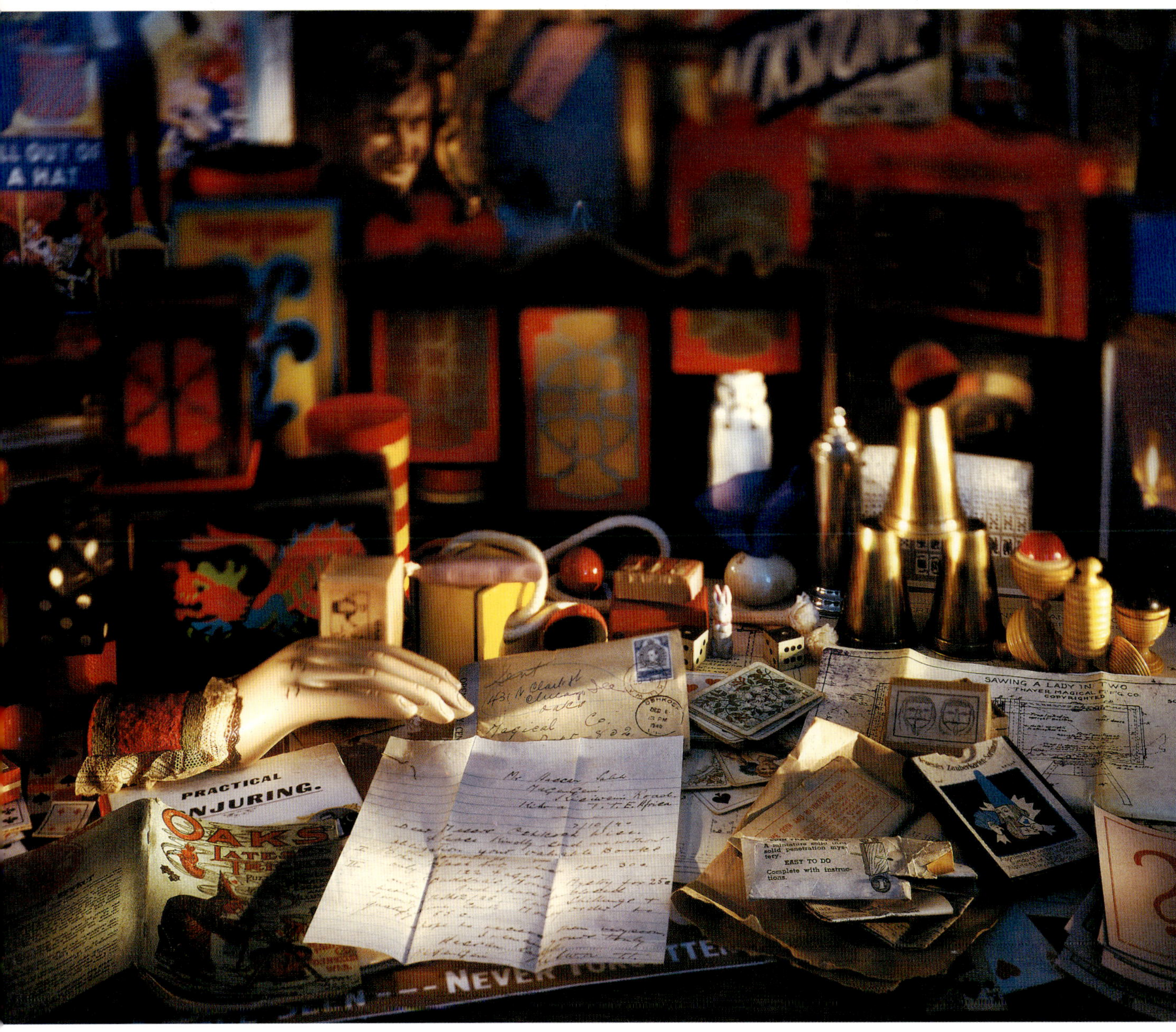




**REPRESENTED BY BARBARA LIVENSTEIN**
**(212) 274-8786**

# WILBY

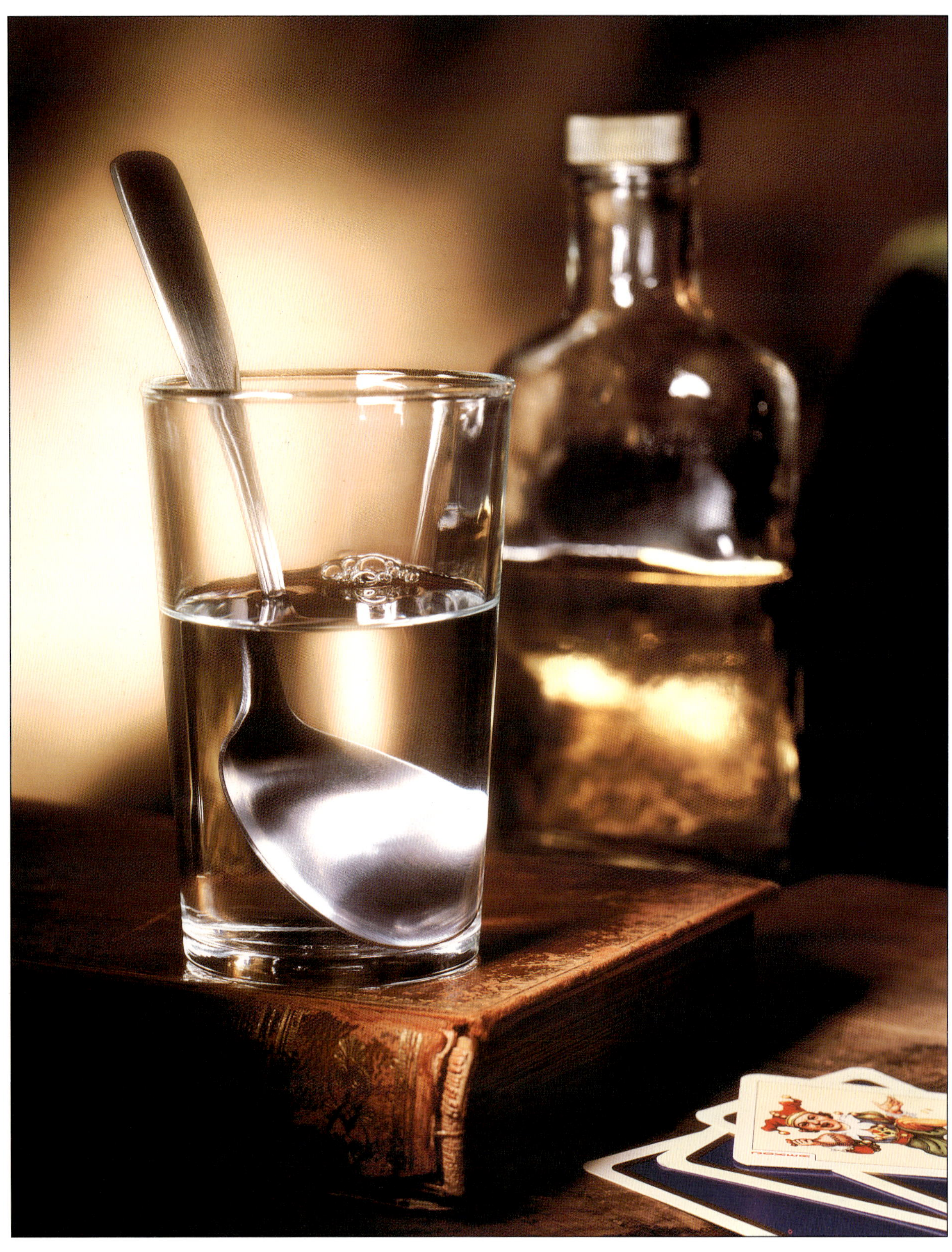

# WILBY

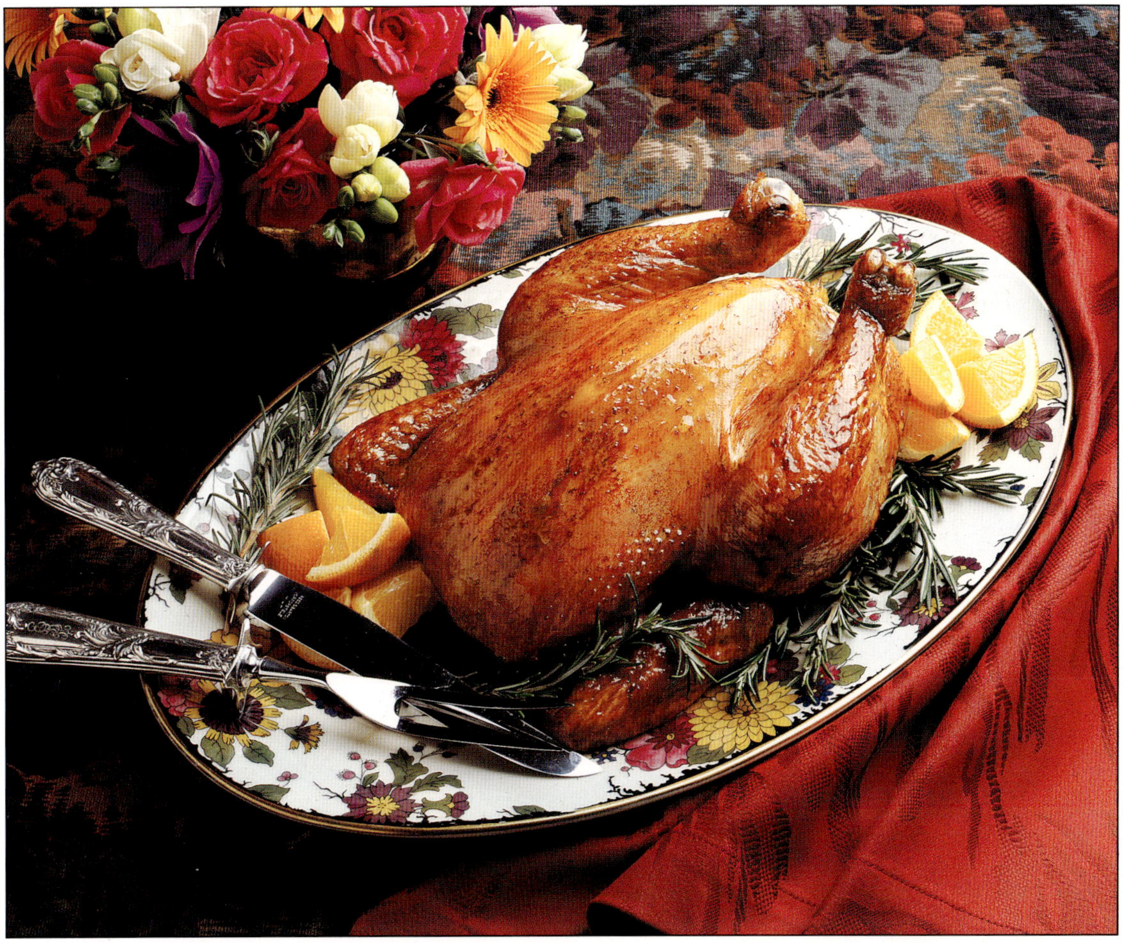

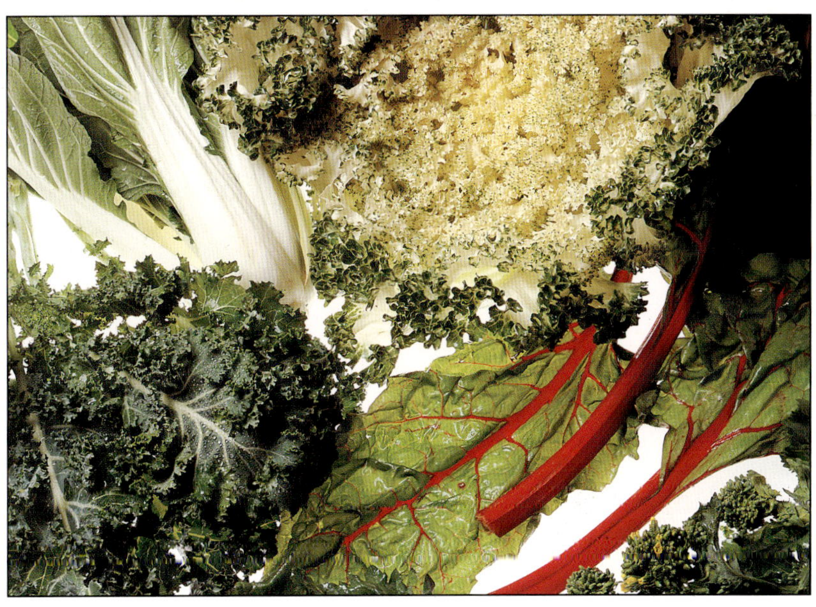


**DAN WILBY PHOTOGRAPHY**
**45 WEST 21ST STREET • 5TH FLOOR • NEW YORK, NEW YORK 10010**
**TEL: 212-929-8231 • FAX: 212-929-8249**

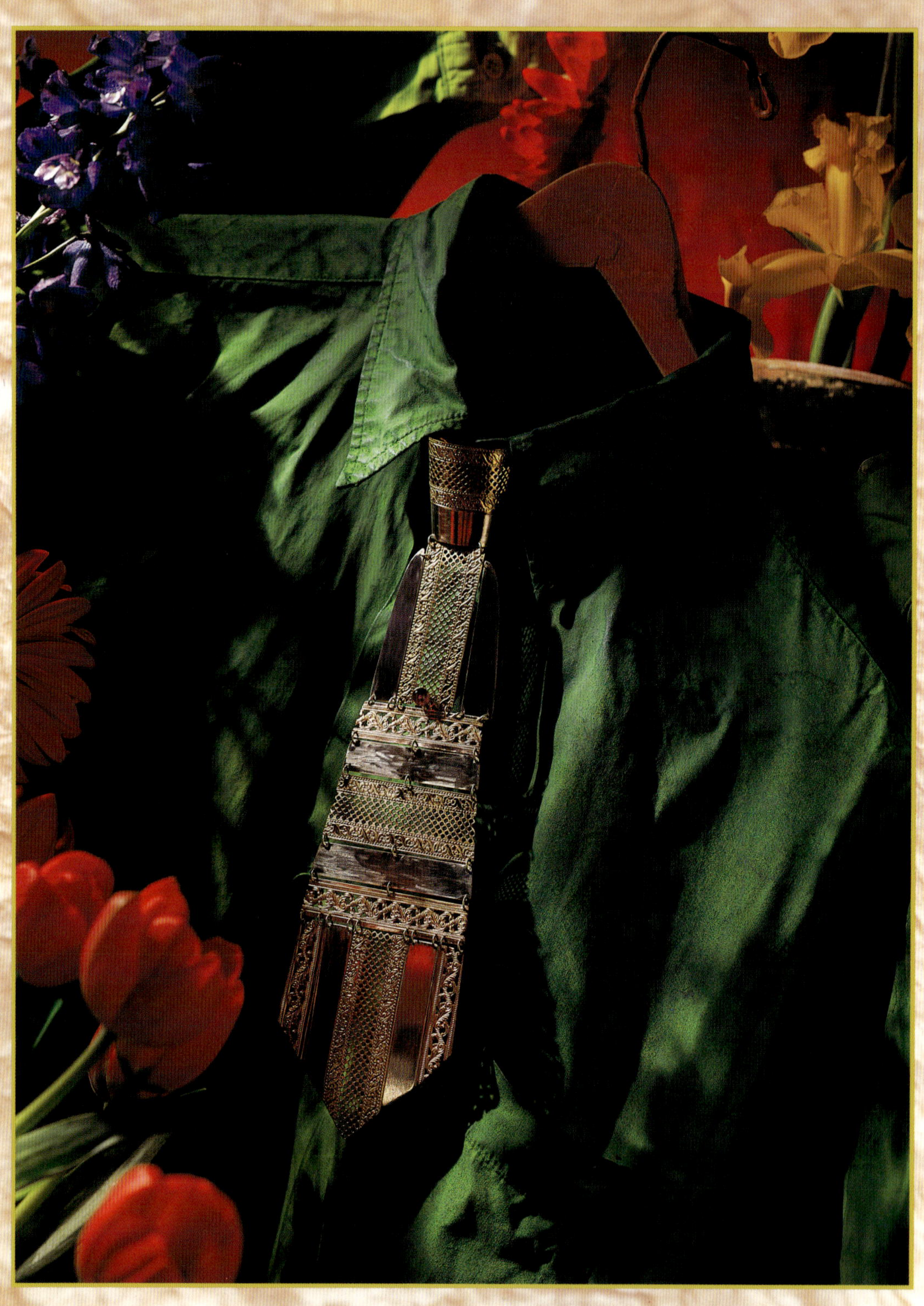

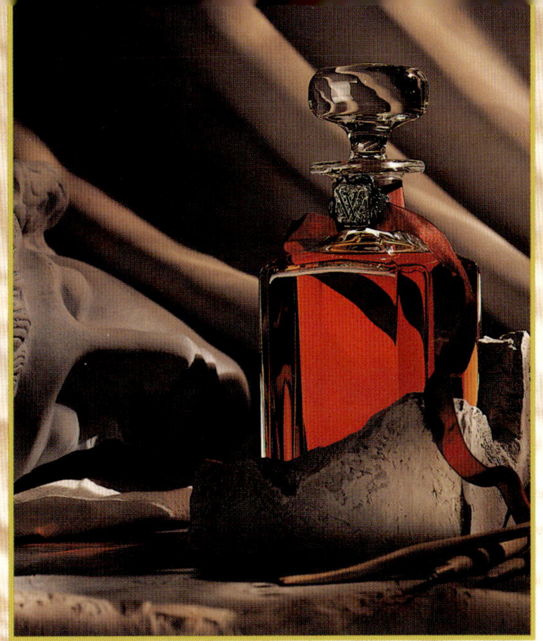

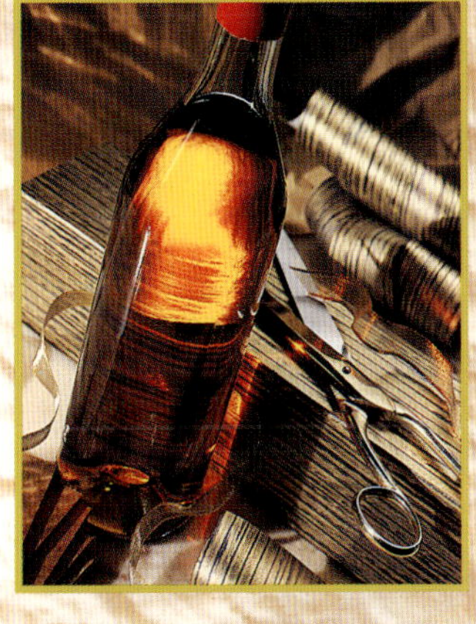

# MATURA

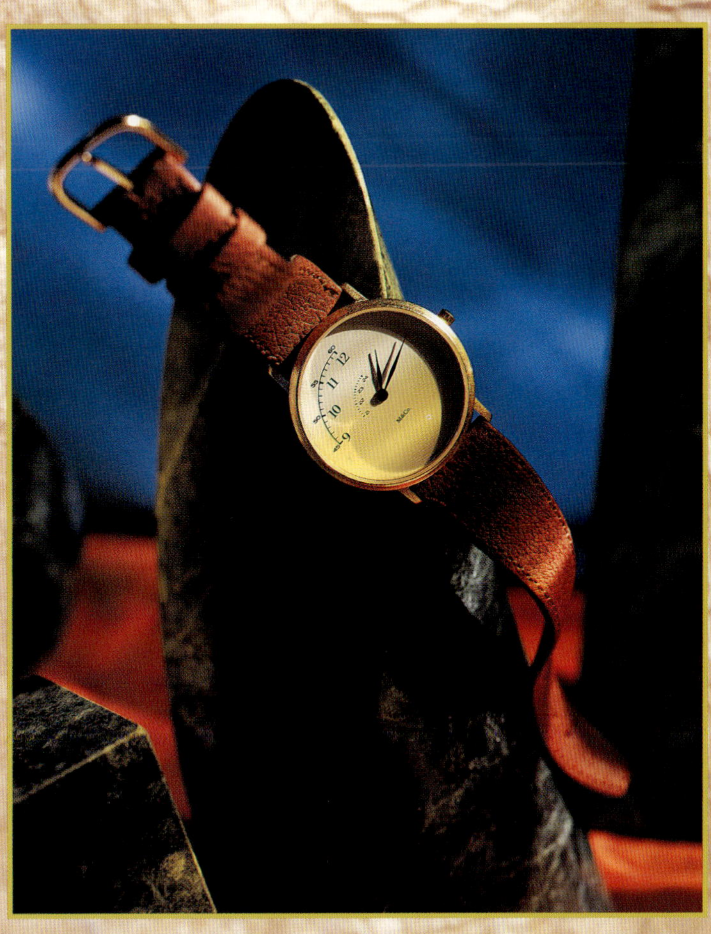

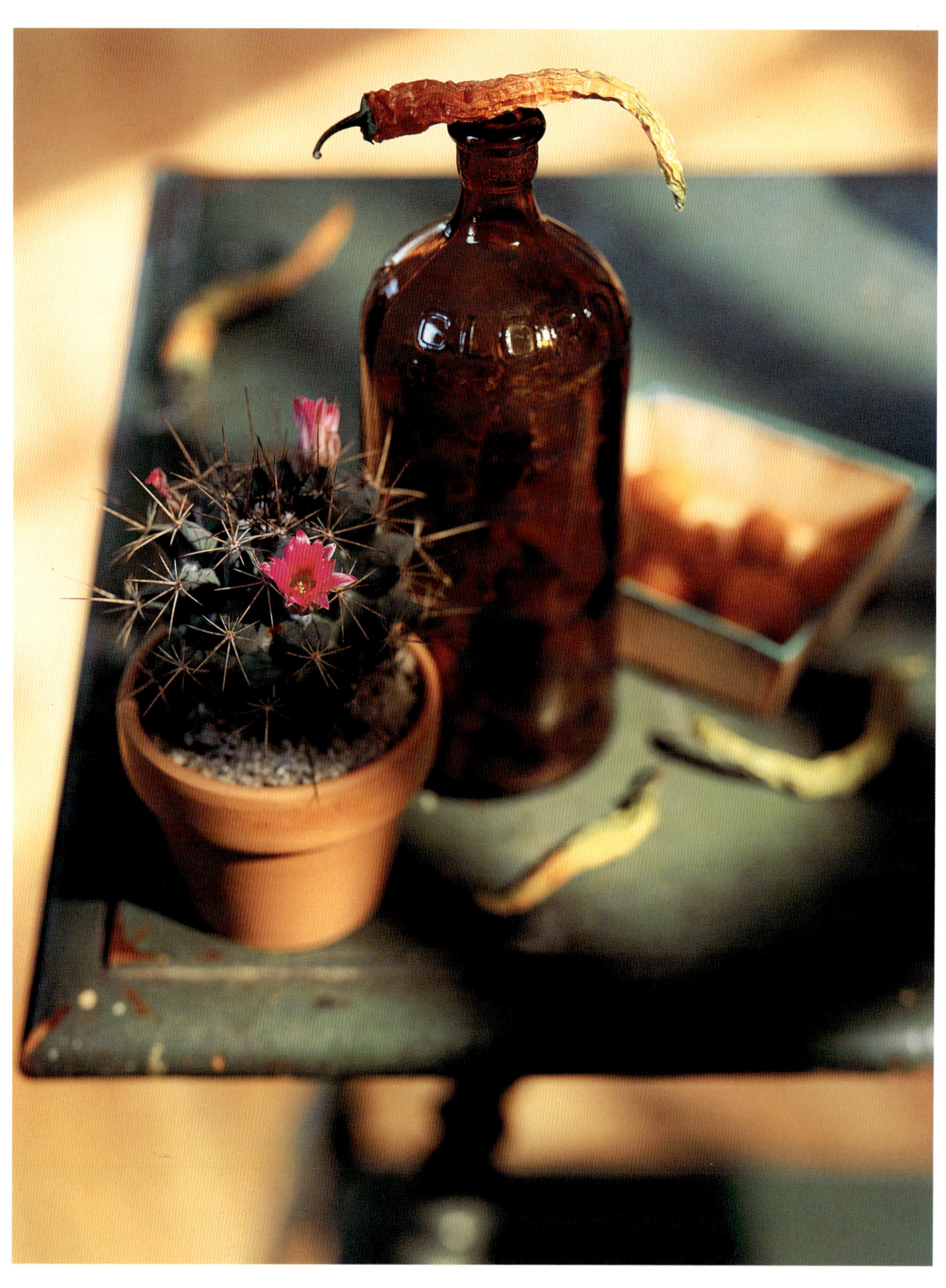

# RITA MAAS

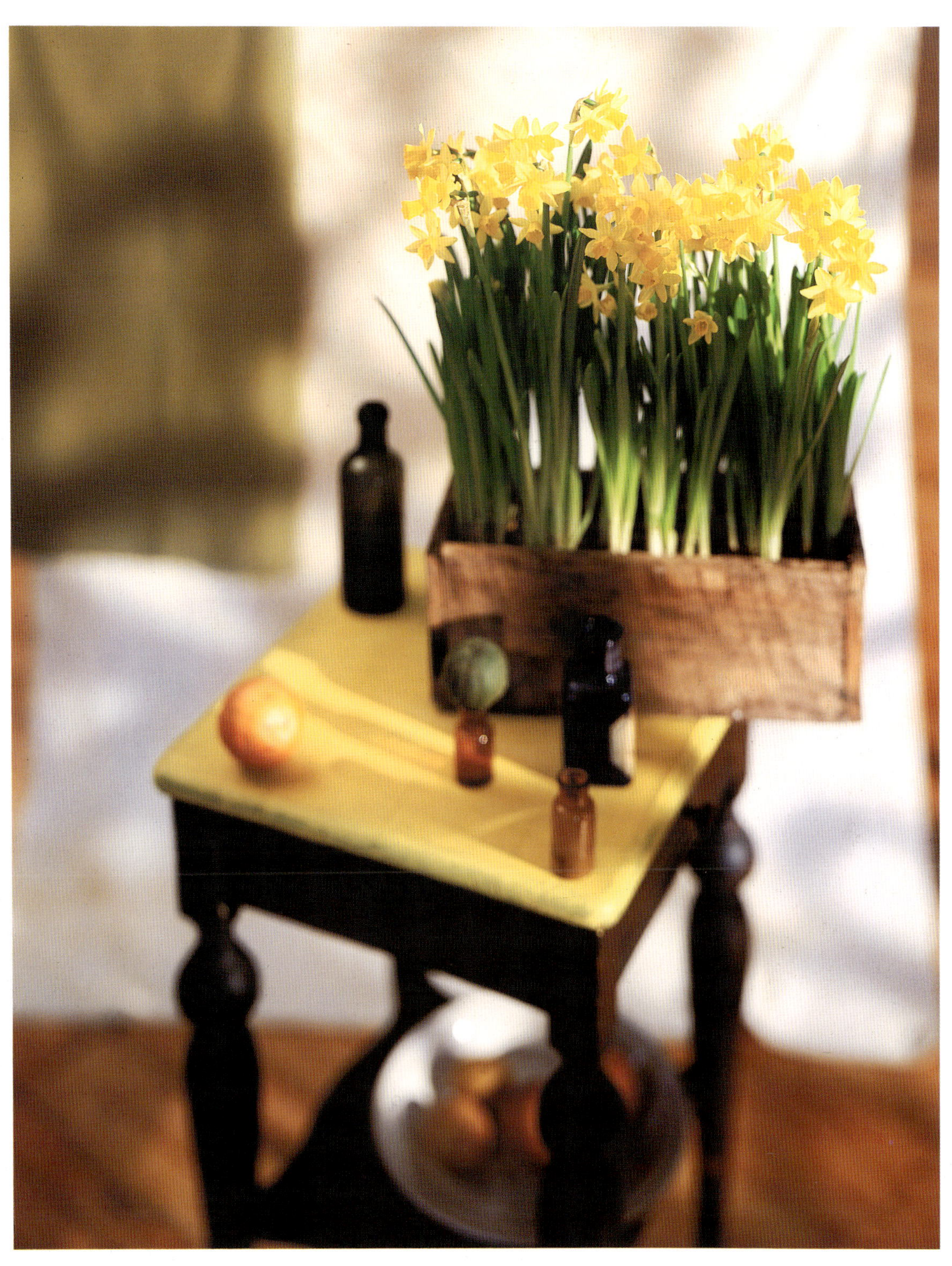

# RITA MAAS

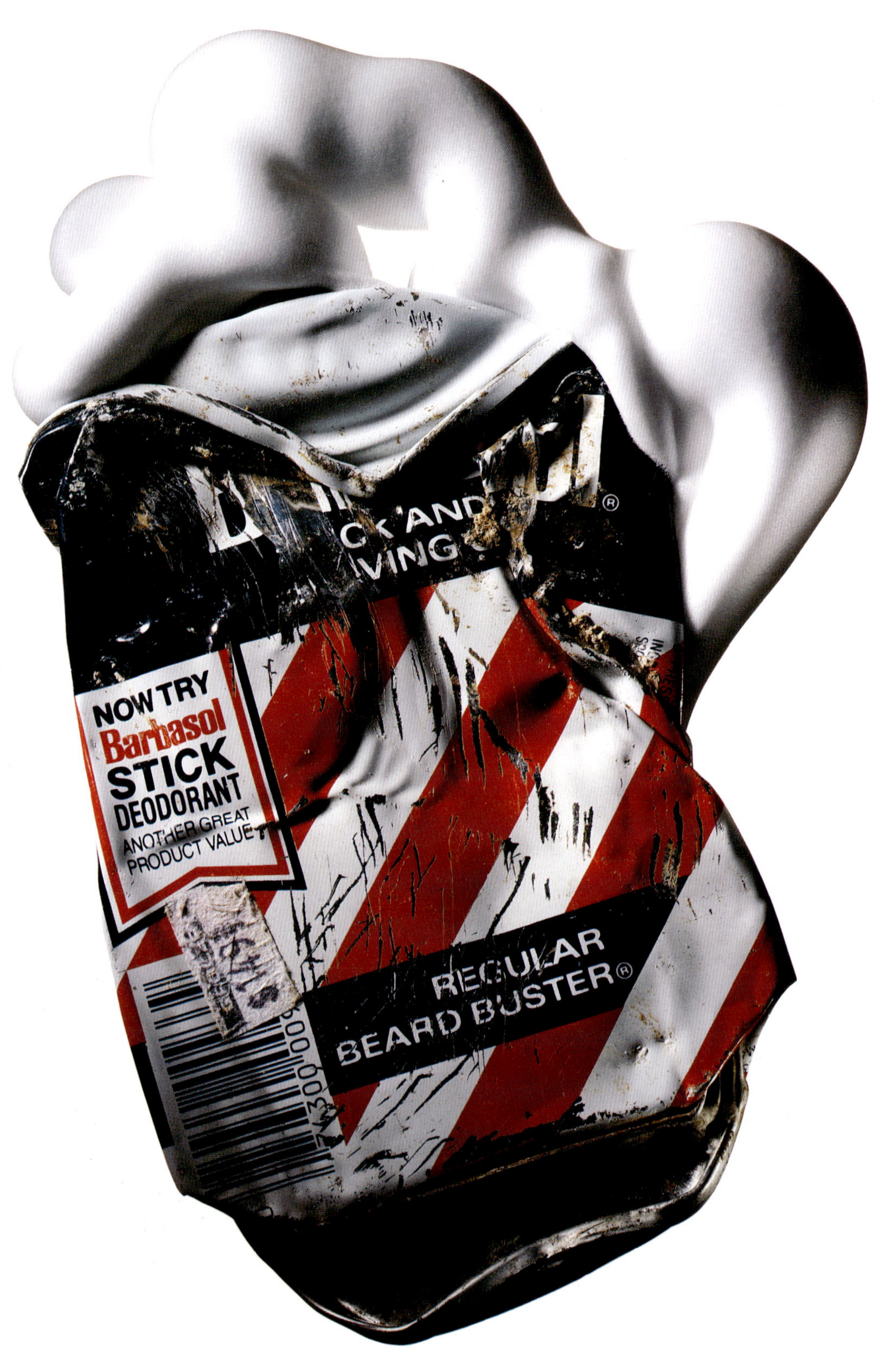


**Represented by Janice Moses  (212) 779-7929**

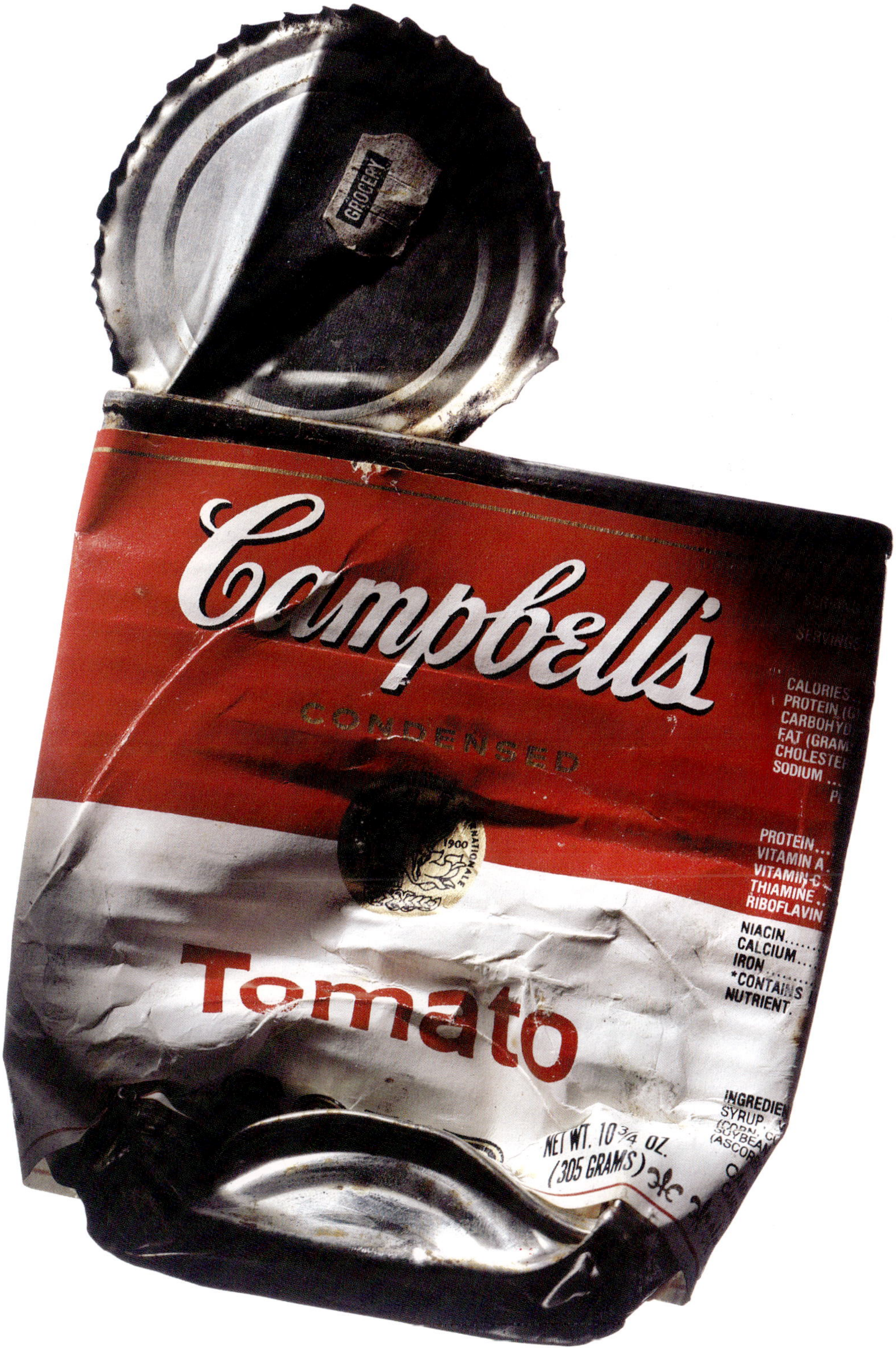

Brad Guice Photography  232 West Broadway  New York City 10013  (212) 206-0966

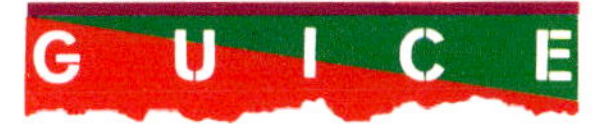

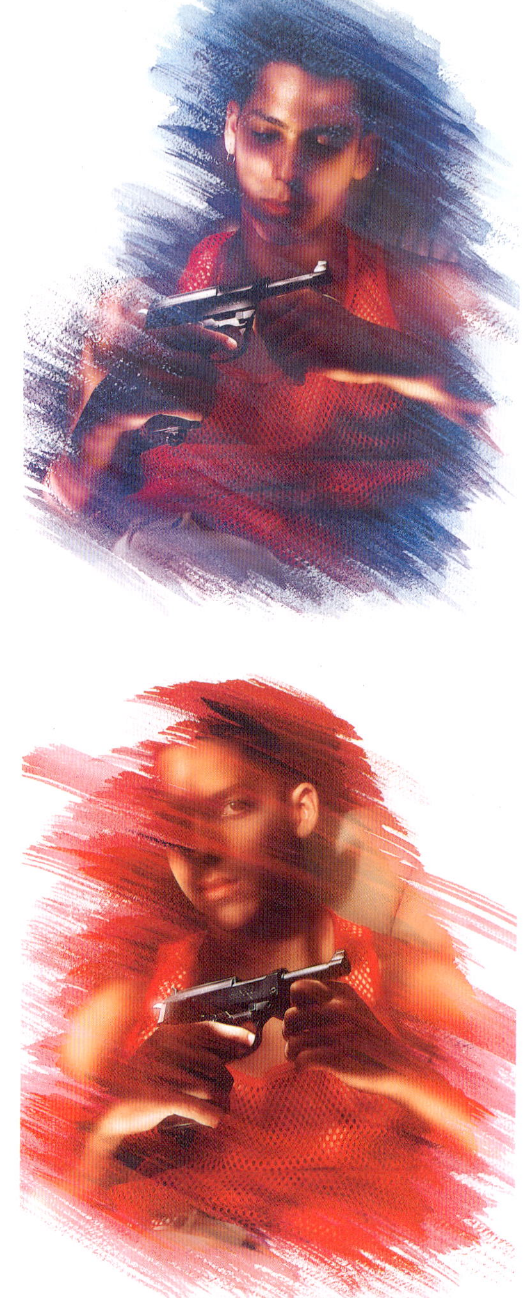

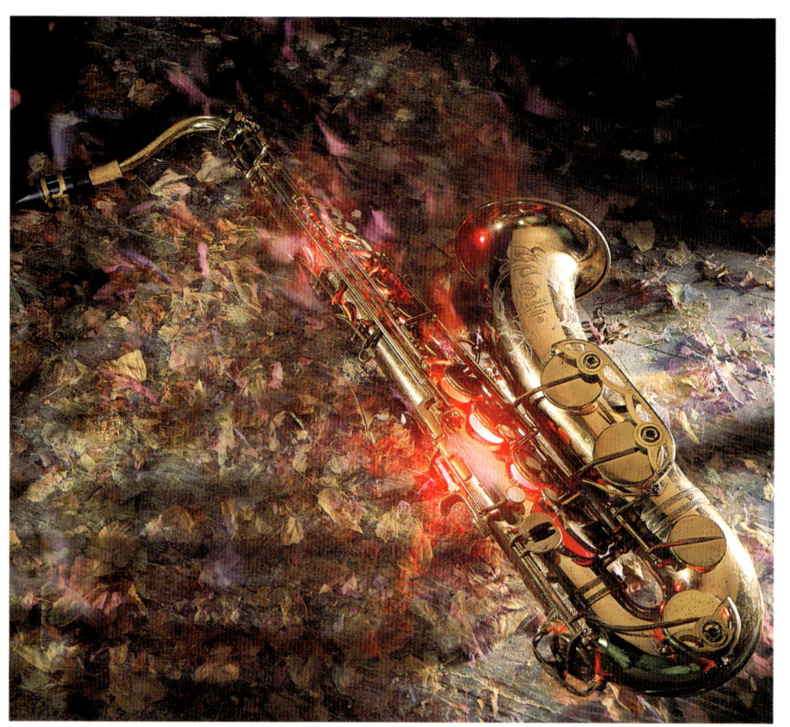

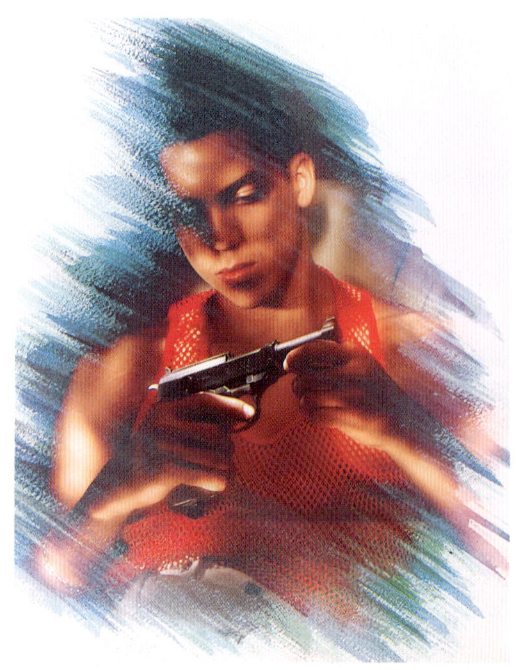

S T U A R T   S I M O N S
201.278.5050

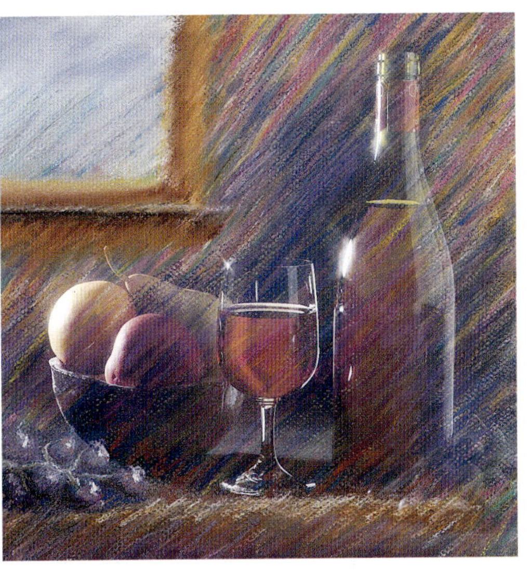

STUART SIMONS
201.278.5050

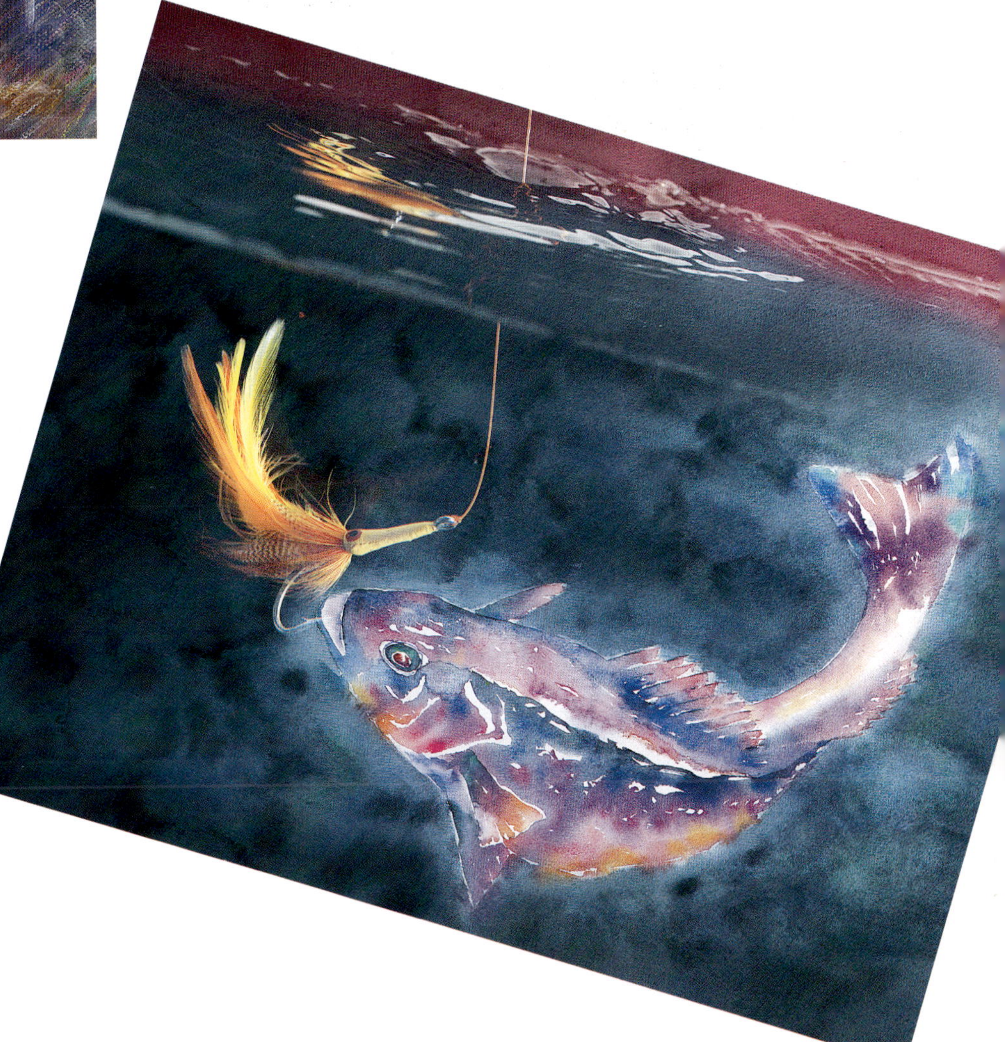

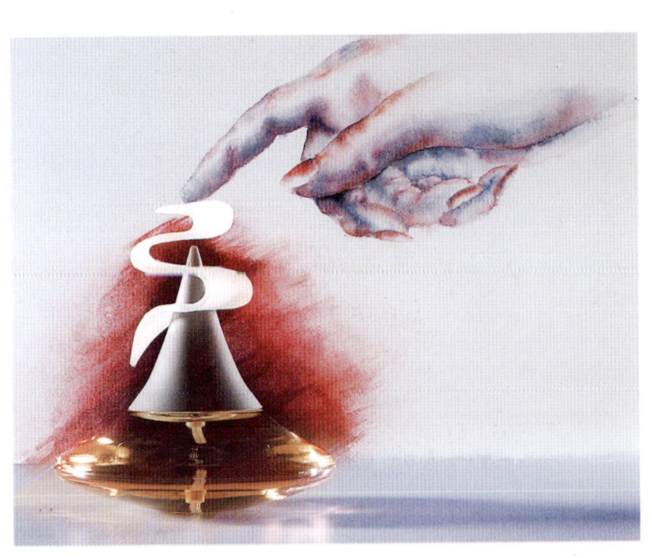

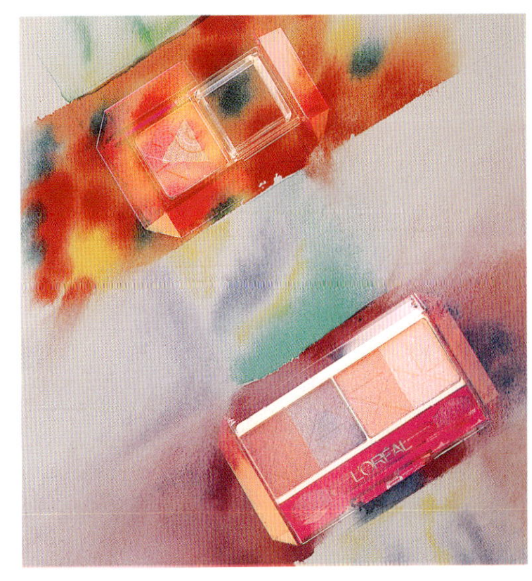

91

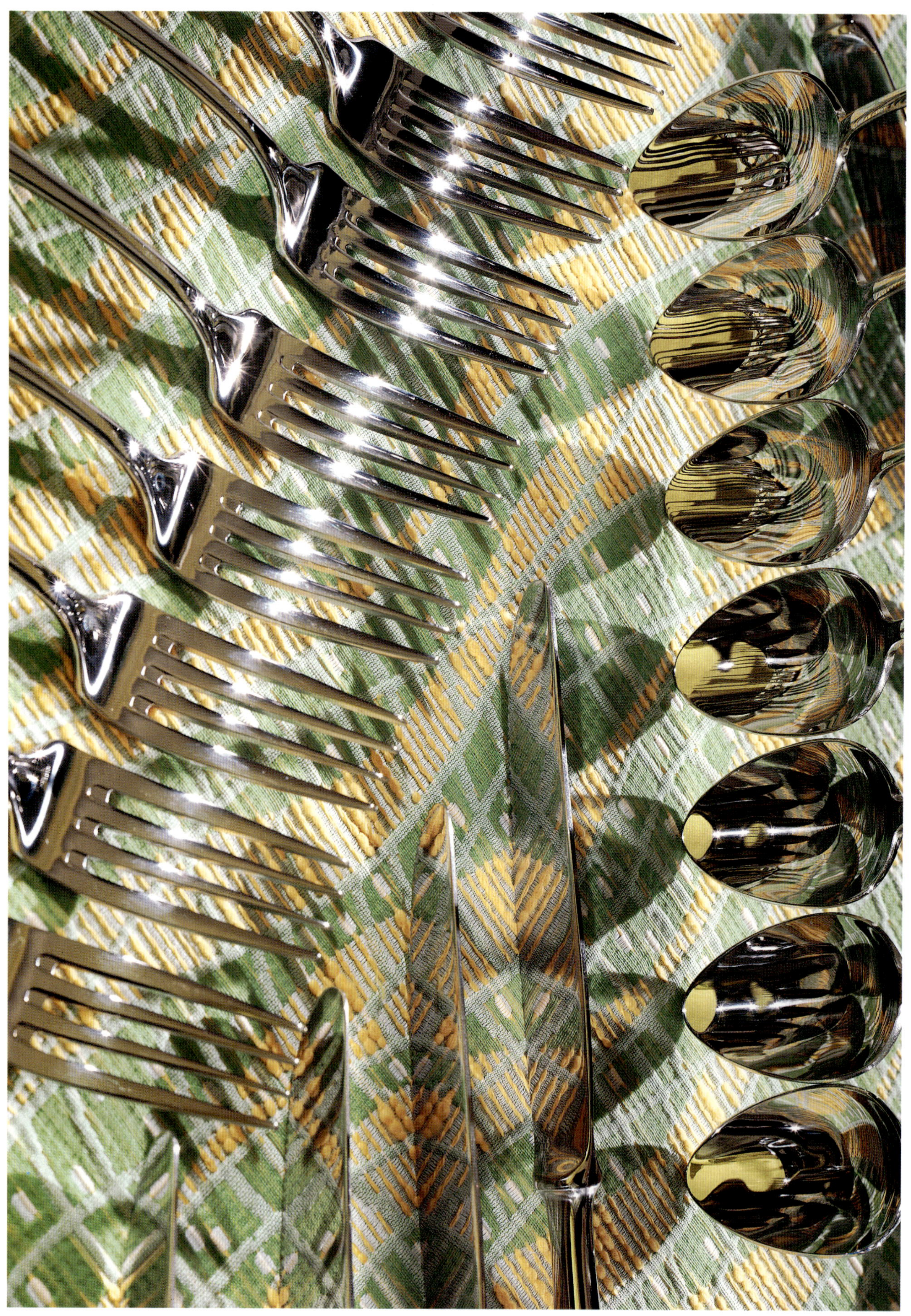

MARK WEISS IS REPRESENTED BY MICHAEL GINSBURG 212 679-8881

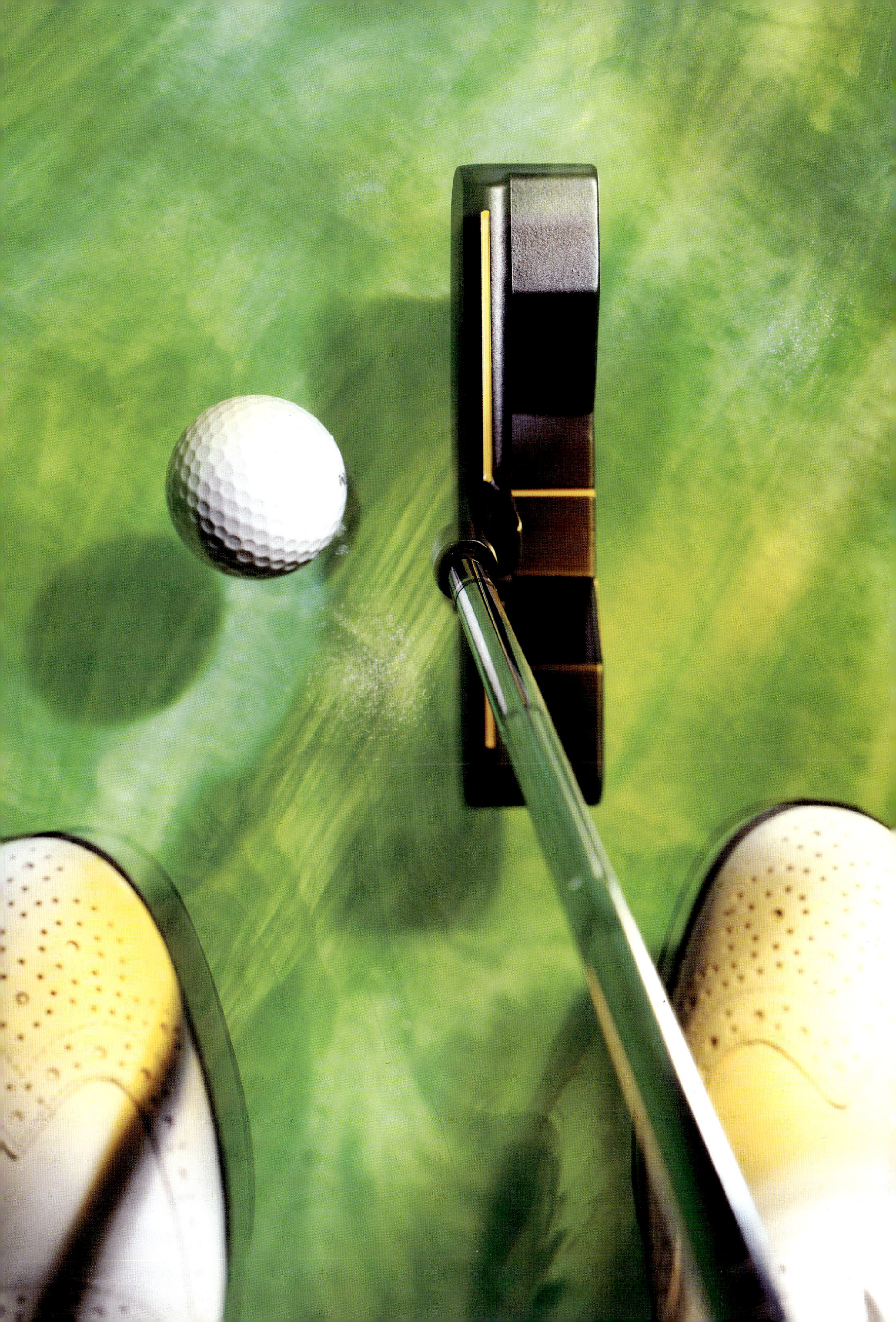

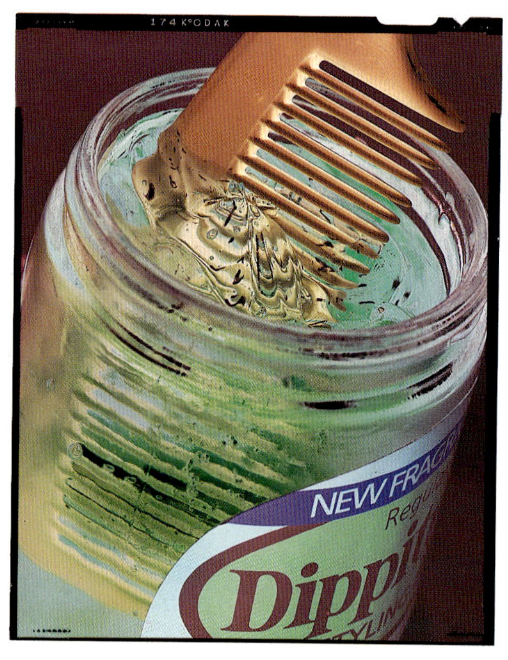


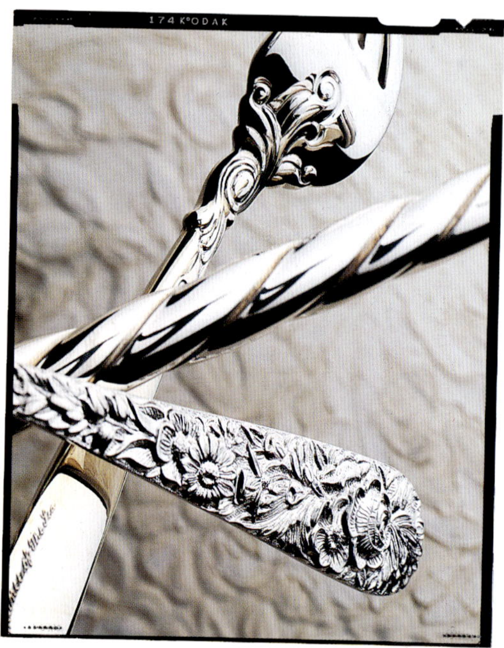


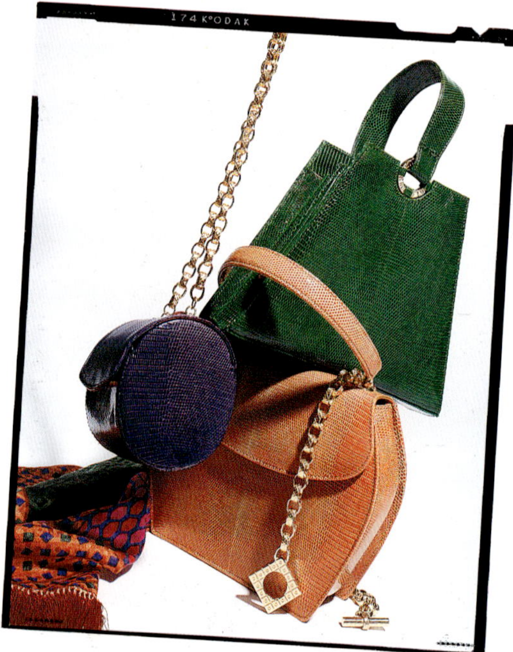


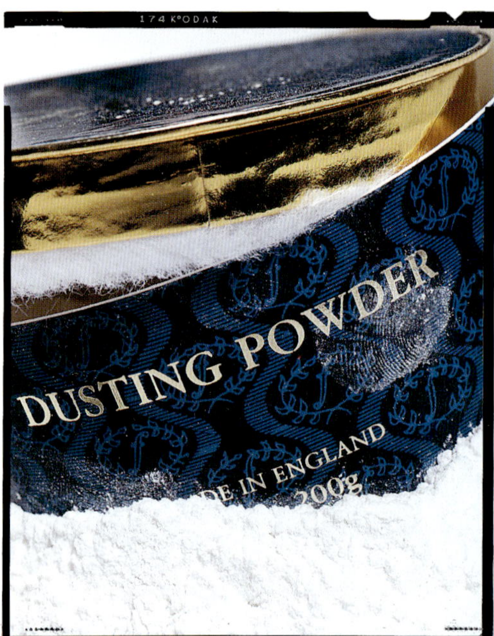


# DAVID LAWRENCE 212·274·0710

*160 Sixth Avenue 2nd Floor  New York, New York 10013*

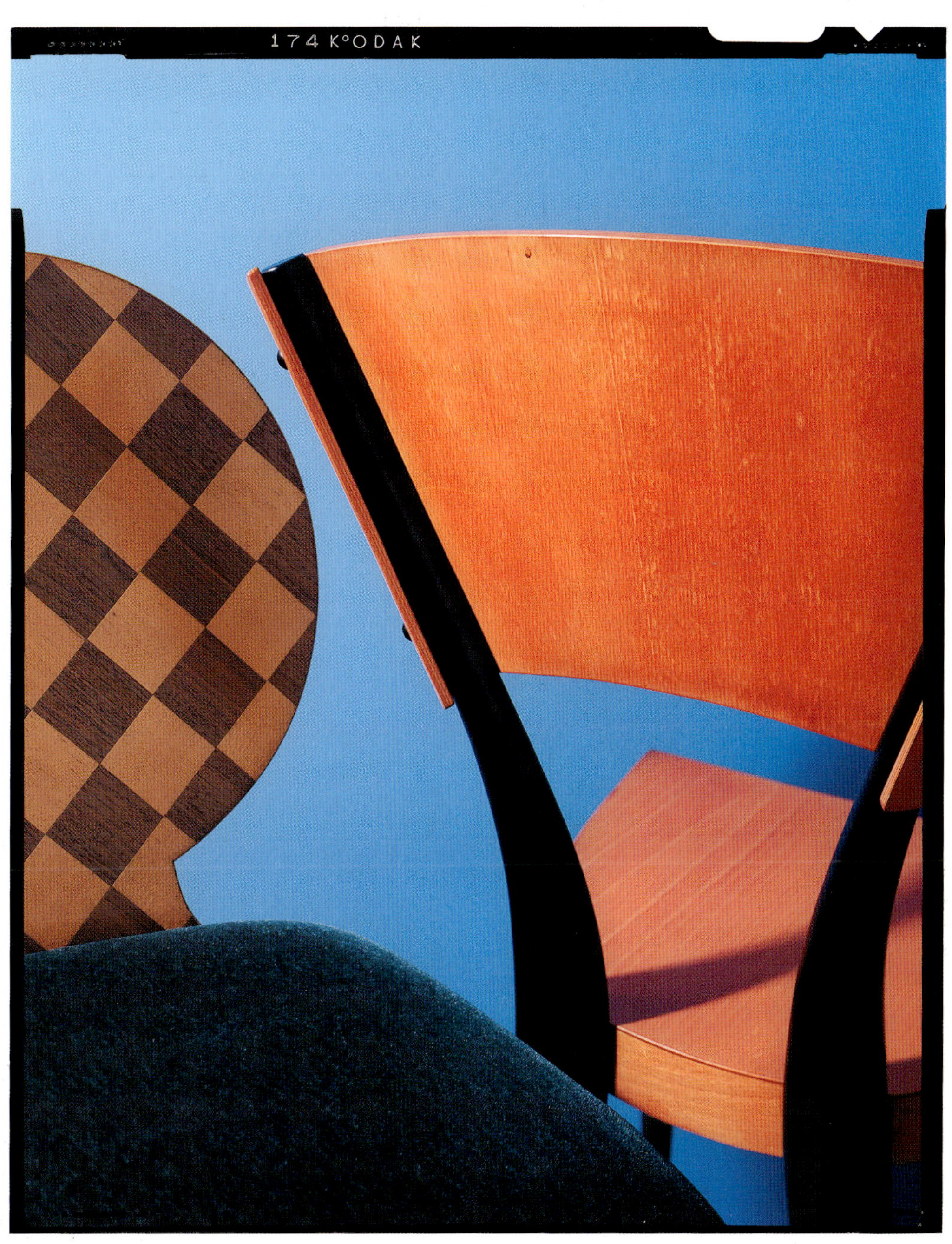

# DAVID LAWRENCE 212·274·0710

*160 Sixth Avenue 2nd Floor  New York, New York 10013*

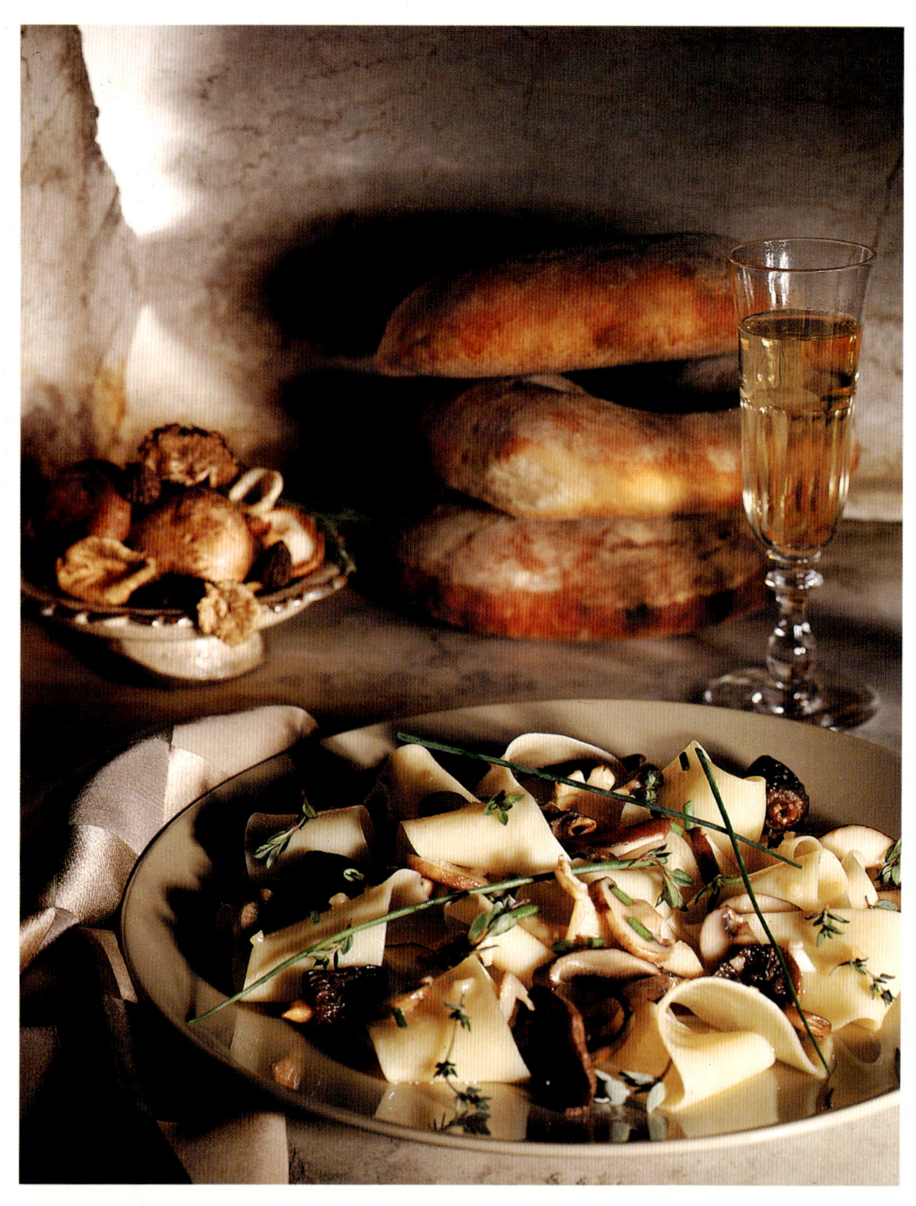

# ELLEN SILVERMAN

## 2 1 2 - 6 7 3 - 9 4 4 9

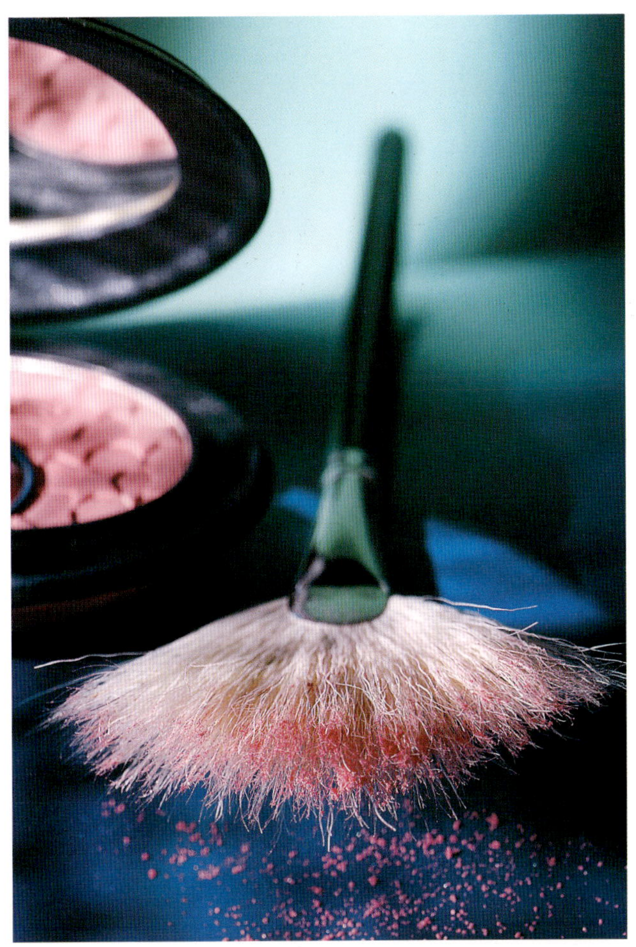

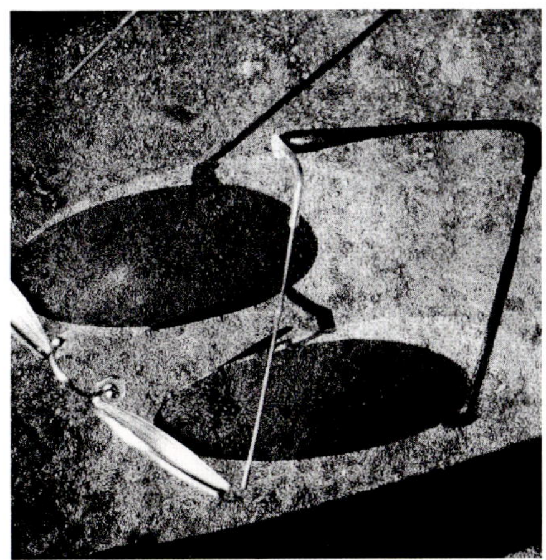

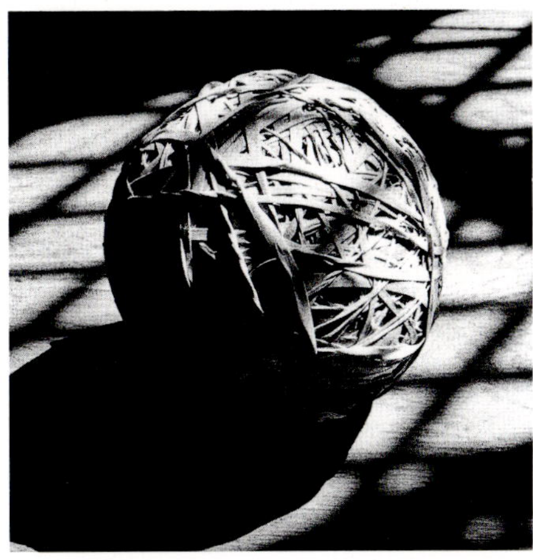

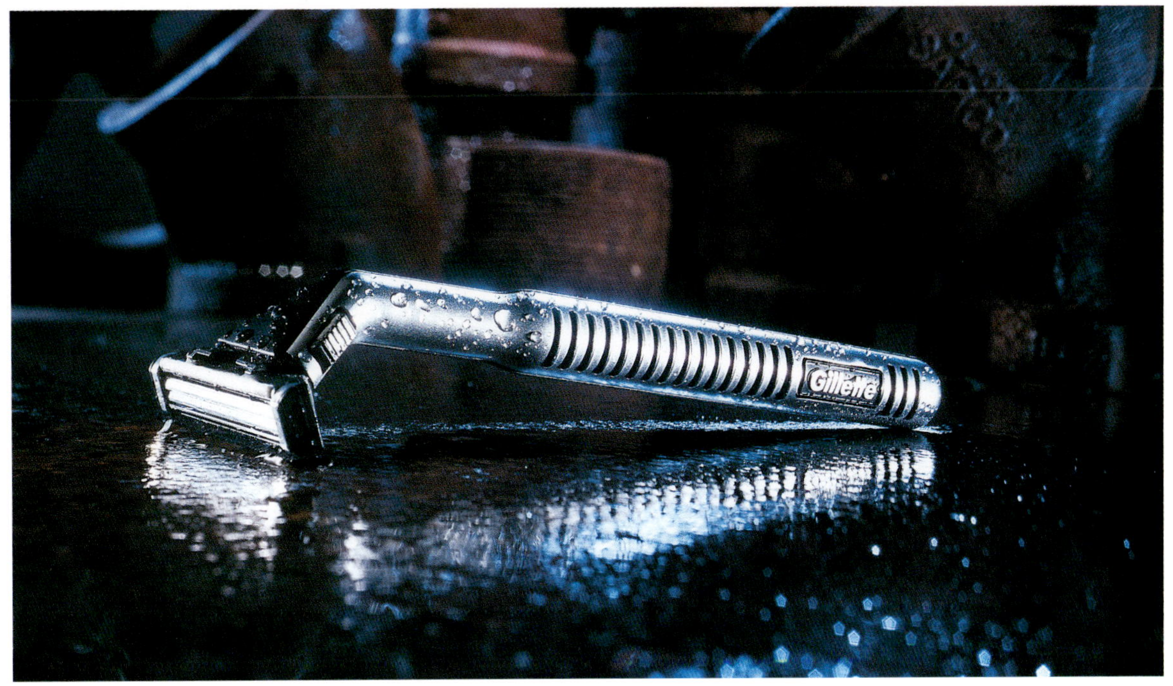


**LARRY BERCOW**
212 · 629 · 9000
FAX · 268 · 7207

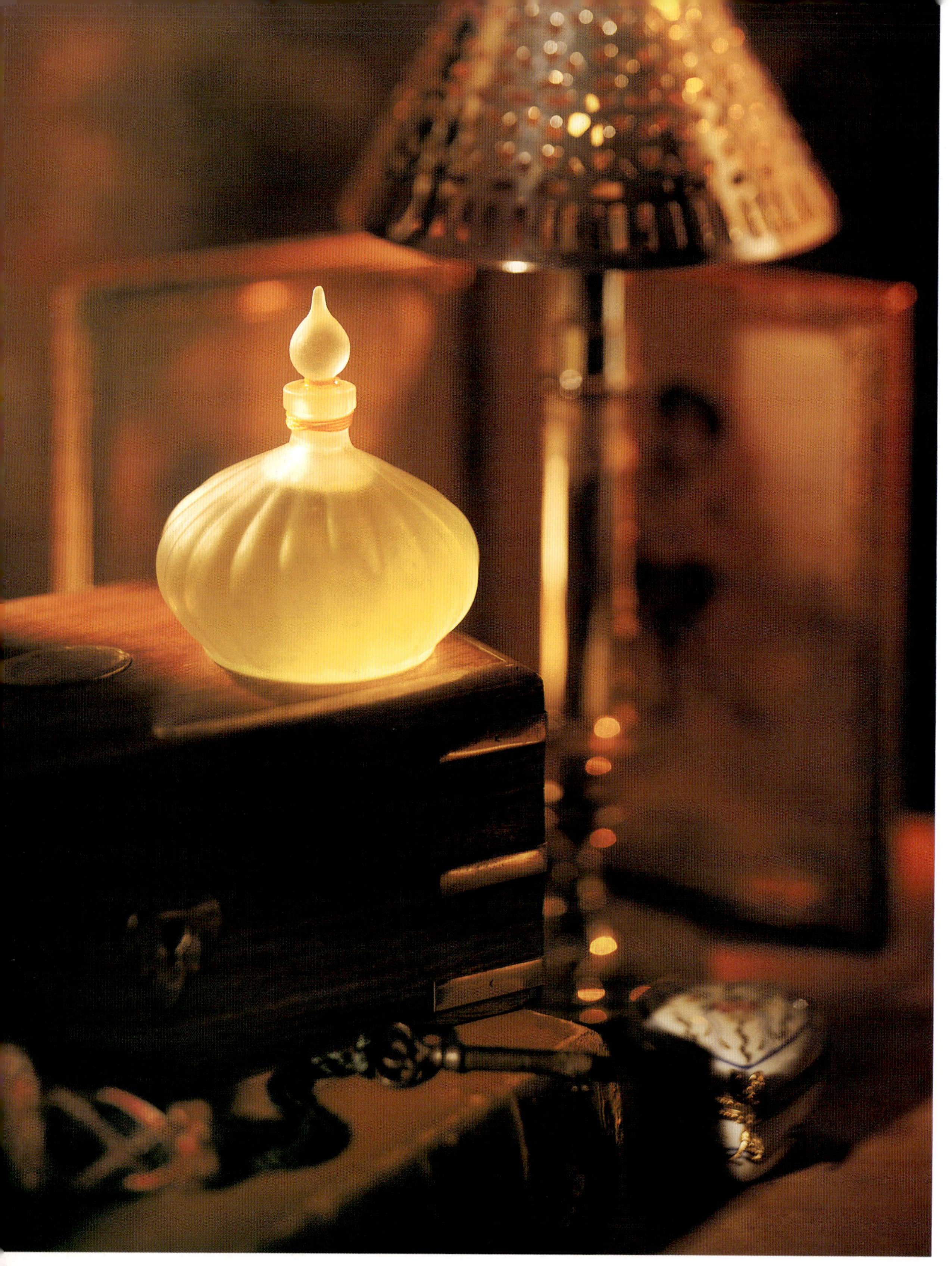

# ALTAMARI

# ALTAMARI

56 WEST 22 ST  NYC 10010     212 645 8484

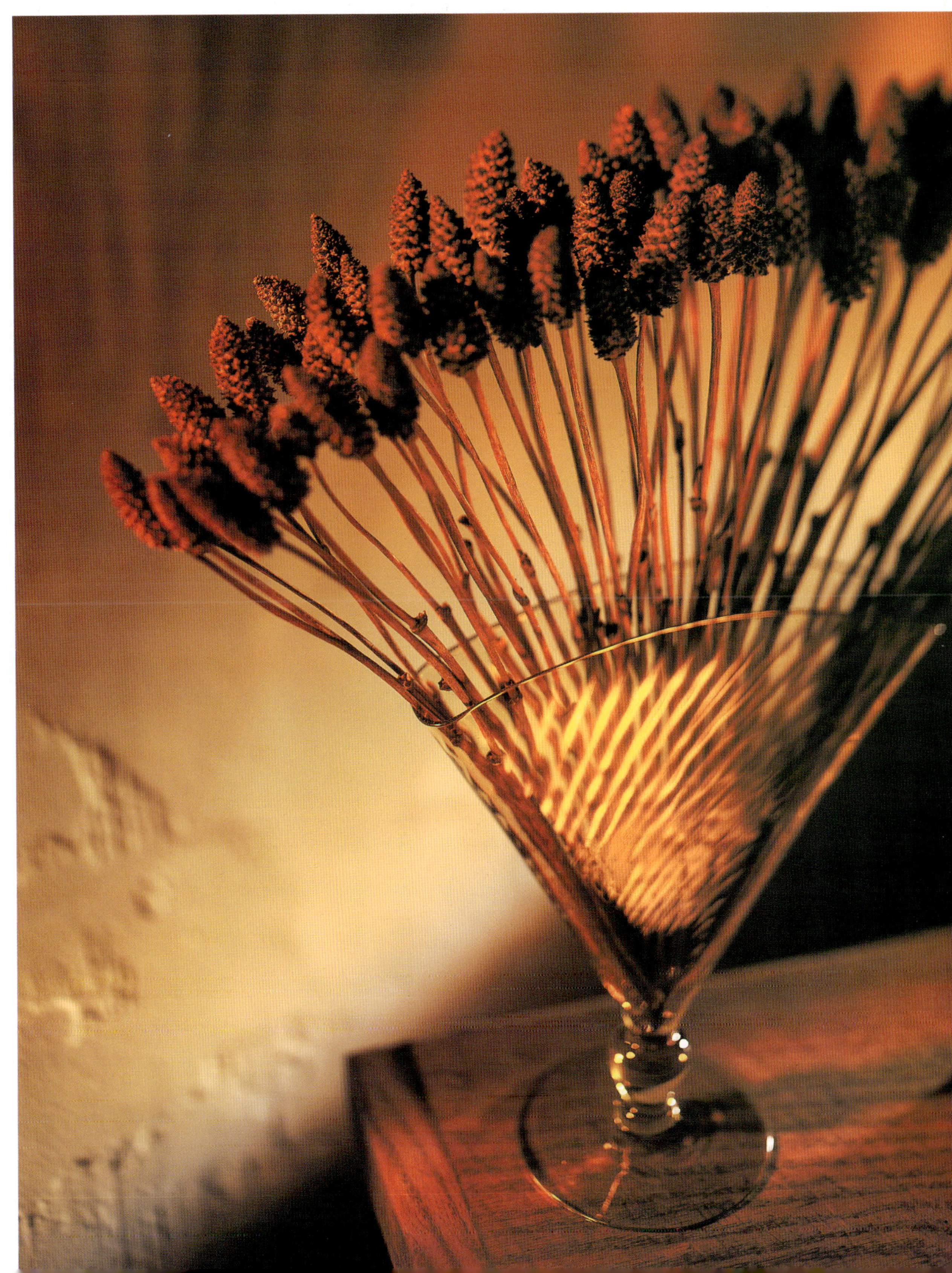

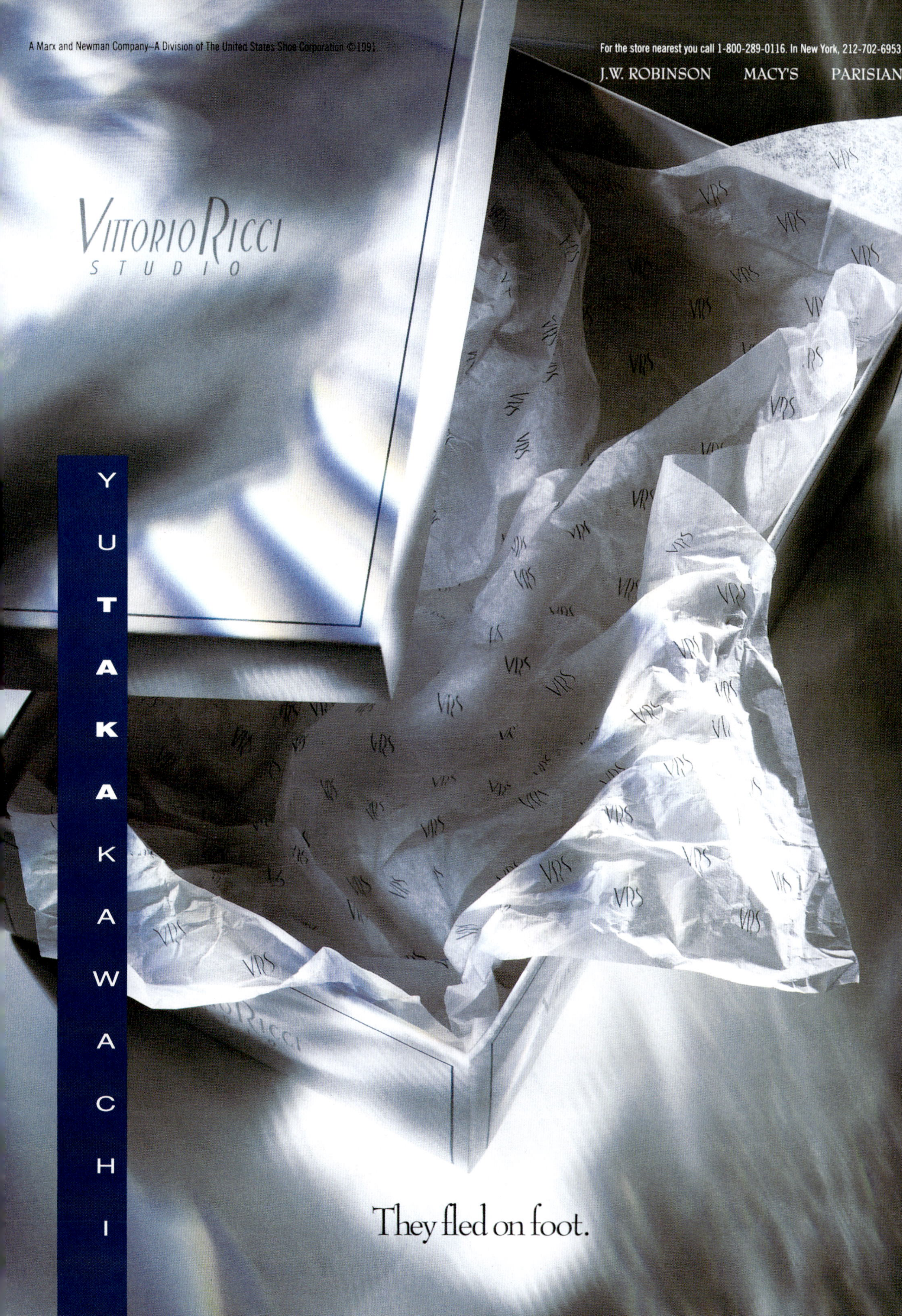

A Marx and Newman Company—A Division of The United States Shoe Corporation ©1991
For the store nearest you call 1-800-289-0116. In New York, 212-702-6953.
J.W. ROBINSON    MACY'S    PARISIAN
VITTORIORICCI
STUDIO
YUTAKA KAWACHI
They fled on foot.

Y U **T A K A**  K A W A C H I  S T U D I O

**2 1 2 - 9 2 9 - 4 8 2 5**

FAX 212-627-1462

R E P R E S E N T E D   B Y
B O B   M E A D   &   J O H N   K E N N E Y

**2 1 2 - 6 2 7 - 3 4 0 0**

FAX 212-633-1228

Y
U
T
A
K
A

K
A
W
A
C
H
I

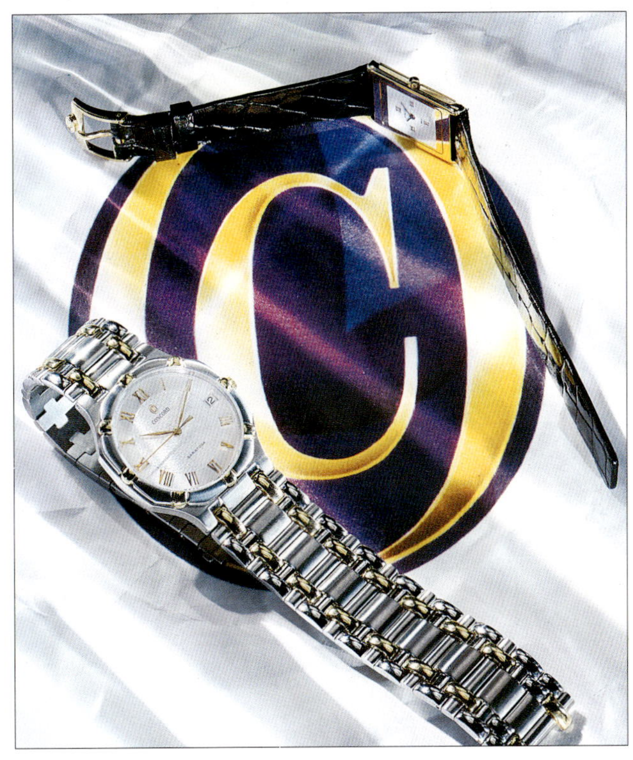

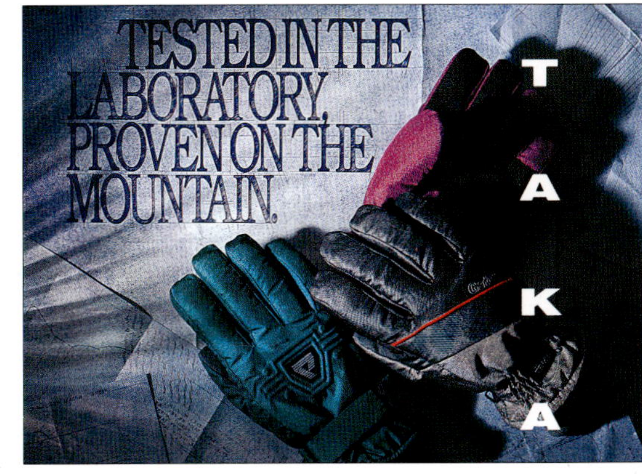


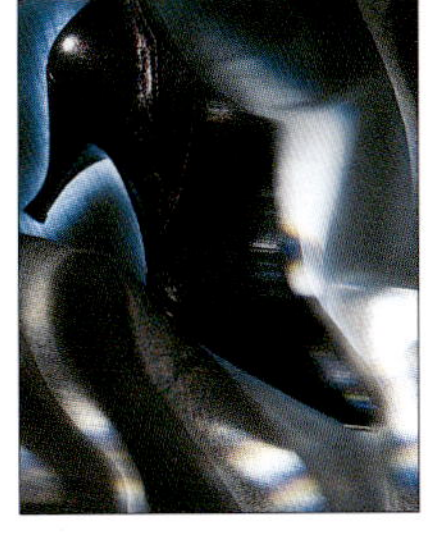

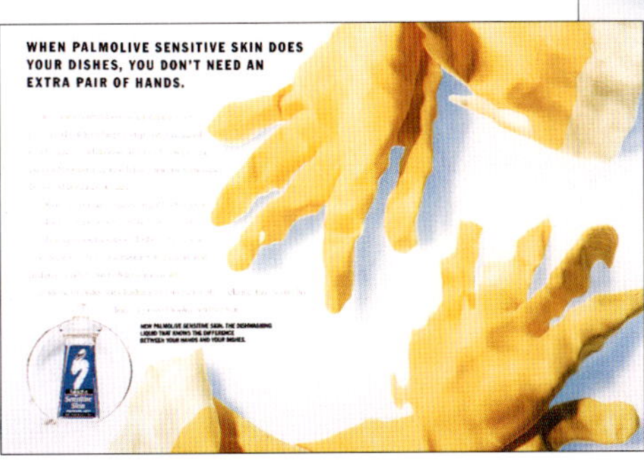




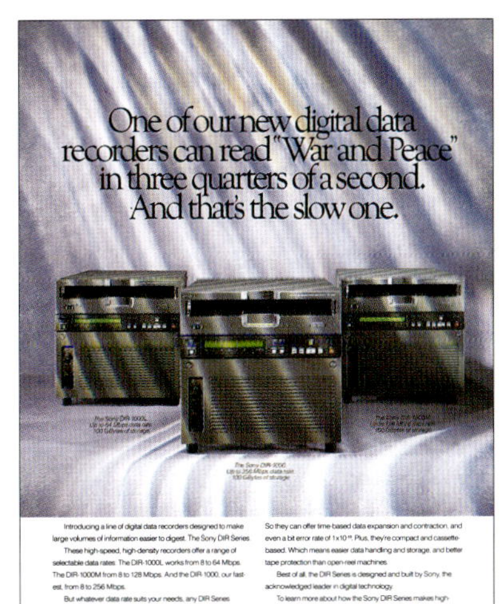

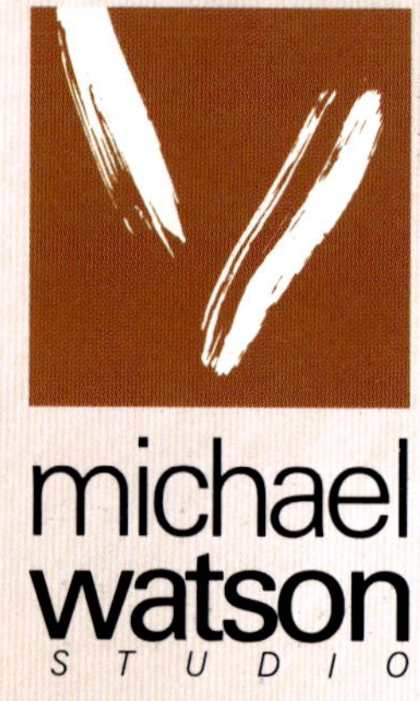

# michael
# watson
S T U D I O

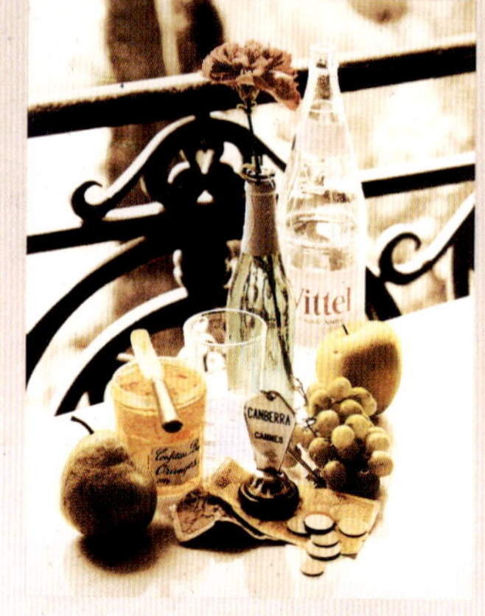

133 WEST 19th

NY, NY 10011

212 620 3125

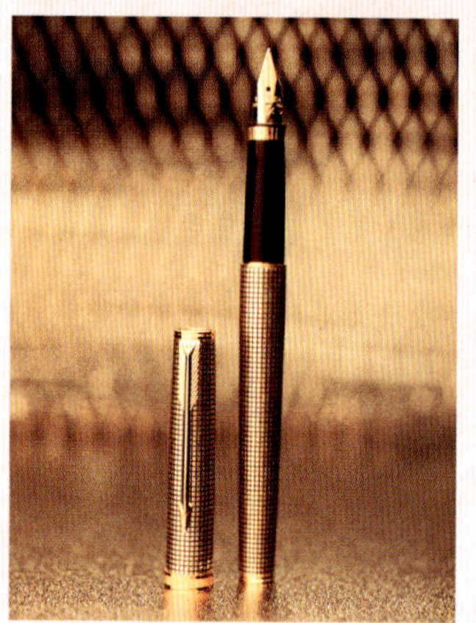

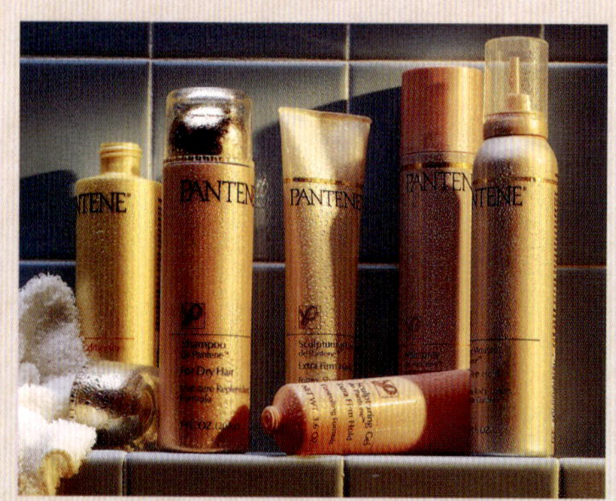

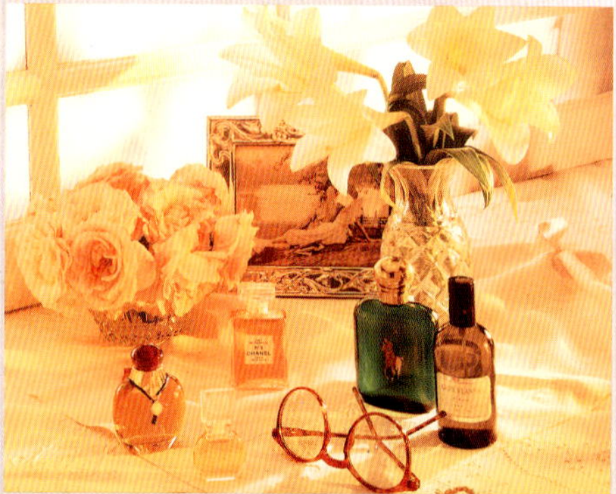

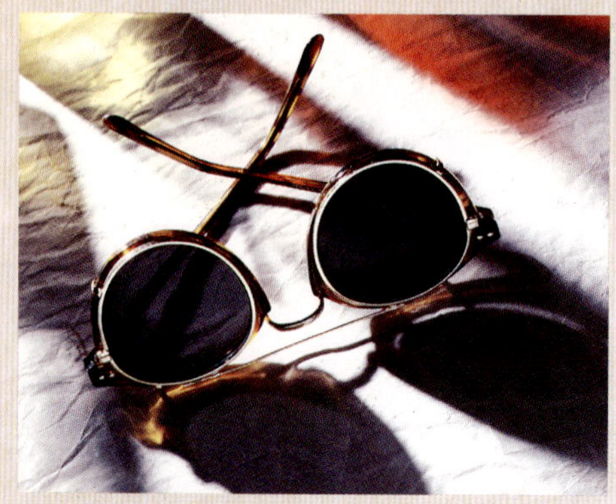

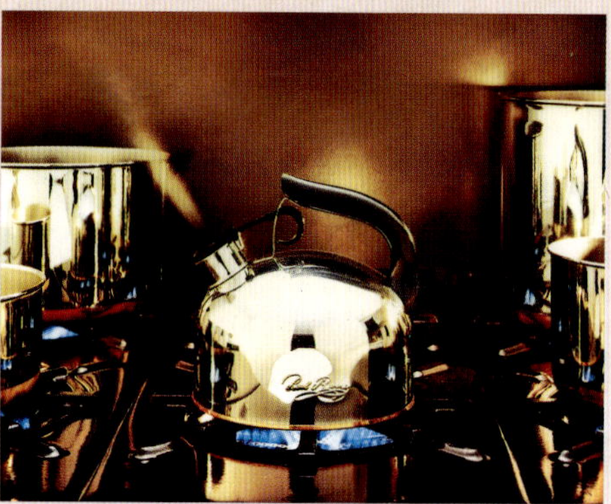

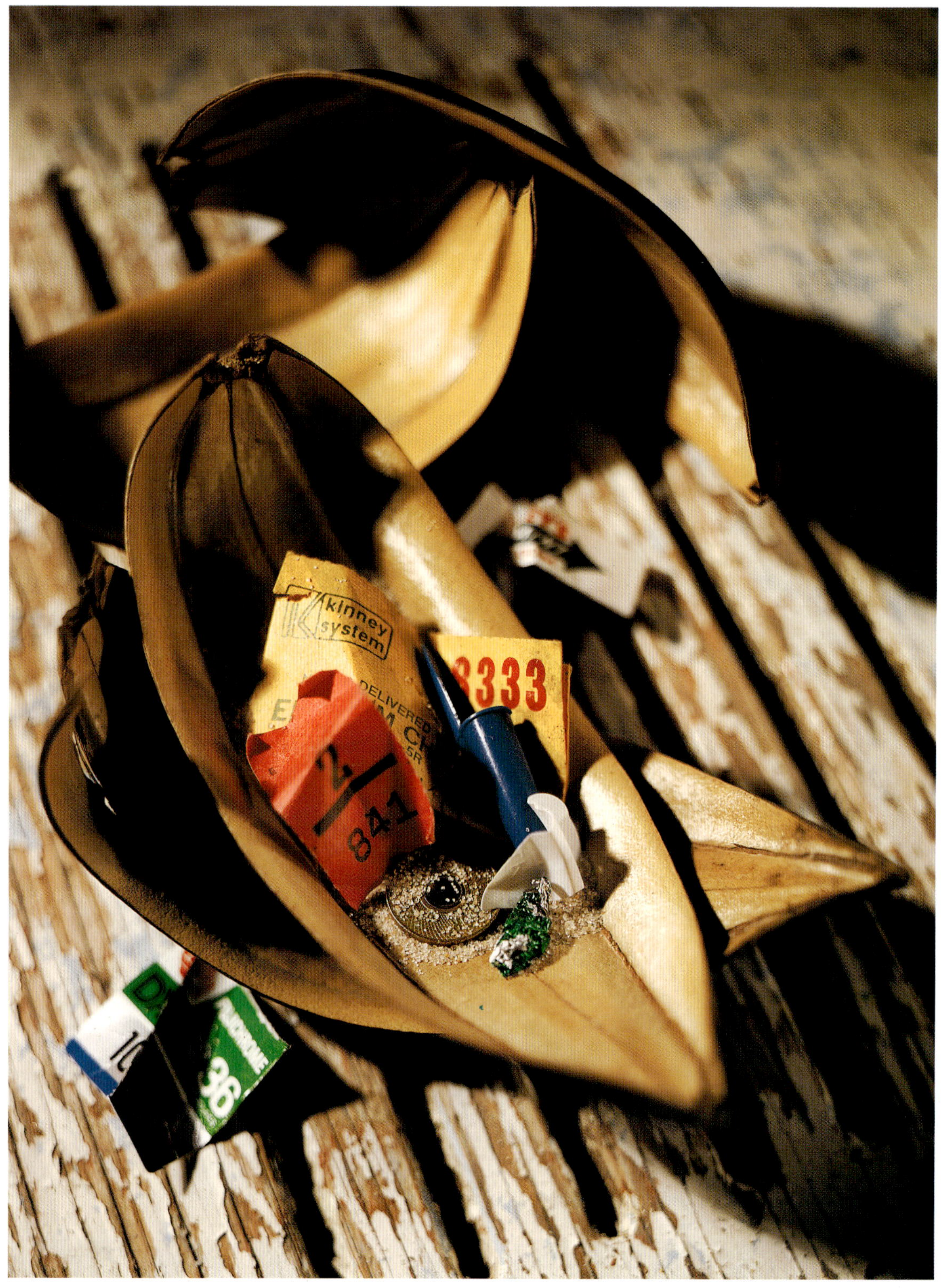
kinney
system
3333
DELIVERED
841
36

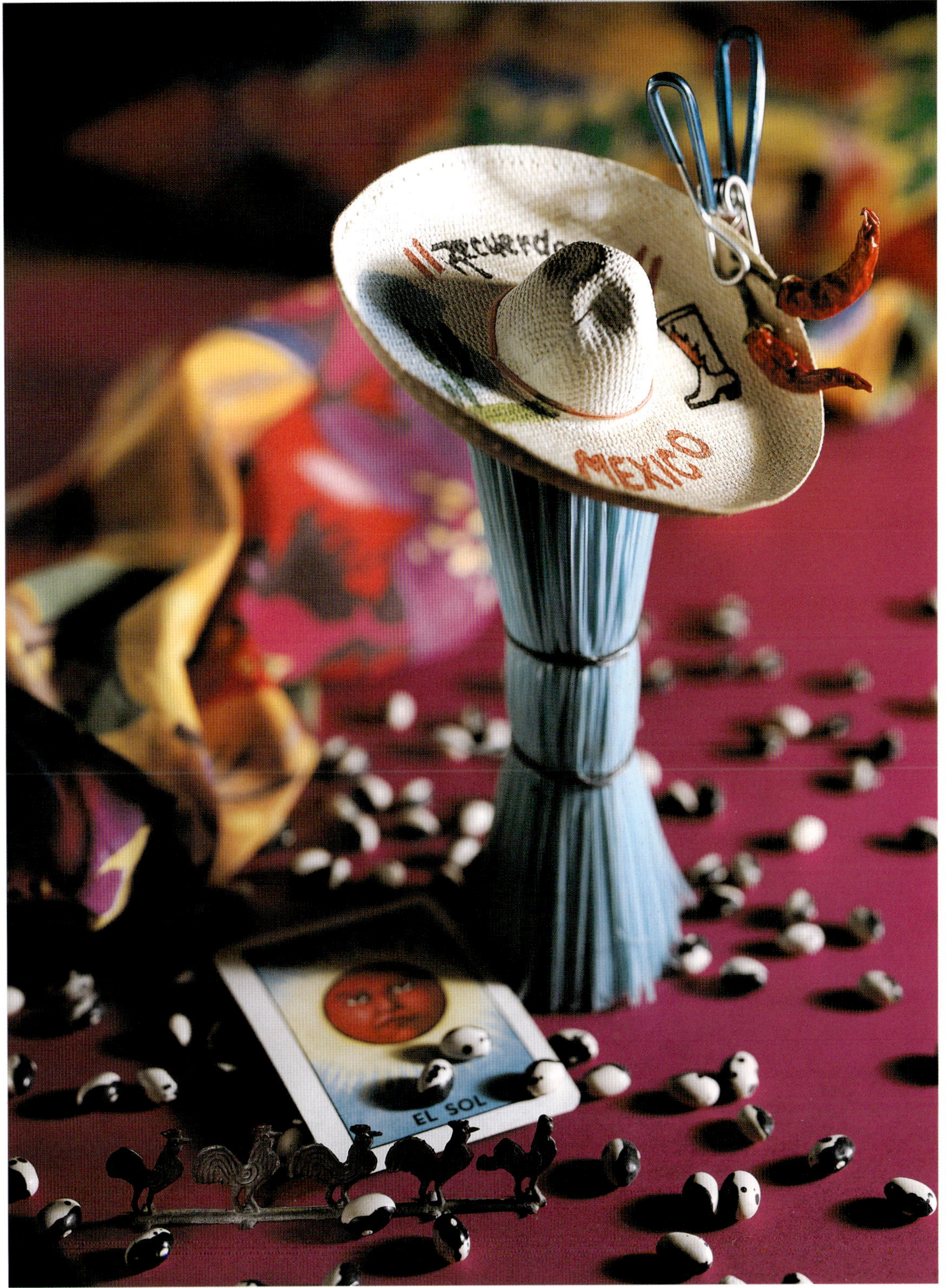


ANDY SPREITZER ■ PHOTOGRAPHER ■ 225 East 24th Street ■ New York City 10010 ■ 212 685-9669

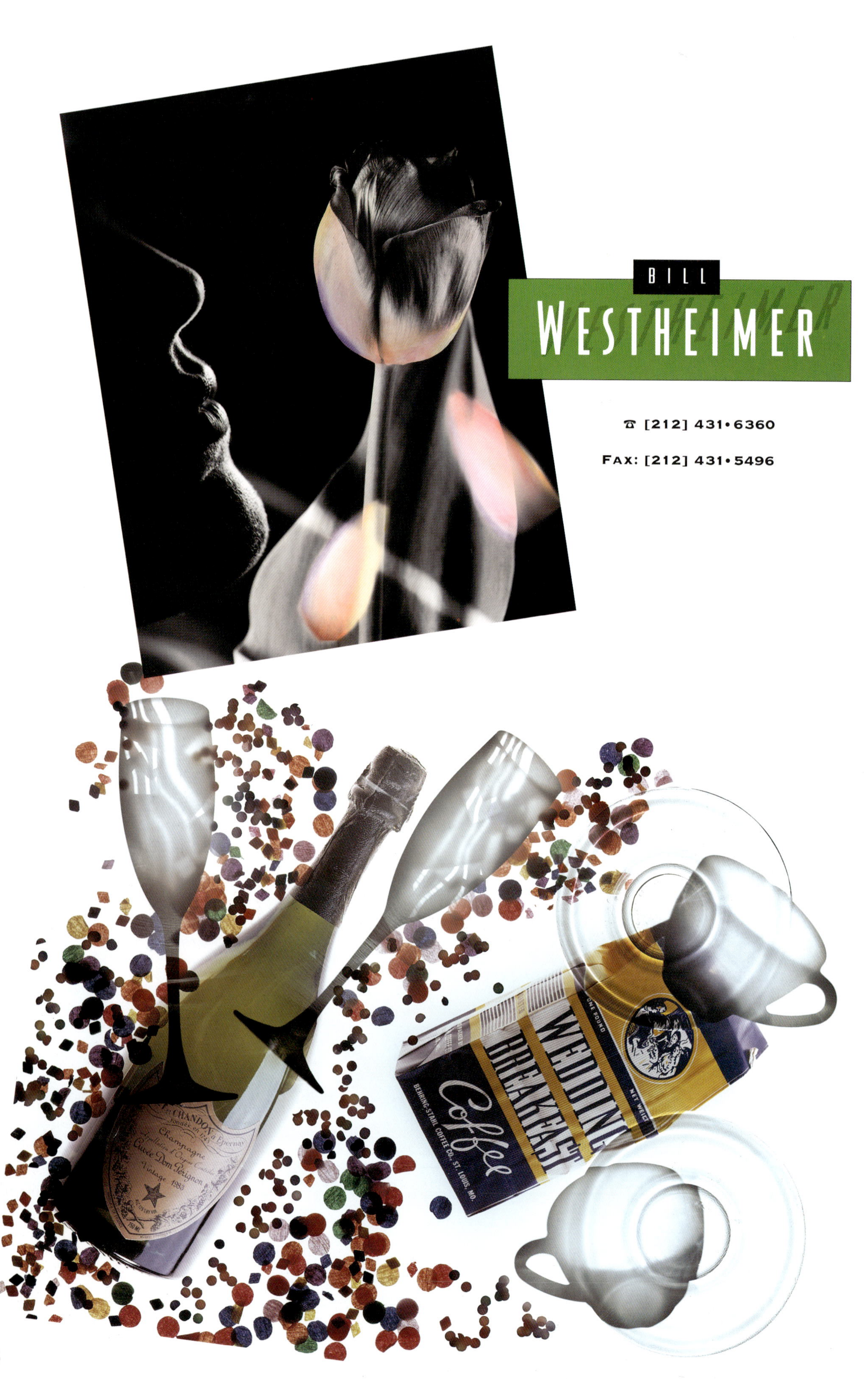
BILL
WESTHEIMER
☎ [212] 431•6360
FAX: [212] 431•5496

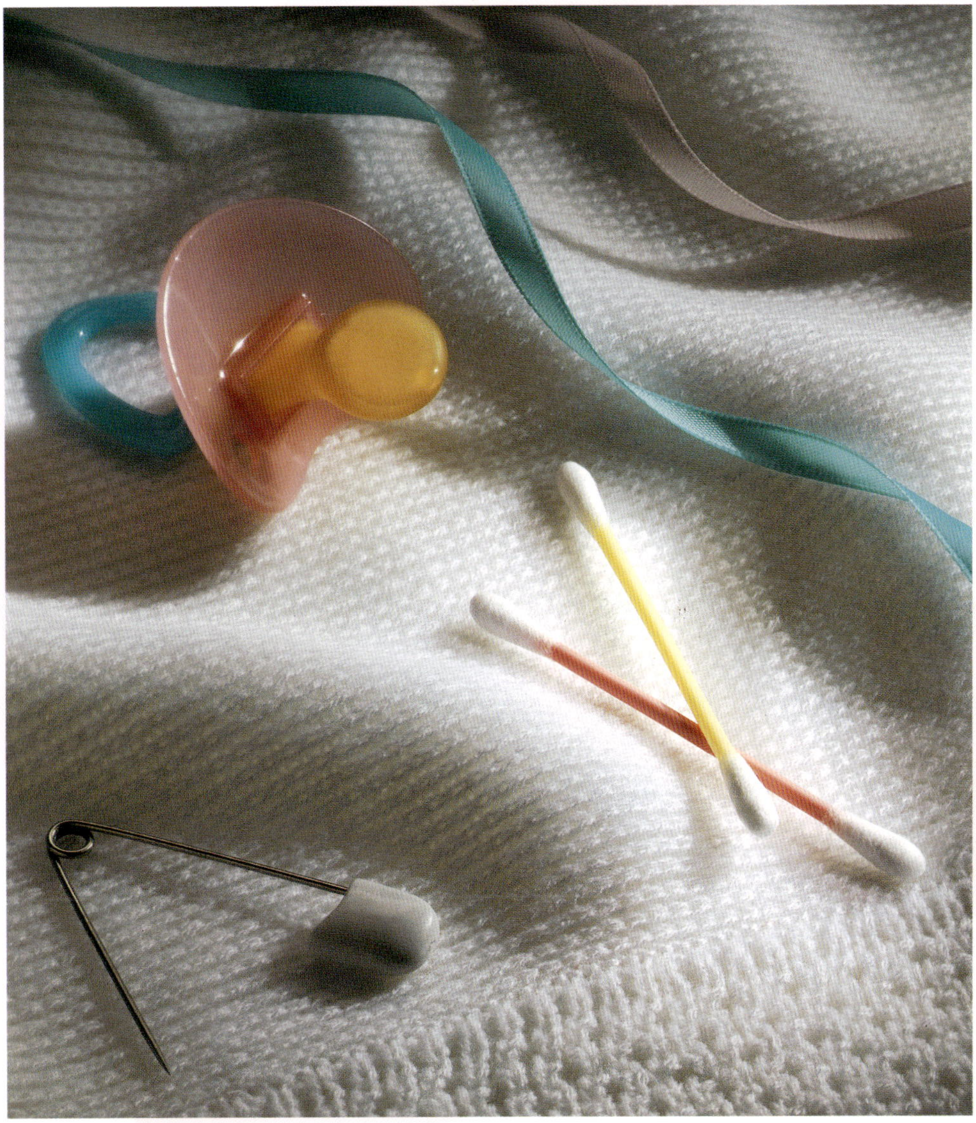

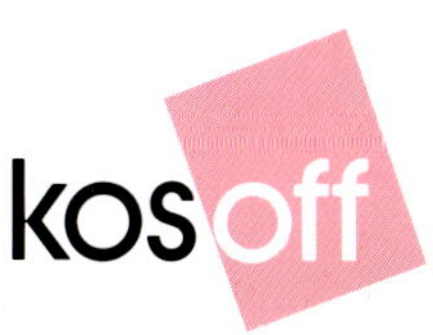

**Brian Kosoff**
28 West 25 Street
New York, NY 10010

212 243 4880
Fax 212 727 2044

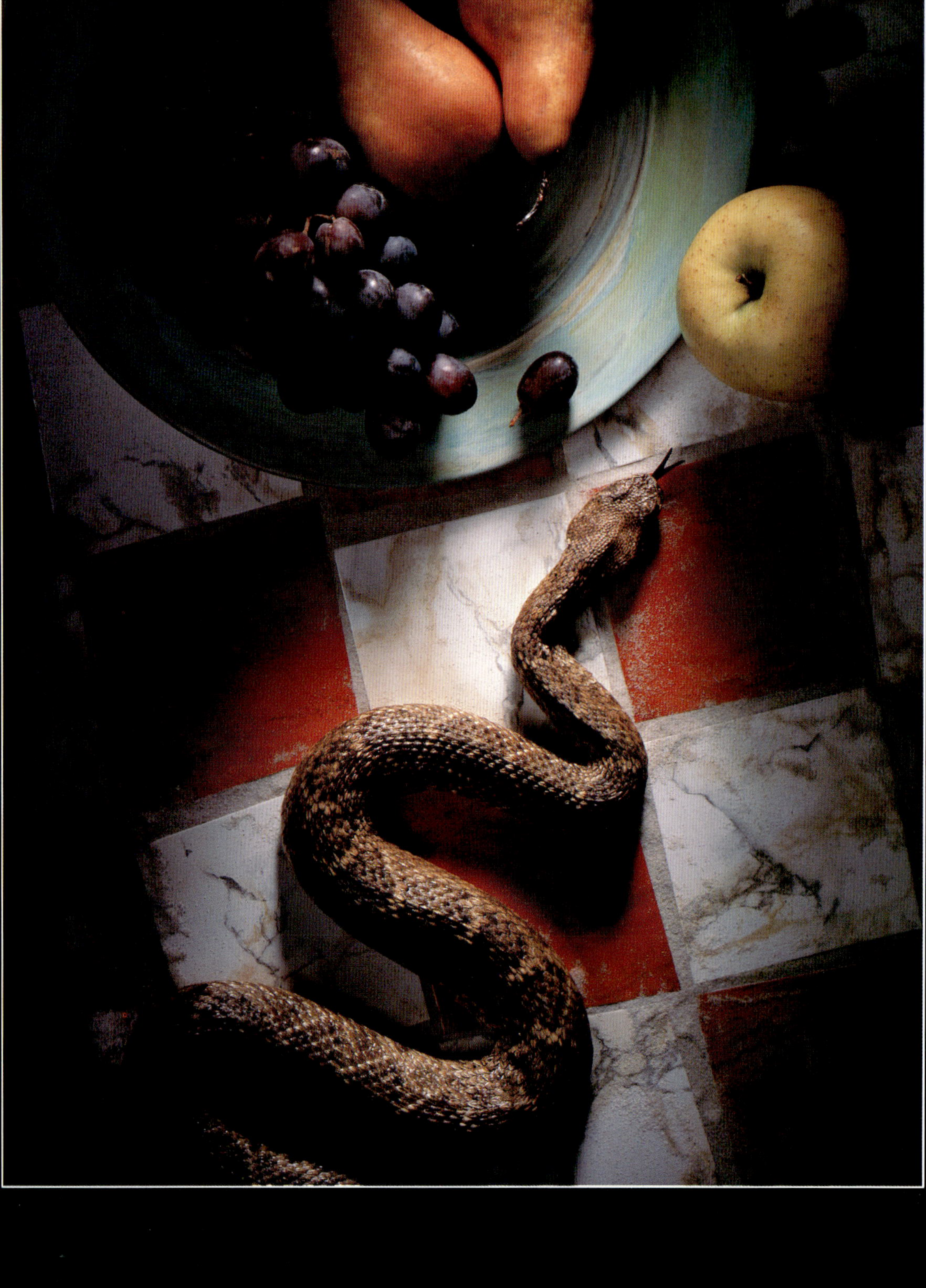

DAVID

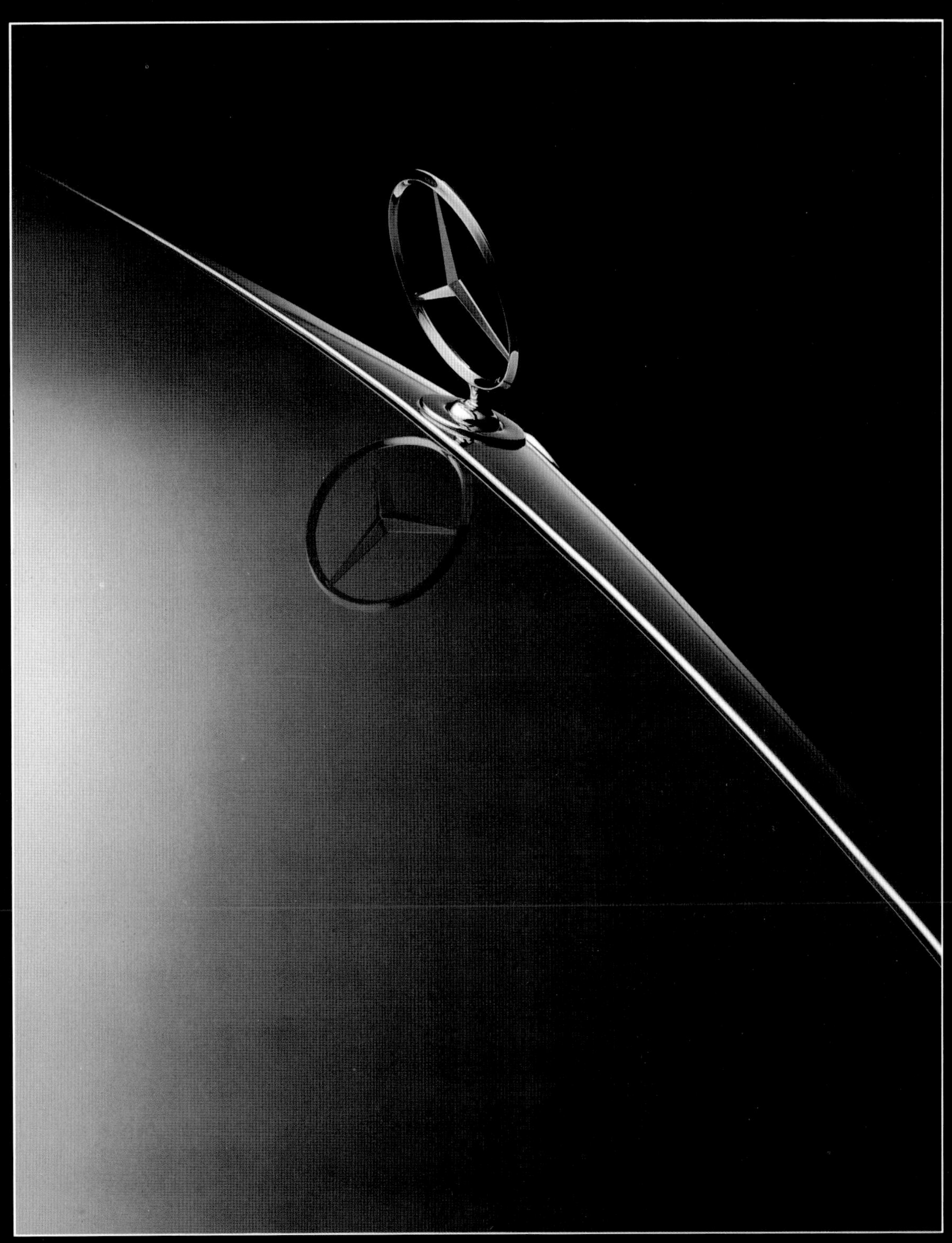WEISS

Represented by Ralph & Co.
212 • 691 • 4277   FAX 645 • 7181

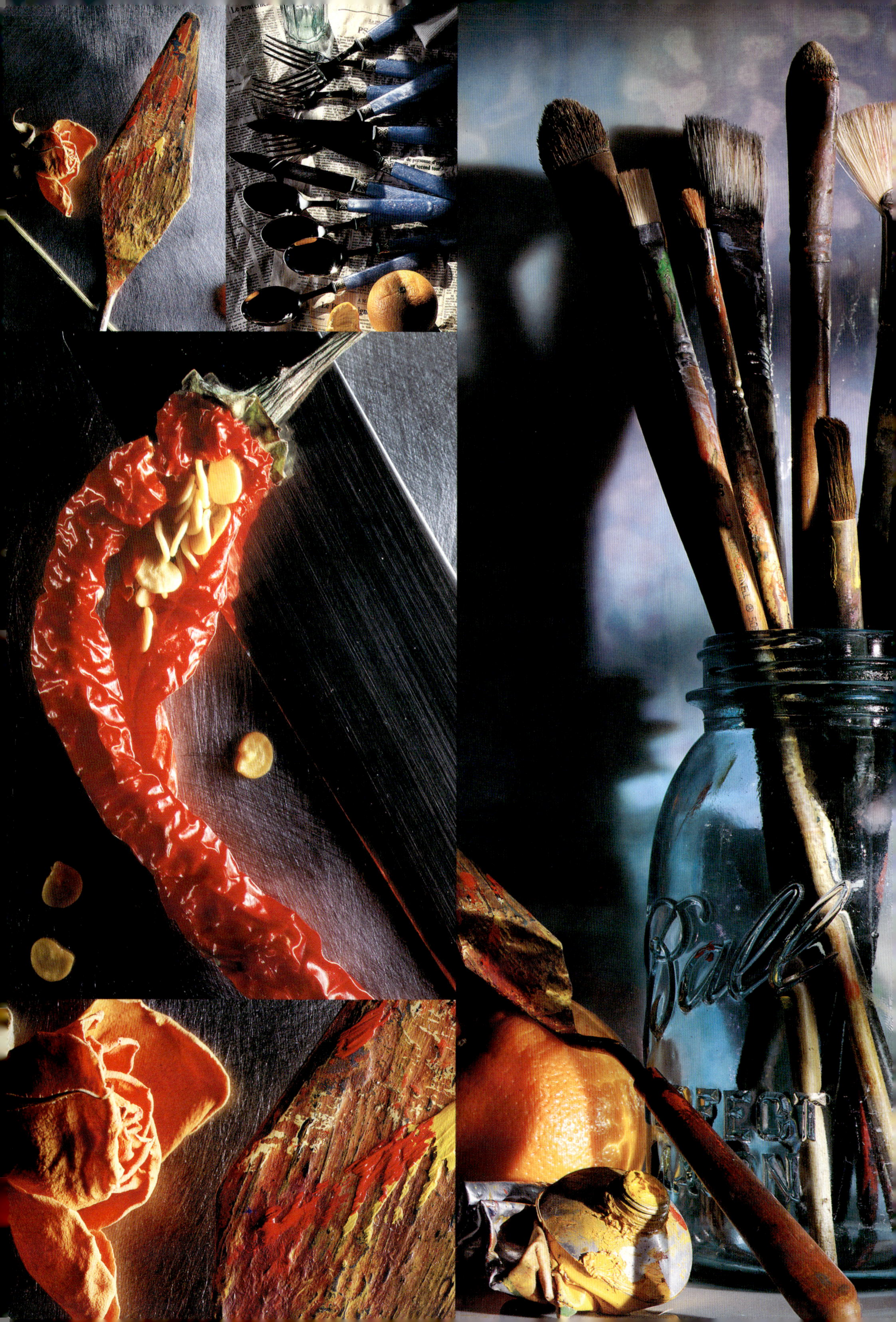

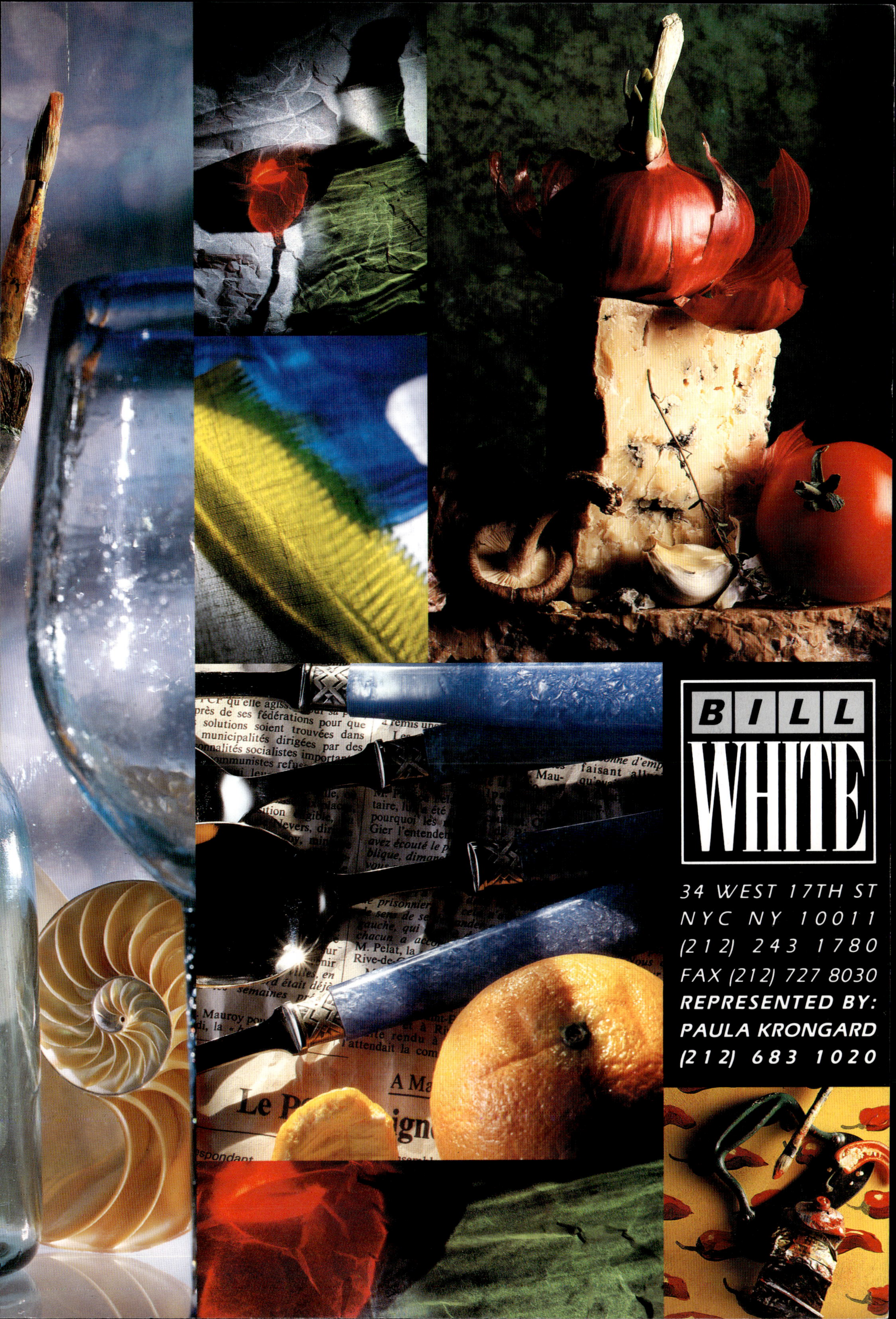

BILL
WHITE
34 WEST 17TH ST
NYC NY 10011
(212) 243 1780
FAX (212) 727 8030
REPRESENTED BY:
PAULA KRONGARD
(212) 683 1020

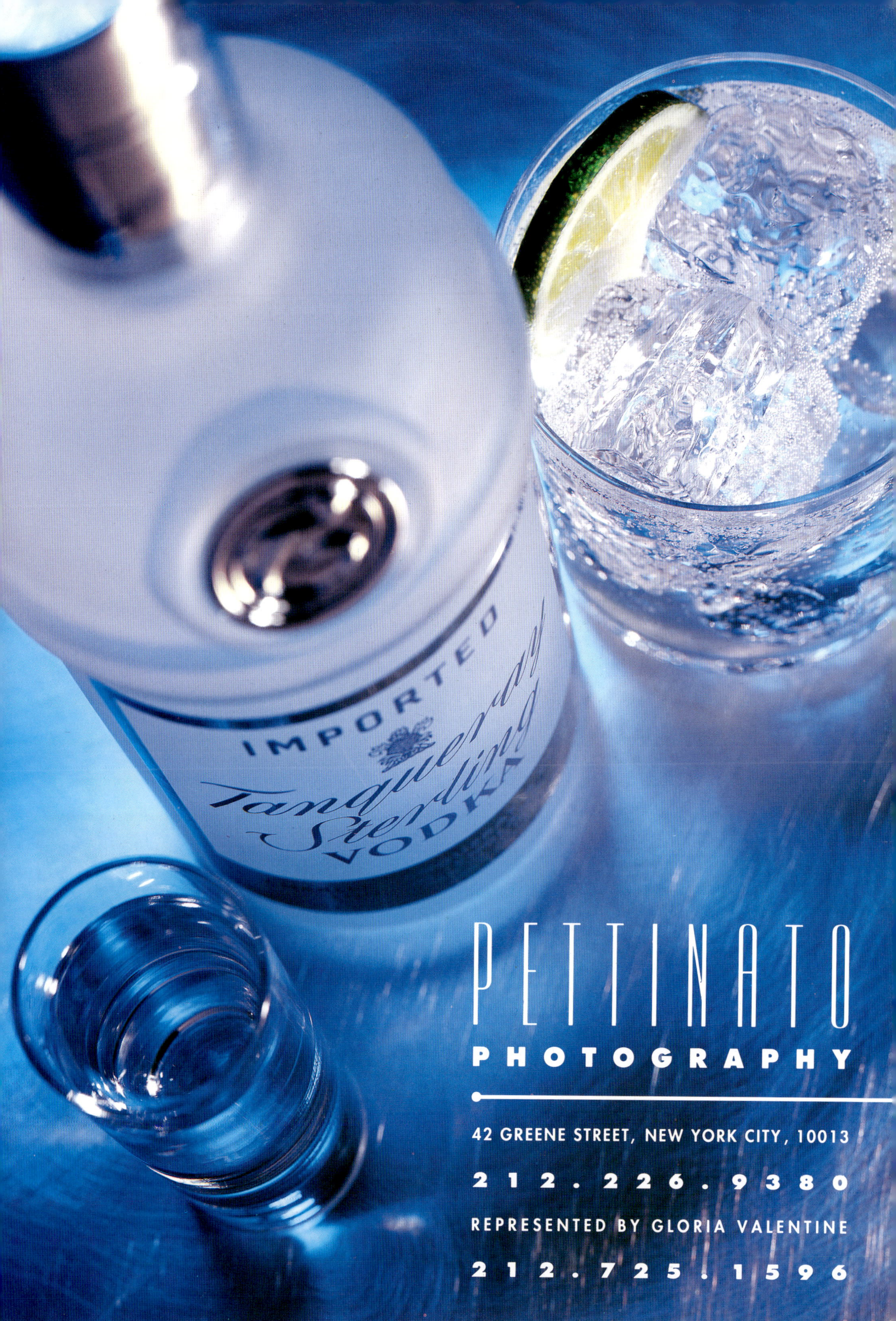

IMPORTED
Tanqueray
Sterling
VODKA
PETTINATO
PHOTOGRAPHY
42 GREENE STREET, NEW YORK CITY, 10013
212.226.9380
REPRESENTED BY GLORIA VALENTINE
212.725.1596

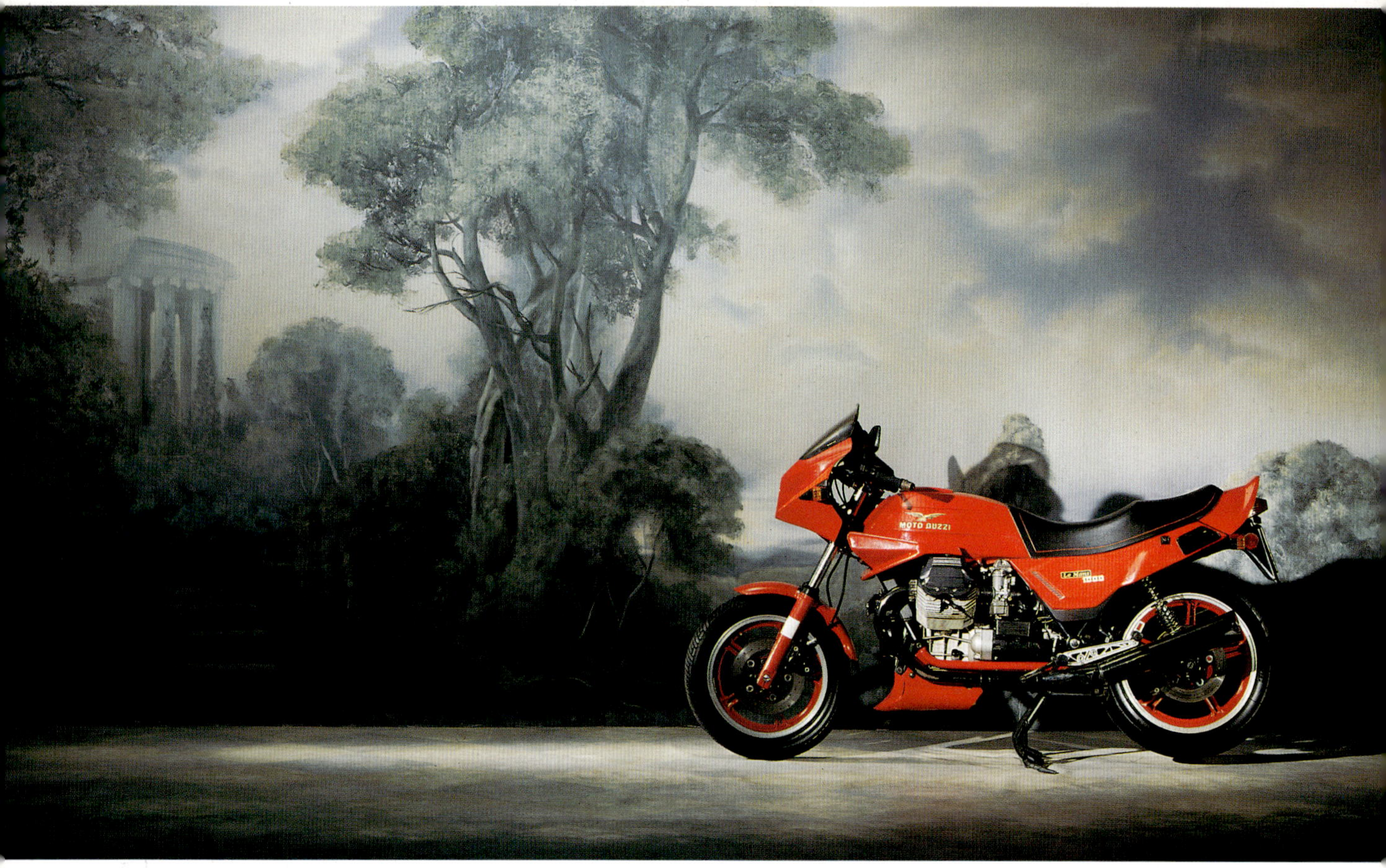

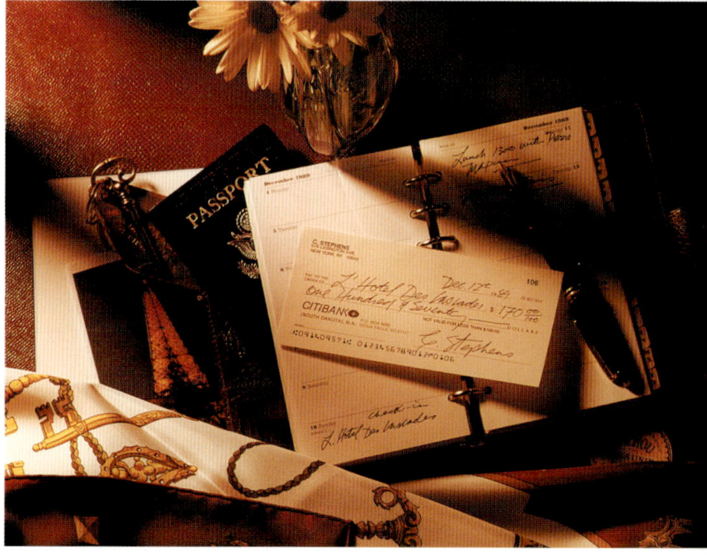

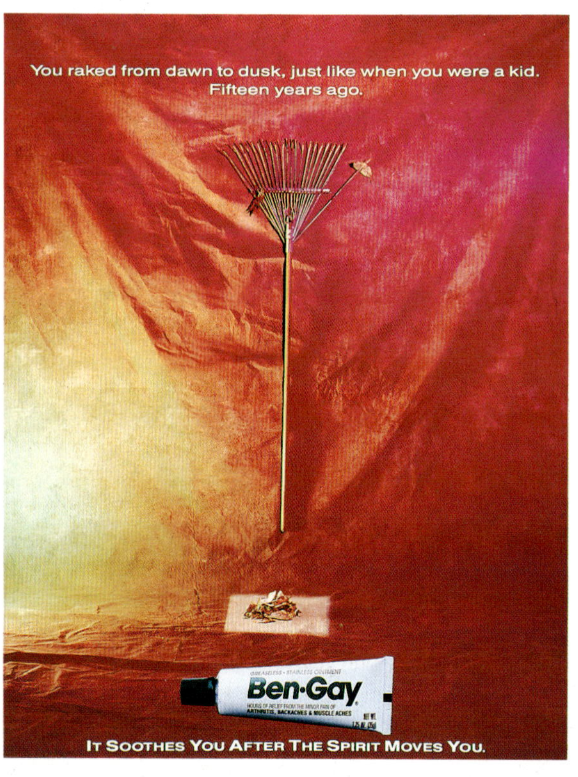


# Daniel Teboul

## PHOTOGRAPHER

146 West 25th Street
New York, NY, 10001
**(212) 645-8227**

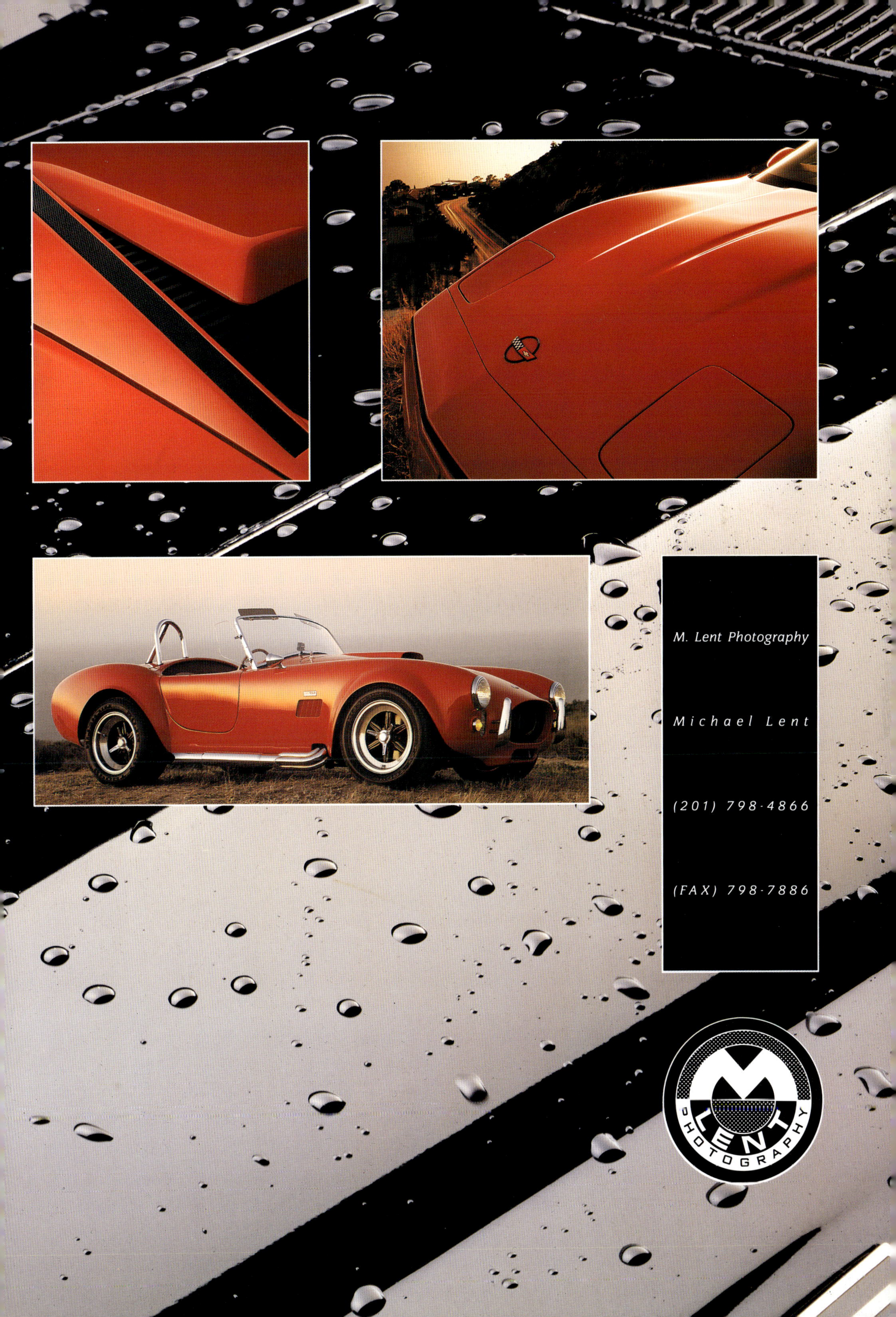

M. Lent Photography

Michael Lent

(201) 798-4866

(FAX) 798-7886

M LENT
PHOTOGRAPHY

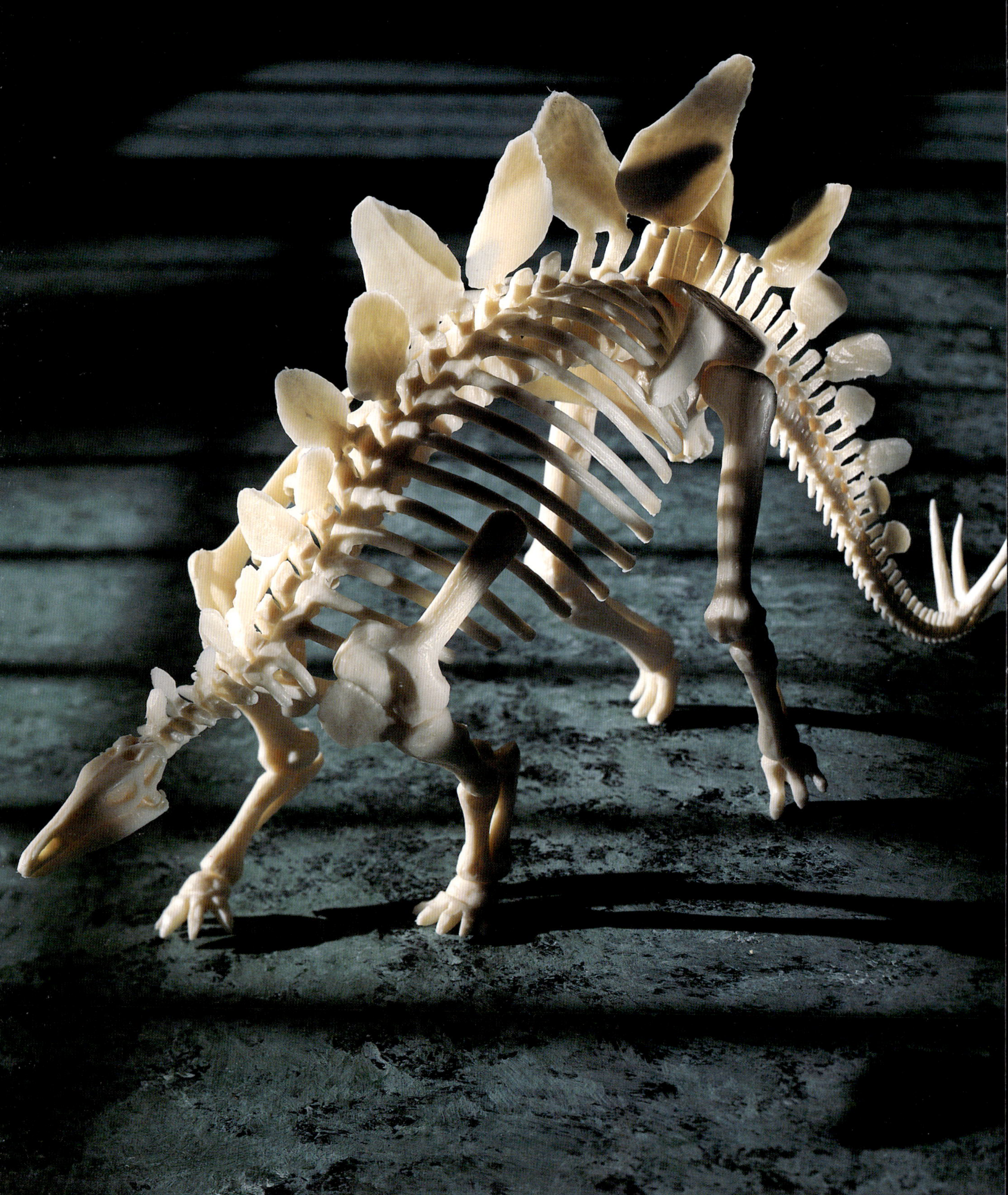
JAY ALAN LEFKOWITZ
PHOTOGRAPHY
212-929-1036 ▲ 5 EAST 16TH STREET, NYC 10003 ▲ REPRESENTED BY CHRIS LYSOHIR 212-741-3187
CHALKIN
STUDIO INC.